CUSTER

CUSTER

From the Civil War's Boy General to the
Battle of the Little Bighorn

TED BEHNCKE AND GARY BLOOMFIELD

CASEMATE

Philadelphia & Oxford

Published in the United States of America and Great Britain in 2020 by
CASEMATE PUBLISHERS
1950 Lawrence Road, Havertown, PA 19083, USA
and
The Old Music Hall, 106–108 Cowley Road, Oxford OX4 1JE, UK

Hardback Edition: ISBN 978-1-61200-889-9
Digital Edition: ISBN 978-1-61200-890-5

A CIP record for this book is available from the British Library

Printed and bound in the United States of America by Sheridan

Typeset by Versatile PreMedia Service (P) Ltd

For a complete list of Casemate titles, please contact:

CASEMATE PUBLISHERS (US)
Telephone (610) 853-9131
Fax (610) 853-9146
Email: casemate@casematepublishers.com
www.casematepublishers.com

CASEMATE PUBLISHERS (UK)
Telephone (01865) 241249
Email: casemate-uk@casematepublishers.co.uk
www.casematepublishers.co.uk

Front image: Brigadier General George A. Custer, U.S. Volunteers, June 1863. (Fort Riley History Museum)

The term "Indians," rather than "Native Americans," has been used throughout, in keeping with the source materials which use "Indians" almost exclusively.

Contents

Preface

No one can consider another biography of George Custer without first addressing the defining event of his life, the battle of the Little Bighorn. How was it possible that the premier Indian fighting regiment of the United States Army, with a national hero leading it, could fall so completely? The answer is shockingly straightforward. The Little Bighorn did happen, therefore, it must have been possible for it to have happened. This simple exercise in logic draws in those who encounter George Armstrong Custer's story and captivates them for life. I was one of those people.

I was first introduced to Custer in 1967 at the tender age of seven, thanks to a children's book titled *Custer's Last Stand* written in 1951 by Quentin Reynolds.

This sketch by seven-year-old co-author Ted Behncke was completed in 1967 after being inspired by reading his first Custer book. The experience launched a lifelong interest in Custer and the Little Bighorn. Like most other artists he got many of the details incorrect save a major one—the Indians far outnumbered the 7th Cavalry at the battle of the Little Bighorn. (Ted Behncke, 7 years old)

To say it captivated me would be an understatement. The colorful cover illustration by Frederick T. Chapman depicted a mounted Custer and a cavalry sergeant at full gallop engaged in a desperate Indian fight. To me the illustration had it all. Custer in his buckskin shirt with the pistol raised, the sergeant with the guidon of Company B, 7th Cavalry flapping in the wind, and the Indian warriors riding alongside firing Winchesters, ignited an unquenchable interest which has lasted five decades. It also, in part, influenced me into becoming a soldier, a decision that ultimately resulted in a 30-year career in uniform. I met the gifted co-author of this book, Gary Bloomfield, while we were assigned to the same unit in 2002. Gary always had some literary project going (maybe three or four at the same time), with an eye for anything else which would just pop into his head. Gary, along with several others of the unit met with me occasionally to talk of Custer, and in time the group came to be known as the "Kansas City Chapter of the Custer Literary Society." I had started to write a book called "The Little Bighorn: Lost, Found, and Remembered," but did not get past a few chapters. I was reassigned to battalion command a few states away and it was not long before I lost focus and the book fell away, the victim of a busy schedule. Years passed, and sadly we lost one of the members of the literary society. I retired from the Army and moved onto an unexpected second career. Time is still short, but a little over 4 years ago, I met with Gary for lunch and my father came along. Unknown to me, Gary and my father spoke about my long-lost literary effort, and the need to get me moving. In 2017, Gary called me about collaborating on a Custer biography, and away we went. It was the twist of fate meeting, and Gary's offer of encouragement which brought this Custer biography to life.

I have had the good fortune to have been stationed at military posts throughout the American west including both Fort Riley, Kansas, and Fort Leavenworth, Kansas, home to the 7th Cavalry during different points in their history. In addition, my position while assigned to Army Recruiting required my travel throughout Kansas to many of the locations (now communities) where frontier forts once existed and were garrisoned by the 7th Cavalry. Two of these forts, Fort Larned and Fort Hays, bear a strong resemblance to their previous existence, and for the student of history, are well worth the visit, walking the grounds, seeing the terrain as it existed more than 150 years ago. Crisscrossing Kansas gave me an appreciation for the environmental demands placed on Indians and the frontier Army who both traveled the area and called it home. Driving in the early morning or twilight, it was not difficult to place myself back in time to the 1860/70s, alone with the lonesome landscape and with my thoughts, imagining myself as a cavalry officer back then. The first thing I noticed was the constant wind, ever-present, and creating a "dancing" movement on the brown prairie grass. Miles and miles of an endless sea of grass in every direction punctuated occasionally by a grove of cottonwood trees announcing the location of a water source. Civilization (now as then) lay a considerable distance apart, often a hundred miles or more. I grew up riding horses, but the thought of riding them for 30–50 miles a day, and for weeks on end on the Kansas landscape was a sobering thought. It was very easy to relate to the challenges of the cavalry and their leadership in this environment and the limited support available to them. As a former Army platoon leader, company commander, and battalion commander, I could easily understand Custer's challenges in maintaining unit cohesiveness in such an environment. Having spent so much time studying Custer over the years, it was an important link to know and understand his feelings at the time.

Likewise, I have made a number of trips over the years to the Little Bighorn National Monument. Each visit had a powerful effect on me because it is both battlefield and cemetery. It is indeed unique, as each headstone placed there closely approximates where a soldier fell and was buried after the battle. For me, the stones represent the "breadcrumbs" of Custer's five companies. In 1996, I hosted a staff ride for leaders of my unit at the Little Bighorn. A staff ride is a military walk of the terrain to better understand the events of a battle. In preparation for the visit, I had the assistance of the National Park Service and their interpretative thoughts of the fight. Together, the blend of park service personnel and the views of Army leaders provided an interesting contrast and confluence of ideas. It was a great experience and we all took away something new. I left there forever changed though. In my mind, I could see the vividness of events as they occurred, the desperate movements of the combatants, the terror of the horses, all wrapped up in an environment of swirling dust, gunfire, smoke, and noise. There was no mystery about those tragic moments, just the latent images of a fight that had ended 130 years previous. It was powerful and it was a capstone event for my understanding of George Custer.

It is a fair question to ask—why do another biography of Custer? Hasn't every bit of material been covered? The answer will always be no. The irresistible enigma of the Little Bighorn has taken care of that, and someone will always seek to answer it. Further, a new generation is always being introduced to the story for the first time. Information old and new is continually being uncovered. In 1984 a wildfire burned off the vegetation on large portions of the battlefield including the Custer battalion area. The resulting bare ground left some artifacts exposed and offered an opportunity to conduct a comprehensive survey. The results were stunning, and subsequent archeological work launched an entirely new perspective on the science of the record exposed. The scholarship evolved has raised new theories and questions about many widely accepted conclusions. Both old scholarship revisited, and new being written, will continue to add clues. Why did Custer make his decisions, and when? What was he thinking in those last critical moments? The quest to know will never end.

Custer's meteoric rise as a leader during the Civil War is so extraordinarily remarkable, it simply is without equal. No other military leader in American history has accomplished more so early in his life and career, and to a greater end. General

Phil Sheridan, Custer's immediate superior at wars' end, could not have been more correct in writing to Custer's young wife Libbie about her husband's performance, "Permit me to say, Madam, that there is scarcely an individual in our service who has contributed more to bring about this desirable result [Confederate surrender] than your gallant husband." Custer was a real, authentic, national hero. He was idolized by the men he led and celebrated in the press. He led from the front, endured incredible dangers, and most importantly, survived. Few Americans or anyone abroad can fully appreciate what an astonishing leader Custer was during the Civil War, and his story has continued meaning in study today. Few leaders survived the war if it began for them in 1861, especially with the kind of action Custer was exposed to. He brought about remarkable changes in the employment of cavalry, the impact of which has continued tactical meaning contemporarily. Plainly, he was extremely fortunate to have survived and his record was authentic—he was the real deal.

This book attempts to bring to readers his deep thoughts and his relationship with Libbie and others. His actions and behaviors, like his tremendous rise in the Civil War to his personal failures which led to court-martial in Kansas, are contrasts so cavernous they defy understanding. Yet, his successes and failures are also amazingly human and relatable. Our attempt in this work is to put the reader there in time and circumstance, to understand the pressures and influences, to be in love and a newlywed, a young man consumed in it all. Custer was totally crushed mentally from the rigors of the campaign, after watching the disintegration of his command, contrasting with the adoration of the American public just a year before. The dichotomies of his life beg explanation.

Of course, every influence and experience in Custer's life was woven into the fabric of his soul, and present to guide his decisions upon his arrival to the Little Bighorn. How did Custer's influences play in the events of the day? Were events influenced by others and how? Was Custer failed by others, or did Custer's luck run out? The five decades of Custer study, and 30 years' experience in the military provide essential assistance. This book attempts to bring insight to the mystery of that day in June of 1876, and Custer's thoughts and experiences are at the center of understanding the events as they occurred. Custer's actions could never be the ultimate answer however, but when combined with cavalry tactics at the time, the personalities of those involved and the dynamic actions of the Indians opposing him, it is much easier to draw the kaleidoscope into focus.

We have been greatly assisted in our work by the use of many sources which are well over 140 years old and contemporary to the events of the time. These numerous sources, like newspaper articles, periodicals of the time like *Harper's Weekly*, and older publications by participants in events, capture what time has forgot, providing the facts and views of the time the way the authors remember them. They are a treasure trove of American culture and necessary to grasp the true nature of events and personalities of the time. Further, our efforts were assisted by letters and official correspondence of the time. George and Libbie's letters in particular, taken from multiple sources, show the endearing intimacy and challenges the couple faced at the time, right up to George's death at the Little Bighorn.

Ted Behncke
Lieutenant Colonel,
US Army, Retired

Brigadier General George Armstrong Custer, the Civil War's "Boy General." (National Archives)

Dare-devil of the class!

JOSEPH PEARSON FARLEY, U.S. ARMY, 1902

There was in him an indescribable something—call it caution, call it sagacity, call it the real military instinct—it may have been genius.

COLONEL J. H. KIDD, *PERSONAL RECOLLECTIONS OF A CAVALRYMAN WITH CUSTER'S MICHIGAN CAVALRY BRIGADE IN THE CIVIL WAR,* 1908

Keeping within the regulations, Custer managed to produce one of the most brilliant and showy dresses out of this hideous uniform.

FREDERICK WHITTAKER, 1876

This officer is one of the funniest-looking beings you ever saw, and looked like a circus rider gone mad!

COLONEL THEODORE LYMAN, *MEADE'S HEADQUARTERS, 1864–1865,* 1922

Custer might not well conduct a siege of regular approaches; but for a sudden dash, Custer against the world.

COLONEL FREDERIC NEWHALL, *WITH SHERIDAN IN LEE'S LAST CAMPAIGN,* 1866

General Custer, who at the outbreak of the war ranked as first lieutenant in the Fifth Regular Cavalry, and has now probably the stars of a major general within his reach, is only twenty-four years of age, and a splendid specimen of the finished soldier.

NEW YORK HERALD, OCTOBER 26, 1864

Throughout the Army as well as among the people, the dashing and never-failing Custer is regarded as the Murat of the war, and well has he earned the title. Ohio has reason to be proud of many things—not least should she be proud of her golden-haired Custer—the full Major General at twenty-six—the right arm of Sheridan—the glory of the old Third Division.

THE CLEVELAND MORNING LEADER, 1865

Although young in years, Custer has fairly won enduring honors as a cavalry leader in the war of the Rebellion; and I hesitate little in saying, that if his life is spared and our country should become involved in another war, the American people may expect to hear again of this promising young officer.

C. J. WOOD, *REMINISCENCES OF THE WAR,* 1880

Introduction

George Armstrong Custer was part of a blended family. Both of his parents had been married previously and had children, so young Autie, as everyone called him, was the center of attention, his eccentricities and tantrums tolerated by his older step-siblings and overlooked by his doting parents. His two younger brothers, Thomas and Boston, were often victims of his outbursts, or co-conspirators in his mischievous bent which was certainly well known, as recalls the minister who wished young Autie found another place to worship: Young Georgie was "the instigator of devilish plots both during the service and in Sunday school. On the surface he appeared attentive and respectful, but underneath, the mind boiled with disruptive ideas."

Not one to leave anyone guessing as to who the culprit was, he boasted of his mischievous deeds, relishing the limelight of notoriety. It was a character flaw—this craving for the spotlight, unwilling to share it with anyone—which cast a long shadow behind him all his life, from unanticipated glory during the Civil War to his tragic demise on the plains of the far west at just 36 years of age.

Despite his Democratic leanings, young Custer asked Republican Congressman John Bingham for an appointment to West Point, which he initially denied, but then granted a year later. There is some evidence this was for a dalliance Custer had with the daughter of Bingham's friend, who had learned of the dandy's desire to attend West Point. The concerned father sought to protect his daughter's reputation, and jumped at the opportunity to get young Custer out of town, as quickly and as far away as possible. He entered West Point in 1857 as an eighteen-year-old probie, just as mischievous and unruly as ever, and never really got out of the doghouse.

Cadet George Armstrong Custer racked up more than 700 demerits at West Point and was threatened with expulsion every year he was there. Known for thumbing his nose at authority and playing pranks on his fellow cadets—some might remember being smeared by his antics, guilty by association—no one considered him officer material, let alone an eventual graduate, distinguished or otherwise. In fact, his only real achievement, after four less-than-stellar years at the military academy, was anchoring his class, by placing last out of 34 graduates ... though it should be noted that at the time, with escalating tensions between the North and South, many of the cadets with Confederate loyalties left West Point when the southern states seceded from the Union, shortly after Abraham Lincoln's election, so there is a miniscule possibility that Custer might have beaten one or two of them in the final class rankings. It can be said that of the loyal Union cadets who remained in school, he was a distant also-ran.

While at West Point, Custer befriended several southern cadets, and participated in spirited debates, without animosity, often sympathizing with their grievances. And even after they stated their intentions to join the Confederate cause, he wished them well in their endeavors, sensing they might one day meet on some future battlefield. This premonition came true on more than one occasion, and Custer's compassion for his former classmates would often influence his actions when he became aware of their presence opposing him. Conversely, when his Rebel counterparts realized who they were fighting, many could not believe the brash Autie Custer, who barely made it at West Point, was now leading the Union cavalry against them.

Confederate and Union forces were enlisting regiments of 1,000 men in the states. They were volunteers, not professional soldiers, and their officers were likely

With war threatening to tear the country apart, men from all walks of life gathered outside recruiting offices to enlist. Some states, such as New York, offered additional cash incentives to bolster their local volunteer and militia units. Initially, many signed up for 90-day terms, but as the war dragged on, new recruits, such as these in early 1864, signed on "for the duration." (Public Domain)

to be political appointments. What were in short supply however, were officers with professional training. Both sides desired the graduates of the various military schools, such as Virginia Military Institute and the Citadel, but also the Naval Academy at Annapolis and West Point. In a short time, this meant the early graduation of classes including West Point. Cadet George Armstrong Custer would become a lieutenant one year early, in 1861.

And this is how George "Autie" Custer went from being a cadet with more black marks on his transcript than exemplary evaluation reports, to become a lieutenant in President Lincoln's Union Army.

Initially, patriotic fervor and the thrill of being bloodied in battle spurred hundreds of thousands of volunteers to swear their allegiance, to leave home and take up arms, for whichever cause they believed in, a cause that sometimes splintered families— fathers against sons, brothers against brothers—especially in the border states.

After proving himself in a few "right place at the right time" moments, Custer was given command of the Michigan Brigade, vaulting over several other senior and seasoned officers, who questioned who this brash upstart was, especially as someone who was last in his graduating class at West Point. And as that less than stellar fact spread through the ranks, they questioned if this dandy was qualified to even join their unit, much less lead them into battle.

A quick assessment revealed that three of the four regiments were filled with green, untested troops, who were already second-guessing their hasty, patriotic decision to enlist. Now they wondered who this Custer fellow was. It was a combination that could only lead to disaster.

Then when the first volleys and artillery barrages cut into their ranks, the thrill of battle suddenly wasn't quite so thrilling, and many of those untested soldiers on both sides tossed aside their rifles and skedaddled for the hills, never to be seen again.

He may not have cracked the books as faithfully as he should have at West Point, but that rapscallion George Armstrong Custer realized his troops needed a leader who could turn their hesitancy, their trepidations to invincibility. Officers with more seniority than Custer provided stability but rarely victory. Safely comforted in the rear, they reacted tediously slowly to events unfolding at the front. And when they did make decisions, they were more likely defensive in nature than taking some initiative. They were rarely offensive in their tactics, a cavalry staple. Custer would change that. He always led from the front.

With the dash and swagger of a musketeer, he mounted his steed, drew his sabre and galloped up and down the line, encouraging them to follow him into battle. With his long blond locks flowing, an oversized wide-brimmed hat and red silk scarf, and slashing that gleaming sabre, he was quite an inspiring sight ... and a tempting target to enemy snipers. And more than often his horses were shot out from under him. But his swagger inspired his troops to follow his lead, with a remarkable first victory at Gettysburg, and then virtually unchecked in every

In the early battles of the Civil War, the Confederate cavalry clearly had the upper hand, and it was rare that the Union cavalry could surprise Rebel guerrillas harassing their pickets and outposts, shown here. When the Union Army's Cavalry Corps was organized, Custer always had the advance, and quickly became a national hero for his exploits. (November 15, 1862 issue of *Harper's Weekly*)

campaign he was involved with. Along the way, he created his own battle flag, and mustered a field band. "Who the hell does these things," his rivals in both the Union and Confederate armies were left to wonder? His men and the press grew to love and admire him. He was, at his core, a romantic and this theme prevailed in most of his actions throughout his life.

In the *Army and Navy Journal*, 29 July, 1876, General A. B. Nettleton recalled the impact and influence Custer had in Civil War battles: "It must be remembered that in fighting with cavalry, which was Custer's forte, instantaneous quickness of eye—that is, the lightning-like formation and execution of successive correct judgments on a rapidly shifting situation—is the first thing, and the second is the power of inspiring the troopers with that impetuous yet intelligent air with which a mounted brigade becomes a thunderbolt, and without which it remains a useless mass of horses and riders."

Custer sometimes questioned his longevity, especially after so many narrow escapes, cheating death, sometimes by inches, or seconds. Twice wounded, it was only a matter of time …

But with audacity and a devil-may-care attitude, and reporters documenting his every move and filling in the blanks with unbelievable exploits, Custer quickly became a celebrity, a darling, outrivaling his contemporaries, his superiors, and even such luminaries as Ulysses S. Grant, Robert E. Lee and Abraham Lincoln. After being promoted to brigadier general in June 1863, reporters dubbed him "The Boy General." Jealous rivals called him other things but he was oblivious to their jabs. Beyond their envy though, he was the genuine article.

He became so addicted to the adoration and the adrenaline rush of skirmishing, that Custer declared, "I would be willing, yes glad, to see a battle every day during my life." For Custer, the Civil War ended with Robert E. Lee's surrender at Appomattox. It was Custer, as a two-star cavalry general, who accepted the Confederate surrender flag—actually just a white rag—only fitting since he had captured the first battle flag a few years earlier at Bull Run.

While others might discredit his accomplishments as merely the "power of the press," Custer's Civil War exploits as a cavalry officer were truly unmatched. In his book *A Complete Life of General George A. Custer*, Frederick Whittaker wrote, "The best cavalry leader America has ever produced, is the only truthful verdict that experience can pass on him: a great cavalry leader for any time or country, history will finally pronounce him; worthy to stand beside Hannibal's thunderbolt Ilago; Saladin, the leader of those 'hurricanes of horse' that swept the Crusaders from Palestine; Cromwell, Seydlitz or Zieten; a perfect general of horse."

If George Armstrong Custer, the boy general, had sheathed his sabre and furled his guidon after Appomattox, returned home to Monroe, Michigan to write his memoirs and live happily ever after, he may in fact have gone down in history as one of America's greatest cavalry generals. He would be toasted and celebrated until his dying day as a Civil War hero. Instead, he chose to remain in the Army and pursue other adventures, wherever he was needed, looking for the next great battle. Tragically that decision—despite opportunities to run for Congress, to become a successful horse breeder, even to be a foreign envoy to Mexico—led to a legacy that wasn't just dragged through the mud. It was ripped to shreds and to this day is still remembered with disdain, disgust and derision.

CHAPTER I

From Boyhood to West Point

George Armstrong Custer … was very intelligent, and, from his earliest years, appears to have had an inclination towards military life.

W. SANFORD RAMEY, *KINGS OF THE BATTLE-FIELD*, 1887

Years before being selected as a probationary cadet at West Point, young George "Autie" Custer was a "soldier" with the New Rumley Invincibles, a contingent of the Ohio Militia. He may have been only four years old, accompanying his father Emanuel to monthly drills, but Autie could mimic the various facing movements—forward march, about face, present arms, parade rest—with enthusiasm and precision. He even had his own toy musket and velvet uniform, with maybe a little extra gold braid and brass buttons, but he loved it, strutting around with a swagger that he never quite outgrew, and all of the militia members looked at him as the unit's mascot. Some of them were veterans of the Mexican–American War of 1846 to 1948. No one could imagine that in less than 20 years, he would become known as the boy general—the most famous and infamous hero of the Civil War. The origins of both his desire for notoriety and for a bit of theater were already present in his early youth.

With two younger brothers and a sister, Autie was the self-appointed ringleader of a band of pranksters, with their blacksmith father often one of the instigators. And when he wasn't an active participant in the kids' latest antics, their father was susceptible to being the brunt of the joke. This mischievous bent was another trait Autie Custer never abandoned, and it would often get him into trouble with his teachers at various schools, his ministers, his professors.

At West Point, he was in constant trouble for his shenanigans and, on the rare occasions when he wasn't working off his demerits, everyone wondered what mischief he was planning next. Custer liked the attention and his ebullient personality had the ancillary effect of popularity. It was difficult not to like him and he became a class favorite.

Even during the Civil War, he thumbed his nose at authority and military decorum and exasperated both his Union Army commanders and his Confederate rivals with his audaciousness.

His thoughts about being a certain kind of leader were seeded quite early and can clearly be seen emerging at West Point and during the Civil War. He would be brave, fearless, audacious, and clear of mind when decisions had to be made. There was definitely a template in Custer's mind, one that came with some deep thought, maybe assisted by all the time spent walking off demerits. Some were quite surprised by his uniform and seasoning as a brigadier general at the young age of 23, but Autie was just displaying what he had prepared for all his young life up to that point.

Young Autie didn't want to be just any soldier. He yearned to be a cavalry officer, riding a glorious steed into battle, slashing his gleaming sword and vanquishing his enemy. Wishing to please the pugnacious Autie, one time his older sister lassoed a heifer on the family farm and plopped him down on its back, only to be promptly bucked off and dumped in the dirt, leaving a permanent scar on his forehead, a "war wound"—the first of several he could impress future young ladies with from his feats of dash and daring. It was also the first of many times he would be tossed from his mount, in battle during the Civil War, on the hunt for buffalo on the great Plains, and while chasing and being chased by Indians.

But that minor mishap with an uncooperative calf didn't dampen his desire for military service. Frederick Whittaker, in his biography *A Complete Life of General George A. Custer*, wrote: "Even then, he had made up his mind to go to West Point when he was old enough. One thing that tended to inflame his martial spirit in those days, was the Mexican War, just then closed. The heroes of that war were almost all West Pointers, and the little regular Army made a very considerable figure therein. However that may be, he had formed the firm resolve to go to West Point when old enough."

Although Autie had a devoted mother, his older half-sister doted on him more. Lydia Ann, 14 years his senior, fell in love, got married and moved to Monroe, Michigan. Soon after that, she convinced her father that maybe the mischievous Autie would do better living with her. She loved and coddled him, when tough love and discipline would have served him better. During the summers he returned to the family farm in New Rumley. For Autie, the change of environs at the New Dublin School in Monroe only gave him new victims for his pranks. By 1855 he was a student at the prestigious Alfred Stebbins Young Men's Academy in Monroe, then it was back to Harrison County in Ohio to finish high school, leaving a trail of broken hearts wherever he alighted between Michigan and Ohio. He had a considerable reputation early on as a ladies' man. He was tall with a strong physique, plus his golden hair, blue eyes, and mischievous charm made him irresistible to almost every girl who came to know him.

In 1856 he was taking classes at McNeely Normal School in Hopedale. McNeely was the first co-educational teachers' college in eastern Ohio. There were plenty of available young ladies, distracted by his attention, which the few men there took notice of. In fact, one former classmate remembered Autie Custer as being

George Custer's boyhood home in New Rumley, Ohio. (New Rumley Historical Society)

kind and generous with those in his inner circle of friends and associates; but bitter and implacable to those he considered his rivals and enemies. Again, traits of the boy which would accompany him into manhood. He would always have his favorites.

With puberty raging, and a bevy of young ladies vying for his attention, the frisky Autie Custer took advantage of the opportunity. But long before any thoughts of married life, young Autie had other aspirations, some carnal, some career-advancing.

After graduating from the McNeely School later that year, and despite teaching credentials to fall back on, Custer hadn't given up on his childhood dream to join the military. But wanting to go to West Point and actually getting there wasn't as simple as hitting the books and getting good grades. It required a nomination by a member of Congress and unfortunately for Custer, whose father was a staunch Jacksonian Democrat, the senator in his district was a hardline abolitionist Republican. Emanuel Custer refused to reach out to fellow Ohioan John Bingham, a junior senator from the fledging Republican Party, which was ramping up for the forthcoming presidential campaign. Appointments to West Point were often used as political favors and, as such, every Republican member of Congress used the nomination to reward their party's supporters.

Still, falling back on his charms of persuasion, Autie Custer figured all he needed to do was prove to Senator Bingham that he was not just a worthy candidate, but the best one, who would excel at West Point if simply given the opportunity. Unfortunately Senator Bingham had already selected another young man for nomination and his second slot was promised to another young man, but young Custer did not give up his quest. He would keep pestering the senator, hoping to eventually win him over.

Despite his persistence, Custer could not secure Senator Bingham's consent and he would have to wait until the following year to try again.

In the meantime, falling back on his teacher's certificate, he took a job as principal of a school in Athens, Ohio. During the spring semester of 1856, Custer was back at McNeely to complete his teaching credentials, then he took a teaching position in Cadiz Township; all of this while waiting a year to ask Senator Bingham for that West Point appointment. To save on room and board, he rented a log cabin, owned by Alexander Holland, the superintendent of a local infirmary and the father of a flirtatious teenage daughter, more than willing to spend time with their handsome new boarder, who all the school girls were infatuated with. Often that alone time was in the mid afternoon, when Autie dashed back to his cabin, and before Mr. Holland came home from work. What started as simple flirtations quickly blossomed to talk of marriage with Mary Jane "Mollie" Holland. She was only 15 and Autie was 17, and when he couldn't explain how he felt, Autie wrote poems and love letters instead, concluding one with "Farewell my only love until we meet again from your true and faithful Lover, 'Bachelor Boy.'" A few days later, he sent Mollie another quick note: "You occupy the first place in my affections and the only place as far as love is concerned … If any power which I possess or control can aid in or in any way hasten our marriage it shall be exerted for that object." Maybe they were in love, but he was writing similar letters and poems to other girls and they all thought they were his one true love.

Whether he discovered one of these love notes to his daughter, or heard about a rumored romp on a trundle bed, or possibly witnessed something he felt was inappropriate, Mr. Holland sought to end things before it went too far. First he kicked Autie Custer out of the log cabin, but true to his nature he simply found another place close by and continued to see Mollie Holland. Then her father found out that young Custer was trying to go to West Point, so he reached out to Senator Bingham and asked him to expedite the nomination.

As soon as the window for nominations opened, Custer reached out again to the senator, unaware that Mollie Holland's father had already sought to have his selection to West Point expedited. Frederick Whittaker, in his biography of Custer, wrote: "That summer of '56, Mr. Bingham came home at the close of the session of Congress, and young Custer went to see him. The result of the interview was that Bingham, pleased with the frank face of the boy, his modest determination, and something in his looks that told him he would yet be a credit to his nominator, promised that he would give him the next year's vacancy, and Custer went home happy." He would report to West Point in June 1857. There is some debate as to whether Senator Bingham was in fact impressed with Custer's "modest determination" or if Mr. Holland had had an influence on his decision.

Young Autie Custer wanted more than anything to be a cavalry officer, much like General Zachary Taylor at the battle of Resaca de la Palma, during the Mexican War. (National Archives)

At this point it would have been prudent for Autie Custer to distance himself from his family's political views, especially since they were diametrically opposite of Senator Bingham's. Instead, as the debate about pro- and anti-slavery state expansion raged in Congress and the newspapers, Autie participated in a public demonstration over the hostilities between Missouri and Kansas, and the many clashes involving "border ruffians." Custer's unwise participation in this event—and choosing a pro-Democratic position over a Republican one that would have clearly put him more firmly in line with Senator Bingham's good graces—would become a detrimental trait demonstrated time and time again throughout his life. Senator Bingham was cautioned about Custer's involvement and was displeased with the news. And yet, one of the senator's constituents and friends was asking him to nominate Custer for appointment to West Point—Mr. Holland became aware that cadets at the military academy could not be married, so if this Custer character was accepted, his daughter would be "safe" for the next five years, and hopefully this marriage nonsense would die a natural death.

In early 1857, Jefferson Davis, the secretary of war, let all members of Congress know who among their many nominees were accepted to West Point. Senator Bingham then reached out to George Armstrong Custer and told him the good news. Custer said goodbye to Mollie Holland, still promising to marry her after he

Ohio Senator John Bingham initially rejected George Custer's request to attend the Military Academy in 1856, then submitted his nomination the following year. Custer reported to West Point in June 1857. (National Archives)

completed his schooling, then embarked on his next great adventure, undaunted by the rigorous academic standards and military decorum demanded of all cadets. Mollie would be forgotten in time, a casualty to his ambition of a soldier.

Custer at West Point

The question was not "Was George Custer ready for the discipline of West Point?" but rather "Was West Point ready for the antics of George Custer?" The boy who attended drill meetings of the New Rumley Invincibles with his father and strutted around the parade field like a peacock; who, with his brothers and father, never missed an opportunity to pull pranks on unsuspecting friends and loved ones, and sometimes each other; and who cared little about applying himself to his studies, always finding out what the minimum requirements were, then barely accomplishing even that, was not about to relinquish any of these tried and true habits, simply because the rigors of West Point demanded something more.

Along with 107 other candidates, Custer arrived at West Point in June 1857. Rigorous examination eliminated more than a third of them, leaving only 67 to begin a six-month probationary period. Frederick Whittaker wrote in his Custer biography: "A great change for the careless young fellow, overflowing with the fun and frolic that comes of magnificent physical organization and keen intellect. There is something in the atmosphere of Western life that seems to rebel against rules and restrictions and everything narrow. With all the differences of race and education, come from the most perfectly republican part of the Union, young Custer was dropped into the midst of one of the most absolute despotisms on earth, the Military Academy at West Point. The poor Plebe comes from the world of freedom, and enters another world, where implicit obedience is the unflinching rule. Instantly, everyone seems to set on him to make his life miserable."

"Side by side stand the lads who have had the most delicate moral nature, or none at all; who are models of truthfulness, or already contrivers of escape from duty and obligations," wrote Joseph Pearson Farley in *West Point in the Early Sixties*, published in 1902. "Every inequality of society is represented in an entering class of cadets. It is necessary to insist upon this point in order to appreciate the results of four years of training. In a few days after entrance, external inequalities vanish as if by magic. Duties, privileges, dress, rooms. Food, all are alike; no one is permitted to have money, or at least to spend it. In a week every sign of external inequality has disappeared. Personal inequalities, of course, there are and necessarily must be."

"Into the midst [of West Point] dropped young Custer. As far as temperament went, he was just the one to get on among his comrades and be happy; and we find accordingly, that he was soon a general favorite," continued Whittaker. "The hardships of Plebe life passed over him lightly. He had the advantage of being a tall strong young fellow, not easily brow-beaten, or physically oppressed, and his good-nature and jolly ways saved him from the more annoying kinds of small persecution." Custer's arrival at West Point and his orientation were experienced by hundreds of newbies—past, present and future—as revealed by Colonel Hugh T. Reed in his book *Cadet Life at West Point*, published in 1896, several decades after his own life as a plebe:

> While one cadet was giving commands with great rapidity, the other one fixed my feet, hands, head and shoulders. "What's your name? Put a Mr. before it. How do you spell it? What's your first name? Spell it. What's your middle name? Have none? What state are you from? What part? Put a sir on every answer. About face! Turn around the other way. Don't you know anything? Now, let's see you about face properly. Steady. At the word about turn on the left heel, turning the left toe to the front, carrying the right foot to the rear, the hollow opposite to and three inches from the left heel, the feet perpendicular to each other. Don't look at your feet. Head up. Stand at attention till I give the command. Now, 'about' (one of the cadets fixed my feet); at the word 'face,' turn on both heels, raise the toe a little, face to the rear, when the face is nearly completed, raise the right foot and replace it by the left. Now, face. Ah! turn on both heels. Draw in your belly. Throw back your shoulders and stand up like a man. Now, left, face. Don't you know your left hand from your right! Face that door; open it. Ah! Why don't you step off with the left foot first? Pick up your things, follow me, and move lively."
>
> All the time that we were in ranks the usual volleys were fired at us, such as: "Eyes to the front. Head erect and chin in." After we were dismissed we were constantly reminded to "carry palms of the hands to the front," notwithstanding the fact that we had been told to go where we pleased for a whole half hour. Some of the candidates went to the sink (i. e., water closet), and some of the old cadets went there, too. A number of them surrounded a poor candidate, called him a plebe or an animal, and fired dozens of questions at him at once. The madder the plebe got the more fun it was for the old cadets.

After physicals, many candidates didn't make the cut, but for those who remained, the verbal barrage of correction after correction from upperclassmen was relentless, and none of the plebes—certainly not George Custer, who didn't take much of anything too seriously—escaped notice. Even the sanctity of their barracks room was ripe with opportunity to do something wrong or put something in the wrong place, and even the most insignificant item—a speck of dust, a smudged window, a wrinkled sheet—attracted attention. And heaven help any cadet who needed a second correction.

Representing all walks of life, nominees arriving at West Point begin to wonder what they had gotten themselves into within minutes of getting there. (West Point Archives)

The "Blue Book" (and other guides such as "Regulations of the U.S. Military Academy") shows the arrangement of rooms, and the exact placement of clothes, necessities, etc. Literally, everything had its place and if it wasn't in the book then it was considered non-essential.

Soon after arriving at West Point, the plebes were pitching tents for the corps of cadets' summer encampment, in July and August. Located in the open expanse where the old Revolutionary War's Fort Clinton once stood on the Hudson River, the camp ground consisted of white tents, in eight rows, ramrod straight, perfectly aligned, pitched over wood slat floors, with woollen blankets for their bedding. "About two weeks after I reported we were directed to prepare to go to Camp McPherson, a half mile or so from Barracks, out beyond the Cavalry plain, near old Fort Clinton," wrote Colonel Hugh T. Reed. "The Yearlings and first classmen, began to take a greater interest in the plebes than ever." Often that "greater interest" took the form of yelling at the newbies at every opportunity, because no matter what they did, it would be wrong.

For many of the young cadets, it was the first time they'd been away from home; first time sleeping under the stars, and without a cushy bed and feather pillow to nestle into until the midday hours of a lazy summer morn. No sir, no mollycoddling for this bunch. Reveille was promptly at 0500 hours, giving them only six minutes to get dressed, perform their ablutions and morning toilet, then scramble to company formation. Roll call, policing of the grounds, breakfast, drills, endless

Plebes arriving at West Point in June endured two months of camp life before moving into the barracks. (West Point Archives)

drills, corrections after corrections, demerits for every infraction, even the smallest of infractions. One former plebe even joked "If my hat or even my head was falling off, I would have no right to raise my hand to save it. Heaven forbid, that would be another infraction, for not asking permission first."

Lunch was inhaled while seated at attention, then there was more policing of the grounds, marching or running everywhere, drill after drill, supper, formation, fall-out, tattoo at 2130 hours, and finally, lights out. Day after day, same routine, same torments. It didn't take long for Custer to start collecting his share of demerits, mostly for lateness and "slothfulness." He did notice that several of the older cadets would sneak out of the encampment after lights out and imbibe on the free-flowing liquors and brews in Buttermilk Falls, a popular watering hole a mile south of the school. He also noticed that those who got caught received severe punishment, some even cashiered without arbitration or appeal.

"This seems hard," he wrote home, "but military law is very severe and those who overstep its boundaries must abide the consequences." An ironic insight, especially from someone vying to rack up more demerits than any cadet before or since!

At the end of August, all of the cadets—plebes and upperclassmen—were given their room assignments, leaving camp life behind, at least until the next summer. With fall, studies and classwork, recitations and exams took over, with the day beginning long before the sun made its grand entrance. Frederick Whittaker wrote about the morning routine at West Point:

> A bright flash and a volume of snow white smoke, as the morning gun awakens the echoes. The smoke goes drifting away on the breeze towards the water, and the sharp boom of the gun reverberates from hill to hill all around the bay, ending in a dull grumble far up the river. Simultaneously, the long roll of the drum-corps, mingled with the sweet notes of the fifes, softened by the distance into a strain of perfect sweetness, comes gaily out on the morning air. As the drummers beat the long reveille, Cadet Custer and his room-mate are sleeping, the sound sleep of the tired plebe, in their little room in the North Barrack, when the long boom of the gun comes through the open window. Up they spring. No rubbing of eyes, stretching or yawning. Outside, the reveille is beating, and the fifes are piping sweetly forth the first tune of the three that constitutes the morning call. Each tune lasts about two minutes, and

at the end of six minutes, every cadet knows that the orderly sergeant will be standing on the company parade ground, book in hand, ready to call the roll. Into their clothes as hastily as possible, little time for toilet comforts, and down the barrack staircase send Custer and Parker. As the rollicking notes of the last quickstep are in full progress, they dart to their places, and a moment later reveille ceases.

Plebes—the Fourth Class—studied French, grammar and mathematics; cadets in their second year—the Third Class—endured more mathematics, including analytical geometry and calculus, French and drawing, both the human figure and topography; those in their third year—the Second Class—studied natural and experimental philosophy, chemistry, and drawing. The Fourth Year—the graduating class—studied civil and military engineering, the art of war—including artillery, cavalry and infantry tactics—mineralogy, and geology.

During that first year, as a Plebe at West Point, Cadet Custer would hardly be what any of his instructors or fellow cadets might consider "officer material." In fact, many wished he would be sent home, and he often came very close to accomplishing just that. But when he needed to buckle down and crack the books, and refrain from the antics, he reluctantly did so. It came to be a pattern seen again and again throughout his years, a strategist regarding what needed to be done and when, and an economy of effort in doing so. He did what was necessary when he had to, but only what was necessary, to not waste effort. While not seemingly connected or associated with his later military success it was exactly these attributes that made him a successful cavalry leader.

"Loaded down with demerit marks" might be a slight understatement, but in fact on numerous occasions, Cadet Custer was on the verge of dismissal, due to exceeding the allowable limit, but always managed to curtail his mischievous antics long enough to see the numbers eventually fall within a manageable amount, thus allowing him to continue tormenting his underclassmen. To be fair, it's actually easier to accumulate demerits at West Point than it is to maintain a spotless record.

J. H. Colton, in *A Guide Book to West Point and Vicinity*, explained that "Offences are classed in seven grades of criminality, bringing from 1 to 10 demerits. For example, an absence from reveille rollcall, is 3 demerits. Introducing spirituous liquors into barracks, is 8 demerits. Disobedience of the orders of a military superior is 8 demerits. The cadets are forbidden to have or to use intoxicating drinks, tobacco, or cards. The following things are prohibited under severe penalties: all cooking in barracks or in camp; damaging or selling public property; absence from quarters, and visiting in study hours, and at night; answering for another at roll call; encouraging or provoking duels, ungentlemanly conduct; combinations against authority; publishing accounts of the Academy, or of transactions in the Institution; receiving money or supplies from home; absence from duty; neglect of study; disregard of the Sabbath; profanity; taking a newspaper without permission; having other dress than that prescribed; lending accoutrements; throwing anything from the windows and doors in barracks; having a light burning after 10 P.M.; running, loud talking, and scuffling in barracks; receiving strangers in barracks in study hours." Cadet Custer managed to violate most of these guidelines, several of them many times over. In fact, some of his fellow cadets wondered if possibly he intended to violate everything that could be violated, just for kicks. Not only did Cadet Custer fail just about every inspectable item in his barracks room and on his uniform, he even found new ways to rack up demerits, also known as "skins."

But while his fellow cadets often kept their distance, not wishing to be smeared with guilt by association, many also admired his flippant defiance of the rules, and his devil-be-damned attitude toward all things military. Like a typical child who knows right from wrong, and is fully aware of the consequences for doing the latter, Custer was more than willing to do the latter with zeal and zest, knowing he would be walking the square for hours on end as punishment. He also knew that if he racked up too many demerits, he would be summarily dismissed from the Academy. During each six-month period, 100 demerits was the limit—101 meant automatic expulsion.

As an example of Custer's class standing, in January of 1858, due to his exam scores in trigonometry, algebra, geometry and English grammar, combined with his demerits, he ranked 58th in a class of 68. Five months later, six of his fellow cadets had either resigned or been dismissed, leaving Custer close to the bottom and very much in danger of being given a train ticket home.

Even in his final semester—when other West Point cadets had accepted the disciplines required to graduate and become a commissioned officer—Cadet Custer remained ever the rapscallion and racked up another 97 "skins." In total, he achieved the distinction of accumulating more demerits than any other cadet in his graduating class. "Custer's pranks at the Academy were those of a high-spirited boy anxious to escape from restraint, but he was always ready to take the consequences," wrote Frederick Whittaker.

By this time Cadet Custer had survived two years at West Point—barely—and had established quite a reputation for himself, as noted by Basil W. Duke when he recalled his first impressions in *The Southern Bivouac*, in the June 1885 to May 1886 annual issue:

> The rarest man I knew at West Point was Custer. The first time I saw him he was about twenty years of age, and had just returned from furlough. [Between their third and fourth years at West Point, cadets can take a summer vacation or furlough, returning in the fall.] I saw only an undeveloped-looking youth, with a poor figure, slightly rounded shoulders, and an ungainly walk. But this was Custer, then considered an indifferent soldier, a poor student, and a perfect incorrigible, who subsequently developed into a splendidly proportioned man, a brilliant cavalry officer, and a writer of no small literary merit, and an exceedingly interesting narrative style.
>
> It did not take me many days to find out all about Custer ... he had no sooner donned the gray uniform of the corps than he at once dropped back into the roystering, reckless cadet, always in trouble, always playing some mischievous pranks, and liked by everyone, and *noticed*

by everyone. He placed great value in his relationships with others and deeply desired the friendship of others. He spent a lot of energy pursuing those intimate associations.

He was a loyal friend and applied great value to it. He clearly did not value the discipline of West Point and conformance with it. Hence, he spent as little time as necessary to meet it.

We, that is, the plebs of that year, had all been "yunked" by our tormentors of the class just above us until they had grown tired of the sport. As a rule, men of the classes further advanced left the sport to the yearlings, but Custer was of that mischievous, restless disposition that he could not refrain from taking a hand if he thought there was any fun ahead. He was a firm believer, too, in the benefits of "running it" on new cadets.

Custer's course at West Point may be described in the remark that he merely scraped through. He was always loaded down with demerit marks, but was not attentive to his military duties, and he was anything but a good student. He told the public in his *Galaxy* article (years later) that he graduated at the very foot of a large class, and that his record at the Military Academy was valuable only as a warning to young men to avoid his evil ways. But he was always sprightly,

Every item in a cadet's room had a specific place, and daily inspections ensured that they were not violating that requirement. A sloppy room, such as leaving a rifle on the floor, meant demerits and punishments. Cadet George Autie Custer was notorious for failing inspections, thumbing his nose at every rule and, as such, racking up more demerits than any West Point cadet, past or present. (Drawing by Cadet George Derby, West Point Archives)

brave, and popular, and everybody wanted to see him get through. If it had been anybody but Custer, the end of the first half year at the Academy would have found him on his way home … but the fact that he was a graduate no doubt greatly aided his advance at a time when, without such an advantage, he might have been considered simply a brave, daring boy, without any of the qualifications of a commander.

Though his class standing may have wallowed consistently near the bottom of the list, Custer remained a popular cadet among his peers, partly because of his defiance and penchant for instigating trouble, but also, despite the national turmoil simmering between the northern and southern states, he was willing to engage in heated discussions and often sympathized with his brethren from those states south of the Mason–Dixon line. He genuinely liked his fellow southern cadets. He liked the military traditions of the south, as they aligned very well with his own beliefs of chivalry, military pageantry, and loyalty. As tensions rose, he understood his southern friends and could continue the relationship with them when others could not.

"During Custer's cadetship, West Point was the scene of constant debates among the students as to the probabilities of war. Talk of secession was rife, and the cadets from the South lost no opportunity of declaring their intention to fight for their own section, should secession lead to war," wrote W. Sanford Ramey in *Kings of the Battle-Field*. "The matter was, however, discussed in a friendly way, and rarely led to ill feeling." Custer recalled years later:

> I remember a conversation held at the table at which I sat during the winter of '60–'61. I was seated next to Cadet P. M. B. Young [Pierce Manning Butler Young], a gallant young fellow, a classmate of mine, then and since the war an intimate and valued friend. The approaching war was as usual the subject of conversation in which all participated, and in the freest and most friendly manner … Finally, in a half jocular, half earnest manner, Young turned to me and delivered himself as follows: "Custer, my boy, we're going to have war. It's no use talking: I see it coming. All the Crittenden compromises that can be patched up won't avert it. Now let me prophesy what will happen to you and me. You will go home, and your abolition Governor will probably make you colonel of a cavalry regiment. I will go down to Georgia, and ask Governor Brown to give me a cavalry regiment. And who knows but we may move against each other during the war."

During the months leading up to the presidential election in 1860, southern politicians forecast the severe consequences if Abraham Lincoln won, promising to abolish slavery, how it would cripple tobacco and King Cotton, both dependent on slaves to plant, nurture and harvest these vital cash crops. Without slaves, the southern economies would be devastated.

Newspapers from Richmond to Atlanta and Memphis to Nashville railed against Lincoln and fomented talk of breaking away from the Union if he became president. Caught in the maelstrom were West Point cadets, echoing what they heard from back home in letters and newspaper clippings. They pledged their unwavering loyalty to the United States, but if the southern states seceded from the Union, those cadets would be faced with remaining at West Point and fighting against their families and

Cadets Autie Custer and his roommate Thomas Rosser were the best horsemen in their class, mastering the use of the sabre. When the southern states seceded from the Union, Rosser left to join the Confederate army. These two close friends, leading cavalry troops in battle, would meet each other several times in future skirmishes, and the sabre was often the deciding factor in determining the victor. (Illustration from *West Point in the Early Sixties* by Joseph Pearson Farley)

friends, or resign from the Academy and volunteer to take up arms against their fellow cadets from the North.

But it wasn't an easy decision. After several years of rigorous training and classwork, adhering to the disciplines and sacrifices that becoming a West Point graduate entailed, should they cast it all aside so abruptly when they were so close to commencement? Some were only a semester from graduation. Or should they proclaim their true loyalties to the South and hope they still warranted a commission in the newly formed Confederate forces?

It was a fractious time, and the corps of cadets was fragmented by discordant discussions that threatened to escalate into fisticuffs. One night, just before the election, cadets from the southern states hung an effigy of Lincoln outside their barracks, but it was taken down before morning formation. Still, word quickly spread of their stunt, and the dissonant rumblings and threats of war reached a fever pitch when Lincoln, with his vow to abolish slavery, won the election in November 1860.

That same night, Custer wrote a letter to his sister, expressing his concerns: "The election has passed, I fear that there will be much trouble." His fellow cadets from the southern states promptly resigned, as they said they would do if Lincoln won, and they were heading home, sensing that war was soon in coming. "You cannot imagine how sorry I will be to see this happen, as the majority of my best friends and all my roommates except one have been from the South," Custer wrote. Unless the South reconsidered its threat to secede, armed hostilities were inevitable, and Custer feared what it would do to the country. It "would be impoverished. I sincerely hope we may be spared this Sorrow," he wrote.

In January 1861 Colonel Pierre Gustave Toutant-Beauregard of Louisiana was appointed Superintendent of West Point and was immediately confronted by cadets from the southern states, asking him what they should do concerning the impending war. Beauregard himself was cognizant of torn loyalties and advised his young charges, "Don't jump too soon. When you see me go, you go." When Secretary of War Joseph Holt learned of Beauregard's intention to return home, if and when the South seceded, he relieved him immediately. A few weeks later, George Washington's birthday became a flashpoint for the

Cadet George Custer was nicknamed "Fanny" by his friends, due to his baby face. Even during the Civil War, his fellow officers teased him about his girlish looks and flamboyant uniform—that is until they saw him in action. (National Archives)

West Point cadets. They assembled in the Academy chapel and listened to a reading of Washington's Farewell Address to his Troops, November 2, 1783. For the most part, Washington was paying tribute to those he'd served with, but some passages in the speech rankled the southern cadets, who felt it was a direct attack on their loyalty to the United States:

> Who that was not a witness could imagine, that the most violent local prejudices would cease so soon, and that Men who came from the different parts of the Continent, strongly disposed by the habits of education, to despise and quarrel with each other, would instantly become but one patriotic band of Brothers? Or who that was not on the spot can trace the steps by which such a wonderful Revolution has been affected, and such a glorious period put to all our Warlike toils? … unless the principles of the Federal Government were properly supported, and the Powers of the Union increased, the honor, dignity and justice of the Nation would be lost forever; yet he cannot help repeating on this occasion, so interesting a sentiment, and leaving it as his last injunction to every Officer and every Soldier, who may view the subject in the same serious point of light, to add his best endeavors to those of his worthy fellow Citizens towards effecting these great and valuable purposes, on which our very existence as a Nation so materially depends.

By the end of the reading, the southern cadets were livid and only military discipline prevented them from walking out en masse. Since no classes were scheduled for the day, the cadets reassembled in small clusters, to express themselves, discuss the inevitability of war and what "duty to country" meant to them. Cadet George Custer, though clearly a "northerner" by birth, was friends with many of those cadets from the southern states and was sympathetic to their cause. In fact, Custer was billeted with Company D, composed primarily of cadets from the South.

As the day dragged on and the fervor increased in both venom and expression, the West Point band marched across the quadrangle, playing "Washington's March" and "The National Anthem." Cadets from every barracks room threw open the windows and cheered or booed (depending on their allegiance) as the band marched back and forth across the parade ground. In between tunes, one of the southern cadets shouted out "Secession. Secession. Play Dixie!" That cadet was Custer's good friend and roommate, Thomas Rosser, of Virginia. The band ignored his demand, so the southern loyalists sang "Dixie" a cappella, while Custer countered with a boisterous singing of "The National Anthem." It was all good-natured banter with serious undertones reflecting the tenor of the country.

By Inauguration Day on March 4, 1861, there were irreparable divisions within the corps of cadets as those from the South, only weeks from graduating, were faced with the difficult decision to feign their loyalty to the Union or withdraw from West Point and take up arms against their Northern roommates and classmates. "When, finally, the secession ordinance passed, and one by one the cadets from the seceding States announced their intention of leaving the academy, a sense of gravity and gloom was felt among the light-hearted young soldiers," wrote W. Sanford Ramey in *Kings of the Battle-Field*. "Nearly all the Southern students left the academy before graduating." In mid-April, Custer wrote to his sister: "War is the main topic here and I have not thought of hardly anything else. The enlisted personnel (assigned at West Point) were leaving for duty with the army. When war is once begun between the states, it will be beyond the power of human foresight to predict when and where it will terminate or who will be prepared to leave, without graduating, to drill the recruits that would pour into the army in the event of war."

Two days later, in the early morning hours of April 12, Confederate artillery shells rained down on the Union-held Fort Sumter, guarding the approaches to South Carolina's Charleston Harbor. The opening salvo was a clarion call to all Southern loyalists to take up arms. The next day, Secretary of War Edwin Stanton demanded that all of the cadets take an oath of allegiance to the Union. Once again, the cadets were marched into the chapel where the Academy staff was lined up in full dress uniform, to witness the oath. Ten of the southern cadets refused to pledge their allegiance, realizing that many of their fellow cadets had already resigned and departed for the South. The only thing the cadets could agree on was the singing of the hymn "When Shall We Meet Again?" with its lyrics ominously predicting what was about to unfold for these friends, soon to be enemy combatants:

> When shall we all meet again? When shall we all meet again?
> Oft shall glowing hope expire, Oft shall wearied love retire,
> Oft shall death and sorrow reign, Ere we all shall meet again.

By the end of that week, the Union commander at Fort Sumter had surrendered, President Lincoln, only a few months in office, called for volunteers and, at West Point, 37 cadets from the South had cast off their school uniforms and headed home.

Custer's sister wrote back promptly to him, hoping he would not be caught up in the conflict, but he let her know he had reached out to the Ohio governor, offering to command a unit of the state's militia, if the secretary of war granted permission to do so. He wrote back to her: "I would not ask for a leave when all are needed. It is my duty to take whatever position they assign me. It is useless to hope the coming struggle will be bloodless or of short duration. Much blood will be spilled and thousands of lives, at the least, lost. If it is to be my lot to fall in the service of my country and my country's rights, I will have no regret."

With the rumblings of war dividing the country, and state militias rushing to enlist and train as many eager volunteers as possible, the War Department took the unprecedented step to graduate what was left of West Point's spring 1861 class six weeks early, in May. With an abbreviated but intensive course load, those cadets who would have graduated in June 1862 would be commissioned instead a year early, if they could survive the gauntlet. Custer was among those early graduates, which proved to be his saving grace, because at the rate he was racking up demerits, there was no certainty he could have survived another year at West Point. But those spring classes of 1861 left the sleep-deprived cadets "thin and pale," Custer wrote. If he couldn't make it to graduation, he would certainly be swept up in the impending war, and accepted whatever fate awaited him. "We are anxious to be prepared fully for the duties of our calling," he wrote, but "if it is my lot to fall in the defense of my country's rights, I will lay down my life as freely as if I had a thousand lives at my disposal."

As the May and then the June graduates got their assignments and departed, those left behind were getting anxious to prove themselves in battle. Custer, being the last in his graduating class, had the humiliating task of welcoming the incoming and returning undergrads to summer encampment. On June 29, he was tasked as officer of the day, maintaining discipline, conducting bed checks—recalling when he stuffed pillows under his blankets so anyone looking in would think he was sound asleep, then sneak off to the local village—harassing the plebes, as West Point tradition dictated. Fortunately, those who knew him best, as the biggest buffoon to ever tramp the grounds of the academy, had already graduated and departed.

But on this specific night, two upperclassmen taunted a plebe, who then threatened them with his bayonet. But when the senior cadets walked off, looking for easier prey, the terrified plebe rushed to the guard tent to report the incident to the officer of the day. An indifferent Custer listened to his complaint, recalling all the harassments and indignities he'd had to endure during his first summer engagement. Noticing this, one of the upperclassmen approached, calling the plebe a coward, who had the audacity to then call him a damned fool, instead of just remaining silent. Just that quickly, punches were thrown, as the two stumbled and grappled between the pitched tents. Soon, other cadets gathered round, cheering on the two combatants. Rather than break up the scuffle, Custer advised everyone "Stand back boys. Let's have a fair fight." Eventually the two were separated and the cadets quickly scattered when they spotted two academy officers fast approaching to see what all the commotion was about.

Early the next morning, the commandant, after hearing of the incident, had Custer arrested. A week later, on July 5, a court-martial was held, charging Custer with negligence of duty and "conduct to the prejudice of good order and military

Cadet life at West Point was rigorous, and for Cadet George Custer, graduation was never certain. He racked up more demerits than any cadets in his class, failed tests, cheated on tests, and while other cadets were leaving to join their military units for the impending war, he was being court-martialed while waiting to learn his fate. His one distinguishing accomplishment while at the Point—besides being an excellent horseman—was to anchor the class standings—last in his class. (*Harper's Weekly*)

discipline." He had failed to "suppress a quarrel between two cadets," and in fact, encouraged them to fight.

The two pugilists testified that the incident was little more than a scuffle. In his written statement, Custer considered it a trifling matter. The court saw otherwise and found him guilty of both charges. Possibly in peacetime his punishment would have been more severe, but instead he was reprimanded and the judge advocate noted that "the court was lenient in the sentence, owing to the peculiar situation of Cadet Custer represented in his defense, and in consideration of his general good conduct as testified to by his immediate Commander."

Congressman John Bingham, who had appointed young Custer to West Point just a few years prior, heard about the court-martial proceedings and appealed to

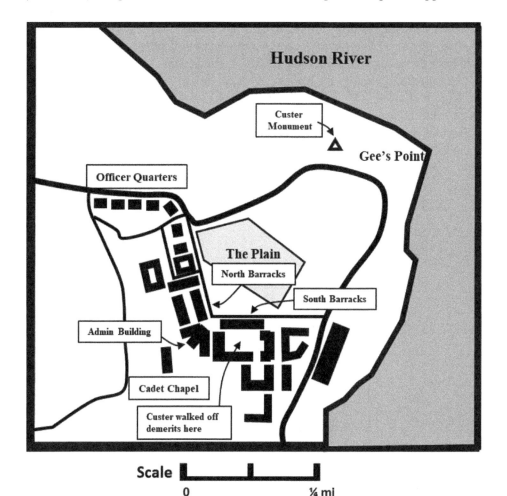

Academy at West Point (main post), 1860. (Map by Ted Behncke)

the War Department, which ordered him to report to DC most promptly. More than a month after his fellow graduates had already left West Point, Autie Custer finally said goodbye. His legacy at the Academy was etched in stone as possibly the worst to ever graduate there. Certainly there were other rapscallions who did worse to disgrace themselves, but they didn't graduate!

"Let us for a moment examine into this phenomenal scholastic performance of Cadet Custer, leading the 'immortals' in a class of one hundred—again of eighty, of sixty, then of fifty, and finally marker of a class graduating with but thirty-four members," wrote Joseph Pearson Farley in *West Point in the Early Sixties*. "Glorious old boy! Dare-devil of the class! How well did you hang on to the tail end—always ahead of the deficients—foot of a class of thirty-four and head of a class of seventy-four."

Later Custer even admitted that possibly his academic achievements were less than stellar. "My career as a cadet," Custer wrote, "had but little to recommend it to the study of those who came after me, unless as an example to be carefully avoided."

He boarded a steamer for New York, where he acquired a lieutenant's uniform, a pistol and sabre, and posed for a photo, which he sent to his sister. He wasn't sure what the future held for him, but young Autie Custer was now free from the rules and rigors of West Point, and was going to make a name for himself, even if it killed him.

CHAPTER 2

The Civil War's Boy General

Custer was the beau ideal of a perfect horseman. He sat in his saddle as if born in it. For his seat was so very easy and graceful that he and his steed seemed one. At West Point he was at the head of all the classes in horsemanship. It is related of him that he could cut down more wooden heads on the gallop than any other one of the cadets.

H. W. BOLTON, *PERSONAL REMINISCENCES OF THE LATE WAR*, 1892

Whacking the heads off stationary dummies while prancing around the West Point training grounds on a majestic stallion was grand sport for the ever-rapscallion "Fanny" Custer—dubbed that by his fellow cadets for his golden locks and feminine good looks—but now he would have to rely on those mock-cavalry drills as a junior officer in the Union Army, knowing he was about to wage war on many of his Confederate classmates, maybe even a roommate or two.

In the coming years, that luck would save Custer's hide—and those of his cavalry troopers who followed him into battle—in many a confrontation with their rebel foes. It was that Custer luck which propelled him to the upper echelons of Army leadership, even skipping a few ranks along the way, aggravating other more experienced but aging officers, who felt they deserved the promotions, without realizing they didn't have the same inner fire which drove Custer from one victory to another, and another.

After weeks of waiting to learn his fate, watching his fellow cadets leaving to join Army units and state militias rapidly expanding their ranks to brace for the impending battles, 2nd Lieutenant George Custer finally had orders to report to the War Department in Washington, DC, in mid-July 1861.

Custer needed a few hours of shut eye and somewhere to prep his new uniform before reporting for duty, so he checked into Ebbitt House, where one of his former roommates was sacked out. 2nd Lieutenant James Parker was glad to see a friendly face, especially since he had recently asked to resign his commission from the Army, to join the Confederate forces amassing near Richmond, a little more than 100 miles south. They wished each other well, both unsure of how they would fare in battle, on opposite sides of the conflict.

Later that day, Custer made it to the War Department, a few blocks from the White House, then sat in the hallway as a steady stream of officers and government officials scurried about. Finally, after hours of waiting, he was ushered in to see the Army's Adjutant General, who started to scribble out orders, assigning him to Company G of the 2nd Cavalry, located at Centerville in Virginia, just east of Bull Run, but then he stopped and asked if this most junior of junior officers would like to meet General Winfield Scott, who had the impossible task of building up the Army and establishing the logistics pipeline to maintain that field force. Everything from weapons and armaments and the various calibers of munitions for each, to uniforms, tents, food, and the means to transport it all were required, and all of his decisions needed to be made weeks ago, before the fledgling Confederacy fired on Fort Sumter and seceded from the Union.

For Custer, he was meeting the hero of the War of 1812 and the Mexican–American War, "Old Fuss and Feathers." As a boy, Custer had listened to veterans in the New Rumley Invincibles, the Ohio militia, many of them battle-tested, talking about Winfield Scott and his exploits. It was then that young Custer, in his pint-sized uniform, dreamed of one day proving himself on some distant battlefield. And now, here he was, about to meet the larger-than-life General Scott, in person. What he didn't know was that he also was about to be thrust into this war splintering the nation.

It was after midnight when Custer was led inside, where he saw General Scott presiding over a gaggle of military and congressional leaders, poring over maps, determining where to position ground forces without verifiable knowledge of where rebel troops were massing near Manassas. Despite the urgency of their strategizing, General Scott stepped aside and met briefly with Lieutenant Custer.

One of General Scott's many concerns was the conscripting and training of thousands of volunteers. Other West Pointers were tasked with training these green troops and so the general asked Custer if he might be willing to fill that vital role. Custer politely declined, wishing to join his unit as soon as possible. The aging general was pleased to hear that, and tasked Custer with finding a horse and reporting back later that night for further instructions.

In the wee hours of the morning, Custer went from stable to stable without success. Not even a flea-bag donkey or sway-backed bag of bones could be found, as every available horse, mule and jackass were mustered to support the war effort. After several hours of frustration, that Custer luck saved him, when he spotted a familiar face, an enlisted soldier who had worked at West Point and was now assigned to an artillery battery near Manassas, which was brewing as the next flashpoint on the battlefield. He too had been in DC looking for horses to pull field guns and caissons. He had a horse and was willing to help Custer with his mission. Together they scoured the city and by seven that night, Custer reported back to the War Department.

General Winfield Scott and his senior officers in 1861. When the southern states decided to secede from the Union, these military leaders had to quickly mobilize the Army, call for volunteers and determine the logistics—food, clothing, weapons, ammunition, transportation, just to name a few of the major issues—in sustaining a field force without knowing how long it would take to quell the rebellion. (Currier and Ives illustration)

"General Scott gave him dispatches to carry to [General] McDowell, then in command of the Army of the Potomac," as it was later reported in *The Cosmopolitan*, in its May to October 1891 issue. Custer "was assigned to duty as lieutenant in the Fifth cavalry and participated on the very day of his arrival at the front in the first battle of Bull Run."

It took all night for Custer and his enlisted companion to get to Centerville, trudging into camp around three in the morning, where General McDowell was preparing to order the attack in a few hours. Custer gave the dispatch he'd been carrying to one of the general's aides, then, hungry and exhausted, he collapsed outside the commander's tent and gobbled down a hasty breakfast of beef and corn bread, before going in search of his unit. The soldiers were already awake and massing for an opening skirmish at Blackburn's Ford—the Union would come to call it Bull Run, while the Confederates called it Manassas.

Bloodied at Bull Run

"On 16 July 1861, the largest Army ever assembled on the North American continent up to that time marched from the vicinity of Washington, DC, toward Manassas Junction, thirty miles to the southwest. Commanded by newly-promoted Brig. Gen. Irvin McDowell, the Union force consisted of partly trained militia with ninety-day enlistments [almost untrained volunteers] and three newly organized battalions of Regulars," wrote Ted Ballard in the Center of Military History's report on the battle of First Bull Run. "Many soldiers, unaccustomed to military discipline or road marches, left the ranks to obtain water, gather blackberries, or simply to rest as the march progressed." General McDowell, who served as a general's aide de camp during the Mexican–American War, was untested in combat. He had gained his current assignment as a political favor from the Secretary of the Treasury, Salmon Chase.

Lieutenant Custer looked around, sleepy-eyed and apprehensive, and as far as he could see, noticed just how undisciplined these conscripts were, thrown into battle with barely a working knowledge of how to fire and reload their weapons, much less how to maneuver as a cohesive unit, or how they would respond to enemy fire, the deafening thunder of massed artillery, the shouting and the screaming and the bugle calls, and the chaos, the sweat and the swirling clouds of dust and smoke, the smell of gunpowder, the sight of soldiers next to them falling, the chaos and confusion of their first taste of battle. Compounding the commitment of thousands of Union soldiers, was the expiration of their 90-day enlistment comrades, on the very day the offensive at Bull Run started. These volunteers were called to arms after the Rebel attack on Fort Sumter in April. President Lincoln was convinced that a decisive victory early on would quell the rebellion, convince the Confederate states that their cause was hopeless, thus restoring the Union, with these patriotic volunteers returning home as heroes. Or so they thought.

Initially, the decision-makers in Washington assumed this rebellion could be put down in a matter of weeks, with a combination of regular Army troops and thousands of the 90-day wonders. But it took that long just to get them into some semblance of a fighting force, outfit them and move into position for the first confrontation with the Confederates, just a day's march from Washington, DC. The Confederates had the nerve to think they could capture DC, and now, here they were, perilously close to achieving just that.

General McDowell expressed his concern about the loss of these temporary soldiers when he wrote to Washington: "In a few days I will lose many thousands of the best of this force." He knew that, without them, his forces may not be able to withstand a Confederate assault on Washington. When his plea for reinforcements was ignored, he turned to the 90-day soldiers and begged them to stay just a few days longer, to put down the rebellion. But their patriotism lasted only as long as they were guaranteed a paycheck, and so, just as enemy guns signaled the start of the battle, thousands of Union volunteers walked away from the fight and headed for home.

Manassas, Virginia was southwest of Washington, DC, approximately 25 miles away. In addition to being situated along a key railway, it was the Confederate army's first line of defense against an attack on Richmond, their "national" capital. The politicians in DC were so confident of a Union victory at Manassas, they had the audacity to muster their friends and family members and converge on central Virginia, for a day-long picnic, and watch the Rebel army get trounced.

From a distance, the Union Army's young conscripts may in fact have looked like an imposing field army, but in reality, they were little more than a rag-tag mob of untested civilians, yearning to taste first blood without themselves getting bloodied. Some wore their state's militia uniforms, in various shades of black, blue, brown and even grey, making it hard to distinguish who was a Union soldier and who was Johnny Reb. The Confederates had this same problem identifying friend from foe, especially in close-quarters combat.

Eventually, around the middle of July, both armies converged on Manassas. Union troops chanted "On to Richmond," confident the war would be over in short order. Because many of the Union forces were outfitted with grey uniforms, McDowell ordered every unit to display the American flag, to prevent them from firing on one another. Resembling unruly mobs, the two sides clashed in a series of attacks and counterattacks, with the Rebels ending up the better, when Union forces withdrew back to Washington.

Possibly a seasoned field force could have carried out McDowell's offensive strategy, but he was dealing with untrained, and undisciplined soldiers, and by the time he realized it, the Confederates had blunted the attack with reinforcements, and thousands of Union soldiers had tossed aside their rifles, and skedaddled to

Union Army commanders expected to easily defeat the rag-tag Confederates at the opening skirmish, at Bull Run, but were stunned by the outcome. President Lincoln and his civilian and military leaders suddenly realized the conflict would last much longer than the few months they initially planned on. (August 1861 issue of *Harper's Weekly*)

safety, to hell with God and country. They left behind several thousand dead and wounded. What started as a Union victory ended with an embarrassing defeat. For the spectators watching the skirmishing from a safe distance, they were soon caught up in the confusion as fleeing soldiers, desperate to get as far away as possible and as quickly as possible, hopped on grazing horses, and piled onto wagons and coaches, leaving the civilians behind to fend for themselves. Back in DC, President Lincoln waited for victorious news from the front. Instead, the news was grim. Jefferson Davis said, "We have won a glorious but dear-bought victory. Night closed on the enemy in full flight and closely pursued."

Lieutenant Custer recalled the chaos at Bull Run, his first experience as a cavalry officer, the Union's first realization that the Confederates could not be so easily defeated. His account of the skirmishing, written in a lengthy letter to his former West Point roommate, Tully McCrea, is filled with the embellishments and exaggerations he would be known for, often veering far afield from the truth. Custer and a former classmate were on a high lookout when they spotted troops approaching and initially thought they might be Union forces, but weren't certain. Part of that confusion was due to the mixture of uniforms, on both sides, the darkness and haze of the morning, the smoke from cannon and rifle fire and the dust from troop and cavalry movement.

> Before doubts could arise, we saw the Confederate flag floating over a portion of the line just emerging from the timber; the next moment the entire line leveled their muskets and poured a volley into the backs of our advancing regiments on the right. I remember well the strange hissing and exceedingly vicious sound of the first cannon shot I heard as it whirled through the air. Of course I had often heard the sound made by cannon balls while passing through the air during my artillery practice at West Point, but a man listens with changed interest when the direction of the balls is toward instead of away from him. They seemed to utter a different language when fired in angry battle from that put forth in the tamer practice of drill.

Anxious to prove himself as a cavalry officer with the 2nd U.S. Cavalry, Lieutenant Custer saw the apprehension in his fellow troopers and attempted to turn the tide, but he deferred to the leadership of his superior, another lieutenant who seemed hesitant to engage with the enemy. Only a few days prior, young Custer had departed West Point and admitted to never having confronted anything more than "a three-foot hurdle, or tried my sabre upon anything more combative than a leather head stuffed with tan bark, it may be imagined that my mind was more or less given to anxious thoughts," knowing his baptism under fire was just moments ahead.

Lieutenant Walker, his fellow officer, had even less experience, having been mustered in from civilian life, with barely a few days' military experience, much less how to handle any sort of weaponry. He asked, "Custer, what weapon are you going to use in the charge?" Custer's weapon of choice was the blade, "in the charge bearing aloft curved sabre, and cleaving the skulls of all with whom came in contact." Their only other choice was the revolver. They both flashed gleaming steel, but halfway up the hill, Custer began to question the decision, and switched over to the pistol. Walker followed suit, but then Custer changed his mind again, still questioning the decision. But before they could be bloodied and taste victory, cries of "We're flanked!" were heard and the raw and untested Union soldiers broke ranks and fled in panic. It was a devastating rout, a decided Confederate victory. "I little imagined when making my night ride from Washington to Centreville the night of the 20th, that the following night should find me returning with a defeated and demoralized Army. Many of the soldiers continued their flight until they reached New York," Custer said. Custer's cavalry unit was tasked with guarding the artillery and, when they beat a hasty retreat, he moved his troopers as a blocking element, a rear guard to blunt any pursuing Confederates. Finally, at Alexandria, the caissons and the field guns were halted, to rest the horses. Pickets were positioned to watch for enemy activity, and Custer hopped off his stallion and found a tree to nestle under. Hours later he woke up, stiff and sore from being in the saddle, for what seemed like a week straight. Just a few days earlier he was itching to get in the fight, confident that he would become the hero he envisioned. But now, after the chaotic and desperate retreat he had just witnessed, Custer wondered if he might end up on the losing side of this conflict, splitting the country in two.

Potential defeat was never mentioned in a letter he wrote to his parents on March 17:

> We followed the retreating Rebel army from Manassas. They had a strong picket posted on a hill about half a mile from us. General Stoneman sent orders to the commander of my regiment to drive the enemy's forces back to their main body … I stepped forward and volunteered to drive away the enemy pickets if I were given enough men. My commander asked how many? I said, "As many as you see fit to give me. Twenty or more." He bade me take my company, about fifty. I took my position in front at a slow trot, so as not to tire horses and men. About halfway I bade the men fire their revolvers. We then took the gallop, and the bullets rattled like hail.

Reality and perception of the truth often got obscured as Custer retold his exploits, whether to an anxious reporter, or to his worried family members. And of course newspaper reports were vastly skewed, depending on their loyalties. Custer noted this in a letter to his half-sister, Mrs. Lydia Ann Reed, on March 28: "They [a Rebel newspaper] say I had 500 men. I had 50. They acknowledge having 300—the number I reported to General Stoneman. They say they killed 40 and took 100 prisoners. The truth is, they shot 3, and took no prisoners."

Bull Run became a disastrous and painful lesson for the Union forces. While the Confederacy could claim victory, they too were able to pinpoint deficiencies which would have to be remedied if they had any chance at ultimate victory.

"First Bull Run demonstrated that the war would not be won by one grand battle, and both sides began preparing for a long and bloody conflict. In the North, Lincoln called for an additional 500,000 volunteers with three-year enlistments, and the men with ninety-day enlistments were sent home," as summarized in the Center of Military History's report on Bull Run. "In the South, once the euphoria of victory had worn off, Jefferson Davis called for 400,000 additional volunteers. The battle also showed the need for adequately trained and experienced officers and men. One year later many of the same soldiers who had fought at First Bull Run, now combat veterans, would have an opportunity to test their skills on the same battlefield."

Convalescence

From his earliest days finagling an appointment to West Point from a rival politician, Custer had an ambitious bent and, after Bull Run, wasted little time securing a position on the staff of Brigadier General Philip Kearny, in charge of the First New Jersey Brigade of volunteers. Dubbed Kearny le Magnifique by the French, for his horsemanship during the battle of Algeria in 1840, galloping into battle with his sabre in his right hand, pistol in his left and the reins clinched tight in his teeth, he later fought in the Mexican War and, during the battle of Churubusco, had his left arm irreparably shredded by grapeshot and had it amputated. Despite his disability, and after the disaster at Bull Run, the hope was Kearny's battle experience and reputation would restore order and discipline to this group of volunteers. Custer was only with Kearny for a short time though. In the fall Custer fell deathly sick, a victim of the rampant diseases raging through many of the encampments, and was hospitalized and sent back to Monroe to recuperate at his sister's home for two months, which was extended another four.

Custer reconnected with the few friends back home who hadn't yet enlisted. As a young officer, and one of the few eligible bachelors, he was a popular guest at many social events in town and attracted the gaze of many young ladies in Monroe. During a night of imbibing hard liquor, while expounding on his brief but heroic war exploits, he got drunk and was spotted staggering down the street by his sister Ann, but others had also spotted him, and gossip quickly spread throughout the town. The next morning, hungover and regretting his transgressions, Custer pledged to never again touch liquor. It would be much harder repairing his reputation as a dandy.

The Virginia Peninsular Campaign

During Custer's absence, the Union Army was radically transformed into a cohesive field force, reconstituted as the Army of the Potomac under Major General George B. McClellan. After Bull Run, both forces regrouped and maintained a defensive posture through the winter months, with the Confederates holding the line near Centerville in Virginia, and Union troops defending DC on the Maryland side of the Potomac River. Union forces had been victorious in other campaigns, such as Missouri, North Carolina and Kentucky, but Virginia held the key to defeating the Confederacy. Failure to capture Richmond had become a double-edged sword for President Lincoln. Not only did it invite criticism of his leadership from northerners, it also bolstered the South's intent to remain defiant and united to secede. With the influx of fresh troops, the lull gave the field commanders time to establish discipline in the ranks, train and hone their battle tactics and prep for the next confrontation. Custer rejoined his unit in February 1862, anxious to get back in the fight.

Another person who was anxious to see some progress made at ending this rebellion was President Abraham Lincoln, badgering McClellan to engage the enemy. But the 35-year-old general known as "the young Napoleon"—who served in the Mexican War and represented the U.S. Army as an observer of the Crimean War—would not be coerced into battle until he felt Union forces were ready, until victory could be assured. Lincoln had put McClellan in charge of the entire Union Army, but after months of postponements, the president reversed course and relieved Mac of overall command, while still allowing him to lead the Army of the Potomac, with the priority to seize Richmond.

Christopher Kolakowski, for the Center of Military History's report on the battle on the Virginia Campaign, March to August 1862, wrote "A superb organizer and motivator of men, McClellan was a vain man and tended to be a secretive and controlling manager. This made for sometimes frosty relations with his superiors in the War Department and with President Lincoln."

The Shenandoah Valley was of vital importance to the south, affording them a clear avenue into Maryland, where they could threaten Washington. McClellan had more than 105,000 troops in early 1862, but the majority of those were untested in battle. Opposing Lil Mac was Major General Thomas "Stonewall" Jackson, his classmate at West Point, who was an instructor at the Virginia Military Institute when hostilities began. McClellan's dual mission was to secure the Valley and if possible, seize Richmond.

The Shenandoah was known as the Granary of the Confederacy, supplying wheat and corn, cows, pigs, and chickens, plus draft animals to haul the caissons and supply wagons. It lies between the Allegheny Mountains on the west and the Blue Ridge Mountains to the east. The valley points like a dagger, from southwest to northeast, aimed at Washington, DC. Without the valley, the Confederacy would not be able to sustain the fight, nor threaten any northward advance.

On March 9, aware that Union forces were about to launch a new offensive, the Confederates around Centerville began pulling back from their winter encampments behind the Rapidan and Rappahannock rivers, where they could better hold the line. The Rebs were dug in, spanning the peninsula from the York and James rivers to the east of Yorktown. General McClellan received reports of the withdrawal and ordered his Union cavalry to mount up and assess exactly where the enemy was positioned.

Lieutenant Custer was among the pursuers and, when they came into contact with the fleeing Rebs, he volunteered to lead a small detachment of 50 troopers to confront the rear-guard pickets. Expecting a small number of Confederates, Custer ordered his troopers to charge, but as they closed the distance, they came under fire, and were faced with approximately 300 Rebel troops who opened up—"the bullets rattled like hail [and] several whizzed close to my head" he would later write to his parents. Clearly outnumbered, he elected to withdraw, with a few of his men wounded. He returned to his unit and informed his commander of his observations, then a hungry press sought him out, eager, after months of nothing, for any news, which he was more than willing to provide.

Those reporters wouldn't have to wait much longer for "action." In a letter to his half-sister, Mrs. Reed, Custer wrote about a typical "skirmish" with the Rebels. "Scarcely ten minutes' interval during the day that the Rebels and our men do not fire at each other. Both parties keep hidden as well as possible, but as soon as either shows itself it is fired at. At night, when it is too dark to shoot or be shot at, both come out of hiding-places, holler at each other, calling names and bragging what they intend to do. Then, when daylight appears, the party which sees the other first, fires, and that puts a stop till night comes, when the same thing is repeated. But we will soon decide the question."

General McClellan was finalizing plans to move more than 100,000 Union troops southward, tasking several hundred steamboats, barges and schooners to lumber down the Potomac River and into Chesapeake Bay with the Army of the Potomac aboard, plus all the horses, field guns, supplies, and accoutrements to effectively wage war, this time with a much-needed victory secured. Their destination was Fort Monroe on the Virginia Peninsula. The journey would take a projected 20 days, sufficient time for Confederate forces to hunker down behind barricades and fortifications to repel any assault. While President Lincoln was fuming about McClellan's deliberations and procrastinations, Lieutenant Custer expressed admiration for his commander in a letter to his parents. "I have more confidence in him than any man that I know. I am willing to forsake everything and follow him to the ends of the world and would lay down my life for him if necessary. He is amongst us now, I wish you could see him, each officer and private worship him, and would fight anyone who would say anything against him."

On March 26, Lieutenant Custer boarded the *Felicia*, moored alongside row after row of vessels, crammed with 120,000 soldiers of the Army of the Potomac, plus everything they would need to sustain the fight. After months of waiting—partially due to the restrictions of winter, but also to reorganize and train—the Union Army was on the move, disembarking at Fort Monroe. The Confederates had been fortifying the peninsula since June 1861 after the battle at Big Bethel. Slaves provided the muscle to prep defensive positions and dam critical waterways to force the Union forces into killing fields. They even built Quaker guns—mock field howitzers fashioned from blackened logs—to fool enemy spotters.

Soon after that Custer was on reconnaissance missions to assess where the enemy was hunkered down. He soon found them, as enemy sharpshooters opened up and he quickly felt the thrill of being shot at. On one occasion he was accompanying Union foot soldiers when the Confederates caught them in the open. Everyone scattered for cover, whether it was a rock, a depression in the dirt, or a sapling. "Everyone got behind a tree and blazed away as hard as he could," wrote Custer. The skirmishing lasted an hour, and many were cut down, then, "I got awful tired of my hiding place." Once reinforcements arrived, the Confederates disengaged. There wasn't much time to tend to the dead, little more than wrapping them in their blanket and burying them there. "It seemed hard," he recalled, "but it could not be avoided. Some were quite young and boyish, and, looking at their faces, I could only think of my own younger brother."

Always one looking for the next opportunity, or another adventure, Lieutenant Custer soon found himself working with Brigadier General William "Baldy" Smith, the Army's chief topographical engineer. Accurate maps were non-existent and Virginia had the potential to become one massive battlefield. It became vital that the Union commanders knew what natural obstacles might hinder their movement, where to anticipate enemy barricades, what potential avenues of approach might turn into killing fields. With his devil-may-care attitude toward probing the frontlines, Custer figured he could surreptitiously reconnoiter the enemy fortifications and the contours of the terrain, sketch what he was seeing, then report back to Baldy Smith. What he hadn't expected was a short introduction to Professor Thaddeus Lowe, and his crazy contraption that could supposedly fly, attached to a long tether. It looked like a large egg basket, big enough for a couple of men to stand in (and fall out of), a tangle of twisted ropes attached to what looked like a pile of tent canvas, and something the professor called a portable hydrogen generator.

The task was simple; hop in the basket, wait for the gas generator to fill the canvas balloon with enough air to lift it off the ground and high enough to see the Confederate array in the distance, all while a tether ensured it didn't float off into the clouds, or worse yet, drift over enemy territory, where sharpshooters could use it for target practice.

"Terrified" might best explain Lieutenant Custer's first venture aloft. In fact, he anchored himself firmly to the bottom of the basket, clutching the sides of the rim as it dipped and soared and swung back and forth. Eventually he mustered enough courage to peek over the rim, a thousand feet higher than he preferred to be, but where he could see the enemy and its fortifications in the distance. He used field glasses, a map, and compass to mark gun emplacements, troop tents and campfires. Once safely back on terra firma, he reported his observations and noted the enemy positions on a map. Despite his better judgment, Custer went up three more times, and during a nighttime reconnaissance—when it was much safer, at least as far as enemy snipers spotting him—he noted that there were no campfires near Yorktown and in fact, the Rebs had pulled out and repositioned further back in the peninsula. Custer's willingness to do what others might consider pure folly—in this instance, his aerial escapades—set him apart from other junior officers, who were maybe just a little more cautious. His superiors, and the press, were taking notice of his bravado.

For the Union Army, the trek across the peninsula was a slow slog, hampered by heavy rains which turned the dirt roads and fields to impassable mud. When mules and horses couldn't budge the heavy field guns, caissons, and wagons, the soldiers had to provide additional muscle. Sometimes the advance was so slow they barely made a few miles per day. During a brief respite, Lieutenant Custer wrote to Mrs. Reed, on April 20. "Our Army is encamped in front of the Rebels. We are getting ready for the expected battle. Our troops are building batteries right under their fortifications. The line of works extends about 5 miles. Our troops threw up

When Professor Thaddeus Lowe presented his crazy contraption to Union Army Brigadier General William "Baldy" Smith, the Army's chief topographical engineer, there was skepticism that it would be a way to spy on enemy encampments and determine troop strength. Baldy Smith needed a volunteer to venture aloft and test the professor's theory. Lieutenant George Custer volunteered, then cowered on the floor of the basket as it ascended toward the clouds. Eventually he mustered enough courage to peek over the rim of the basket and make notes of the Rebel army in the distance. (October 1861 issue of *Harper's Weekly*)

breastworks in the night, and mounted guns about 400 yards from them. Also we have rifle-pits for our sharpshooters about the same distance. When we first came the Rebels would fire a shell at our men, then jump on the parapets to see where it struck, then cheer and jump down. But our artillery men and sharpshooters have taught them better manners."

Advance scouts continued to search for safe passage up the peninsula, and so when a former slave who was familiar with the area told of an alternate path cutting through the trees, General Smith needed confirmation. Baldy Smith reported on May 10:

> On the morning of the 4th instant, soon after daylight, General Hancock rode up to me bringing two contrabands [escaped slaves], who informed me that the works in front of us had been evacuated. I immediately directed General Hancock to call for a few volunteers from each regiment of his brigade to cross the dam in front of us, and made the necessary dispositions of my artillery and infantry to cover as much as possible the crossing of these men, in case the work should still be occupied. Before, however, the troops arrived at the points designated, at about 5.30 a.m., Lieutenant Custer, Fifth Cavalry, and Captain Bead, assistant adjutant-general to General Brooks, had crossed the dam and taken possession of the works. The Fifth Vermont being near at hand, I ordered it forward at once to occupy the works, and other regiments were immediately ordered in as a support.

Wherever he showed up, Lieutenant Custer was looked at with curiosity. He was one of the hundreds of junior officers who were part of the reorganized Army of the Potomac, but he managed to distinguish himself, not so much by his actions, as yet little known or heard of, but simply by the way he looked.

"A queer figure Custer then was, according to the accounts of eye-witnesses," wrote Frederick Whittaker in his comprehensive biography of Custer. "One officer took him for a dashing newspaper correspondent, out to see the fun. He wore an old slouch hat and a cavalry jacket, with no marks of rank, the jacket flying open, while his muddy boots did not look worth more than a dollar. His hair was beginning to grow long, and aided his careless dress to give him a slouchy appearance, but even then there was something peculiar about him that made people ask, 'Who is that young fellow?' It was not for more than a year after, that he came out as a dandy."

Union forces were in pursuit when the Chickahominy River temporarily halted their advance. Major General John G. Barnard, in his report by the Army engineers wrote that the river, "at the season we struck it, was one of the most formidable obstacles that could be opposed to the advance of an army—an obstacle to which an ordinary river, though it be of considerable magnitude, is comparatively slight. The distance from New-Bridge to Bottom's Bridge, is eight miles. In this space there were two or three indifferent summer fords, or places where a pedestrian could make his way through the swamp and stream, but it was currently reported at the time of our arrival, that the stream was nowhere fordable."

Barnard was tasked with finding safe passage across the river, and scouted potential crossings with Lieutenant Custer. Barnard reported: "The knowledge of the Chickahominy gained at Bottom's Bridge showed me that the stream might be reached at almost any point, with little risk, and thoroughly examined, provided the enemy's pickets did not actually hold our sides. Taking with me Lieut. Custer … I reached it at a point three-quarters of a mile below New-Bridge, and caused him to enter it. He waded across without any difficulty (the depth being about four feet), and a few days afterward, emboldened by this experiment, he caused the length of the stream to be waded, from the bridge for half a mile down. The attack and capture of the enemy's pickets by him and Lieut. Bowen, was founded upon these reconnaissances, to which the successful results are due."

General Barnard's report revealed little of Lieutenant Custer's escapade, but Frederick Whittaker wrote about it: "Arrived at the other side [of the river], Custer peered through the bushes and cautiously ascended the bank, being rewarded for his explorations by a distinct view of the enemy's picket fires, some distance off, and by the sight of their nearest sentry, lazily pacing his post, quite unconscious of the proximity of any foe."

Without attracting attention from the Rebel sentries, Barnard motioned for Custer to get back across before he was spotted. But first, Custer wanted to get an accurate assessment of the enemy positions, so he could give a detailed description once he got back among friendly forces. Barnard promptly reported back to General McClellan but when he was too vague responding to one too many questions, he finally admitted that it was young Custer who made the crossing and saw the enemy encampment. McClellan wanted to meet this young officer, who was "dirty and muddy, with unkempt hair, coat not brushed, but all creased from being slept in, trousers far from guiltless of rags [fruit of hard riding], boots more russet than black, with red reflections, cap once blue, now purple from many rains and suns," wrote Whittaker. "Such was the figure that presented itself before McClellan—general, as always, neat as a pin—boy's face as red as fire with shame at his own carelessness. But McClellan knew how to conquer 'mauvaise honte' as few other men could. He pretended not to notice Custer's confusion, told the lad to ride with him, that he 'wanted to hear all about this crossing of the river and what was on the other side.'"

The general was impressed with Lieutenant Custer's spunk, his attention to detail, and his enthusiasm. Without a second thought, he invited this ragamuffin of a junior officer to join his staff. And just like that a life-long adoration began.

McClellan referred to him as Captain Custer, even though it was not yet official, and consented when asked if he could lead the detachment across the river.

With Rebel troops positioned at Williamsburg, Union Brigadier General Winfield Scott Hancock ordered a cavalry charge to break through the ranks. Hancock tracked down Colonel Amasa Cob, commander of the 5th Wisconsin Regiment, and wanted young Captain Custer to show them the way. Whittaker wrote, "He says that he has found a place where he can cross the stream and turn the enemy's left flank; you

Pickets from the Army of the Potomac keep a watch on the distant approaches, aware that the Rebels were constantly probing the perimeter for any weakness. (November 1861 issue of *Harper's Weekly*)

will follow him with your regiment and effect a crossing if possible. Keep a sharp lookout for surprises and keep me advised of everything of importance." Custer "was absorbed in thought and anxiety about this, his first serious expedition, and consequently did not take much notice of the troops with him, till they came to the ford. Then, as the light was growing stronger, he heard a voice say 'I want to know … if that ain't Armstrong!' Custer started and looked at the dingy blue-grey crowd of soldiers, and was greeted in a moment by animated cries. 'Why, it's Armstrong.' 'How are ye, Armstrong.' 'Give us your fiat, Armstrong.' He had, by a strange chance, fallen into the midst of Company A, 4th Michigan Infantry, a company raised in Monroe, and composed almost entirely of his old school friends and playmates."

A McClellan Man

Few others knew who this Custer guy was, but the Monroe boys knew him, and just seeing familiar faces gave him the confidence to lead the way. The path was just wide enough for a wagon, cutting through the trees and across the dam, and up a rise above the village of Wheatfield, where field guns were soon in place to rain down thunder on the Confederates at Fort Magruder, just outside of Williamsburg. The Rebels countered by calling up reinforcements and soon Wheatfield was a killing field.

A cavalry charge was ordered but the Union troopers were hesitant to leave the safety of the wood line. Captain Custer charged ahead on his own. Reckless? Maybe. Foolish? Definitely, if he continued on by himself, but his actions inspired his fellow cavalry troopers to follow close behind, and soon the Confederates scattered in retreat. A triumphant Captain Custer soon returned with a Rebel captain and five soldiers in tow. More importantly, the Union's Golden Boy waved a Confederate battle flag—white silk with a red cross—the first for the Army of the Potomac, and the first of many he would personally add to his war chest. On May 15, he wrote a letter to Mrs. Reed. "The Battle of Williamsburg was hard fought, far more so than Bull Run. I captured a Captain and five men without any assistance, and a large Rebel flag. It was afterwards sent up by McClellan to the President at Washington."

The *Cosmopolitan* newspaper reported the victory under the title "Two Modern Knights Errant."

> In May 1862, McClellan was so impressed with the energy [Custer] displayed in crossing the Chickahominy alone, in search of a ford for the army to pass over, that he was appointed aide with the rank of captain. Custer applied for permission to attack the enemy's picket post, and at daylight he surprised them, capturing prisoners and the first flags taken by the army of the Potomac.

In *Heroes of the Army in America*, Charles Morris wrote about the audacious Custer:

> In the pursuit of the enemy on their retreat from Williamsburg he was in Hancock's corps, reaching the Chickahominy in the advance of the army and being the first officer to wade that stream. He traced and marked the ford and reconnoitered the enemy's position before returning, and on the next day, June 16, at the head of two companies of cavalry and one of infantry, he daringly attacked a large detachment of the Louisiana Tigers acting as a picket guard, stampeding them and capturing their colors with his own hand. This, the first trophy of the kind taken by the Army of the Potomac, was a feather in the cap of the young dragoon, and when General McClellan heard of his exploits he at once appointed him an aide on his own staff.

Custer Meets a Former Classmate Wearing Confederate Grey

After the battle of Williamsburg, on May 5, 1862, Custer was given the grim task of combing the killing field for Confederate survivors. There were so many bodies, it was difficult to avoid stepping on or tripping over the dead and wounded. While canvassing the area, he came across one of his West Point classmates—Confederate Captain John "Gimlet" W. Lea of the 5th North Carolina Infantry—and was stunned to see he was, by some miracle, still alive. If another Union soldier had found Lea, his fate would have been much worse, but instead, Custer carried him to a field hospital.

On May 15, Custer recounted the incident in a letter to Mrs. Reed: "A classmate of mine was captain of one of the Rebel regiments and was taken prisoner after being badly wounded in the leg. I took care of him, and fed him for two days, but then had to leave him when I went on with the army, while he would be sent North. When we first saw each other he shed tears and threw his arms about my neck, and we talked of old times and asked each other hundreds of questions about classmates on opposing sides of the contest. I carried his meals to him, gave him stockings of which he stood in need, and some money. This he did not want to take, but I forced it on him. He burst into tears and said it was more than he could stand. He insisted on writing in my notebook that if ever I should be taken prisoner he wanted me treated as he had been. His last words to me were, 'God bless you, old boy!' The bystanders looked with surprise when we were talking, and afterwards asked if the prisoner were my brother."

Lea was then transported to the Williamsburg home of a Rebel colonel and was cared for by his 17-year-old daughter, Margaret. During lulls in the Peninsular Campaign, Lieutenant Custer would journey back to Williamsburg to check on his friend and former classmate. Lea reciprocated by writing in Custer's notebook, "Wmsburg. 5-6-62. If ever Lt. Custer U.S.A. should be taken prisoner, I want him treated as well as he has treated me."

After Margaret's care, "Gimlet" proposed and she accepted. During the Army of the Potomac's withdrawal from the peninsula in August, Custer was granted a final visit to the home, to say goodbye to his old friend and his new fiancée. Instead, they decided to rush the wedding so that Autie Custer could serve as groomsman. Standing at the altar in their military uniforms, one in dark blue, the other in heather grey, these two "enemies" would not allow their friendship to tear them apart. After the wedding, Custer remained a few days longer, while Union forces assembled at Fort Monroe awaiting transport. He enjoyed the company of his secessionist hosts, specifically Margaret's sister, and jokingly considered switching sides, if she asked him to. He would later write to his sister, "I never had so pleasant a visit among strangers."

But eventually, Custer had to return to his unit, and the two friends reluctantly said goodbye, knowing they were duty bound if they ever met again on some future battlefield. It would not be the only time Custer met a former classmate wearing Confederate grey.

Richmond remained the prize for the Army of the Potomac and, as he had already exhibited, Autie Custer was not about to be a casual bystander. But Richmond was heavily fortified and the Rebels braced themselves for a lengthy artillery barrage to weaken them. And maybe a more seasoned Union officer would have brought his batteries on line, dismounted his cavalry and arrayed his infantry to block any attempts at retreat. C. J. Wood in *Reminiscences of the War*, published in 1880, wrote:

Not so, with the intrepid Custer. The usual cautions and preliminaries were too tedious for his impetuous nature. Quickly forming his command in line, he ordered them to draw saber and charge front. In the face of a galling fire from the Rebel artillery, these daring cavaliers, under Custer's lead, rode headlong on the enemy's works, brandishing their burnished blades and yelling like demons. Although the works were temporary in their construction, the Rebels little expected a cavalry charge on regular military fortifications. Bewildered by the dashing recklessness of the charge, they rapidly but wildly continued firing their guns, and attempted to make good their defense against an attack made in violation of all the known rules of regular warfare. On came the cavalry like a resistless torrent, riding over ditches, parapets and embankments, and began furiously to cut and slash among the garrison on the inside of the works. The astonished Rebels fled in wild confusion, leaving their guns and fortifications to fall into the hands of the victors. In vain Rebel officers attempted to halt and form the retreating ranks.

During the advance on Richmond, Custer was rapidly making a name for himself. After probing the Chickahominy River for suitable crossing points, he would guide a detachment across, while enemy skirmishers fired on them. The Union troops from the 4th Michigan forded the river, often up to their armpits, holding their cartridge boxes on their shoulders, sometimes even higher, all while under fire from the Rebel pickets. Fellow Lieutenant Nicolas Bowen, of the Army's topographical engineers, wrote the following in his report, on May 25, at Cold Harbor, just east of Richmond: "Lieutenant Custer, Fifth U. S. Cavalry, who was the first to cross the stream, the first to open fire upon the enemy, and one of the last to leave the field."

"First to charge the enemy, last to leave the field of battle" would become a Custer staple. He knew no other way. His regimental commander also commented that Custer "can eat and sleep as much as anyone when he has the opportunity. But he can do without either when necessary!"

While Lieutenant Custer—not yet officially a captain—enjoyed the rush of battle, General McClellan hated the carnage, and by the end of May, with the Seven Pines campaign, he wrote to his wife, "I am tired of the sickening sight of the battlefield, with its mangled corpses and poor suffering wounded! Victory has no charms for me when purchased at such cost." W. Sanford Ramey in *Kings of the Battle-Field* wrote:

In July Custer was appointed aide-de-camp to General Philip Kearny, an appointment which was soon afterwards annulled by a general order forbidding officers of the regular Army from serving on the staff of generals of volunteers. In February, 1862, [Custer] was assigned to the Fifth Cavalry, then serving in the Army of the Potomac. Near Cedar Run he ordered his first charge in one of the slight skirmishes which passed for battles at the beginning of the war. He served through all the Peninsular Campaign under McClellan. At Williamsburg Custer distinguished himself, and was mentioned in General Hancock's official report. He led a charge on the brigade commanded by General Early, which cost that officer four hundred men. Shortly afterwards he made a reconnaissance of the enemy's lines, which brought him under the notice of General McClellan, who offered Custer a position on his staff. This was the commencement of a very warm attachment on his part to McClellan, which lasted all his life. At the same time of his appointment as aide to McClellan, he was promoted to the rank of captain. (Later McClellan would recall: "In those days Custer was simply a reckless, gallant boy, undeterred by fatigue, unconscious of fear; but his head was always clear in danger and he always brought me clear and intelligible reports of what he saw under the heaviest fire.")

Rebel Lieutenant James Washington was a former classmate of recently promoted Captain Custer. Now, after the Seven Days' Battle, he was a prisoner of war. The two chatted briefly about old times. Soon after this shot was taken, the photographer grabbed a "contraband"—African American boy—and had him sit on the ground, between the two. The photograph was published nationwide, under the title "Both Sides and the Cause." (Photo by James Gibson, Public Domain)

Custer's promotion was promptly reported back home, in *The Cadiz Democratic Sentinel*, in its June 11 issue, "Bully for Custer—A Harrison County Boy Promoted":

> It will be seen by the … General Order of General McClellan, that Lieut. G. A. Custer, of this county, has been promoted for gallant conduct, to a Captaincy, and placed on General McClellan's staff. Lieutenant Custer, of your county … was promoted for having been the first person to cross the Chickahominy River, which he did *alone*, while the enemy's pickets lined the opposite shore, and ours were a half a mile from this side. During the Seven Days' Battles Custer was noticed for the dash and impetuosity with which he joined in the eventual fighting of that stormy period.

As part of the media fascination with Custer, James Gibson shot a staged photograph after the Seven Days' Battle, showing the dashing Union officer and aide to General McClellan, with his Confederate counterpart, now POW Lieutenant James Washington, aide to Lieutenant General Joseph Johnston. Custer and Washington had been classmates at West Point, and even though Custer had many southern friends, Washington was not one of them, but they had many friends in common, and were catching up on any snatches of news or gossip about those friends. As he was posing the two young officers, Gibson, a member of Matthew Brady's staff, spotted an escaped slave and had him sit on the ground in front of the two. The photograph was titled "Both Sides and the Cause" and was published in numerous newspapers and illustrated magazines.

At Malvern Hill, during the Seven Days' Battle, Custer had been in the saddle four days straight, with only a few hours of shut eye in brief snatches. He ate breakfast—hard bread dipped in coffee—and little else. His stamina was boundless, and while others were ready to drop, he was itching for a fight. Soon after the battle at Malvern Hill, Custer gave chase to a Rebel officer separated from his detachment, all of them fleeing in desperation. A letter home recaps the incident:

> By avoiding some soft ground which I saw was retarding him, I was enabled to get close upon him when I called him to surrender, or I would shoot him. He paid no attention and I fired, taking as good aim as was possible on horseback. He sat for a moment in his saddle, reeled and fell to the ground, his horse ran on and mine also. Before the "rally" was sounded, however, I saw the horse … a red morocco breast strap which I had noticed during the chase. He is a blooded horse, as is evident by his appearance. I have him yet and intend to keep him. The saddle, which I also retain, is a splendid one, covered with black morocco and ornamented with silver nails. The sword of the officer was fastened to the saddle, so that altogether it was a splendid trophy.

The Union forces were positioned on one side of the Chickahominy River, the Rebels were on the other, with pickets positioned up and down the river to watch for enemy activity. When it became necessary to determine the depth of the river, and where it would be safe to cross, without detection, Custer volunteered. Not only did he make it safely across, he snuck around the underbrush, for a quick look see, noting the exact location of the enemy encampment. (Public Domain)

One night, Custer was helping to evacuate the wounded, encouraging those who could still walk to evacuate the battlefield, while there was still time. Some were waiting for stretcher bearers and horse-drawn ambulances, which were already over-committed and would not be coming any time soon.

"Who says no ambulances are coming for us?" one wounded soldier asked. Custer recognized the voice as that of Kentuckian Julius Adams, a former roommate from West Point. Custer hopped off his horse and ordered four soldiers to use a broken fence gate to carry his wounded friend over a bridge and for another few miles to a staging area where wagons were being loaded, for departure the next morning. Custer accompanied them and assumed his injured friend would be cared for, but the next morning, he returned and everyone was gone, including the wagons, leaving his mortally wounded friend, an enemy soldier, there to die. Custer saw that there was little more could be done. Julius Adams was still conscious and understood his fate. He asked for Custer's journal so he could leave a few notes for his mother and his sweetheart back home. Custer promised to see that they got his messages, then he left his friend.

He would later write to his sister, "I lost several friends in the various engagements and lament their loss. It is better to die an honored death than to live in dishonor."

But by July 1, President Lincoln ordered the Army of the Potomac to withdraw and return to Washington in anticipation of a second battle at Bull Run and the upcoming Northern Virginia Campaign. General McClellan ordered his forces to pull back to Harrison's Landing, board anything afloat, and leave the peninsula. Union gunboats were positioned on the James River to repel any Rebel troops in pursuit.

During the four days it took to evacuate thousands of Union troops, Custer spurred his steed from McClellan's headquarters to numerous field commanders and back, carrying messages and guiding the units to the rescue boats. As he hurried down the line, from one unit to the next, the weary soldiers cheered him on, welcoming the news that the Peninsular Campaign was over. It was an inglorious end.

The president and his field commanders quickly realized that this conflict would be much longer and more difficult than they hoped. In addition to enlisting thousands more troops and mobilizing the north's industrial machine, Lincoln contemplated a change in military leadership. Most notably, he was very dissatisfied with McClellan, who seemed to oppose the president's directives at every opportunity. On July 8, Lincoln travelled to Harrison's Landing and noted that the officers and soldiers wanted to renew the attack on Richmond. The only hesitancy came from McClellan.

"Sensing the push for sterner measures, McClellan presented Lincoln with a letter in which he advocated that the government continue to adhere to 'the highest principles known to Christian Civilization' in waging the war," wrote Christopher Kolakowski of the Center of Military History in a 2016 report of the Virginia

After the debacle at Bull Run, Union forces felt they were prepared for a better showing the second time around, but it turned into another disaster. (September 1862 issue of *Harper's Weekly*)

Campaigns. "Although the government had to destroy the political and military forces of the Confederacy, the general argued that the conflict should not devolve into 'a war upon [the] population.' Rather, the North should respect the rights and property of Southerners, to include the right to own slaves."

Three days later Lincoln appointed Major General Henry Halleck as commander in chief of the Army, bypassing McClellan, then the president briefed his cabinet that he intended to proclaim freedom for all slaves. He was advised to wait until a major battlefield victory, otherwise the move would look like an act of desperation. In fact, there was very real concern that the Rebels could attack and seize DC.

"For the first time," stated the *New York Tribune*'s Washington bureau chief on September 1, "I believe it possible that Washington may be taken."

The Army of the Potomac had pulled back to DC, to lick their wounds, re-group, again, and brace for a Rebel assault on the nation's capital. But Jefferson Davis and General Robert E. Lee were not attempting to defeat the much-larger Union military, but rather to demoralize the northern populace, possibly convince the British and French to side with the South, then hope for a negotiated peace which would allow the secessionist states to create their own unified government and country. Ted Ballard, for the Center of Military History's 2008 report on the battle of Antietam, wrote:

> Although the year had seen one Confederate victory after another in Virginia, months of campaigning had taken its toll on the Army of Northern Virginia. [Confederate General Robert

E.] Lee's command had suffered many casualties who would be difficult to replace. It was also short on rations and supplies, and literally thousands of Lee's troops were without sufficient clothing, especially shoes. As the Army of Northern Virginia prepared to embark on another major campaign, only its military organization prevented it from resembling a mob of hungry vagabonds. In the days after Second Bull Run (also known as the Second battle of Manassas, August 29 and 30), the government in Washington prepared for an expected Confederate assault and Lee pondered his options. Insufficient numbers of troops, rations, ammunition, and other supplies prevented him from either attacking or engaging in a siege of the city. Washington was surrounded by extensive fortifications, bristling with artillery, and defended by large numbers of troops.

Robert E. Lee saw the deplorable condition of his field army and informed Rebel President Jefferson Davis, "The army is not properly equipped for an invasion of an enemy's territory." They certainly couldn't penetrate the defensive posture around Washington, DC. Instead he planned to advance into Maryland just east of the Blue Ridge Mountains and hit Frederick, then probe the outposts near Baltimore and swing north into Pennsylvania. Lee's hope was to divert the massed Union forces from DC to stem multiple attacks, and thus have a better chance at defeating the much smaller Union defenders. What hindered the Confederate war plan was the pitiful condition of thousands of troops, who were underfed, emaciated, wearing thread-bare rags for uniforms, some without even footwear, who fell by the wayside, or just drifted off to forage for anything to eat. Many Southern soldiers succumbed to diseases more so than battle wounds.

In Washington, President Lincoln was reassessing his decision to leave General McClellan in place, especially after the disaster at Bull Run, the second defeat there. It was Little Mac who took an exasperatingly long time to even kick off the campaign to capture Richmond, which ended without success. Some Republican politicians and cabinet members in DC even wondered if McClellan, an avowed Democrat, had openly defied the president's orders at every opportunity. They went so far as to inform Lincoln that they didn't trust the general to command any military force in the country, much less the crucial defense of DC. But with the Confederates moving into Maryland, the president had no choice but to stick with McClellan for the time being. Lincoln also knew his proclamation to give freedom to slaves could very well turn the tide of war, but he wanted to make the announcement with a victory in hand.

Lincoln was aware that many northern civilians and soldiers were ambivalent about emancipation, McClellan among them. In fact the general had already made his position very clear: "I am fighting to preserve the integrity of the Union and the power of the Govt—on no other issue. To gain that end we cannot afford to mix up the negro question—it must be incidental and subsidiary." Lincoln didn't agree. The "negro question" was pivotal to devastating the economy of the southern states, which depended on the slaves to harvest King Cotton and tobacco, and to free up southern whites to take up arms for the Confederacy. Not only was emancipation vital to bringing the secessionist states back to the Union, it was the right thing to do, for the thousands of slaves in the South.

Lincoln desperately needed a victory in the East but he wasn't sure McClellan was the field commander to get it done. Other campaigns, out West, and down South were more successful, but closer to DC was becoming perilous.

Robert E. Lee was on the move and had invaded Maryland and planned to attack multiple Union fortifications in an effort to divide and conquer, then threaten DC. Personally, he knew his troops were in pitiful condition, on the verge of total collapse, hardly up to an all-out war, on all fronts. But he could focus his troops on smaller enemy concentrations, such as at Harper's Ferry and, hopefully, overwhelm them. For McClellan, it became a guessing game, trying to figure out what those Johnny Rebs were up to. Advancing or retreating? From reports he was getting, McClellan wrote to this wife, "From all I can gather secesh is skedadelling."

But then, on September 13, while scouring a recently abandoned Confederate encampment, soldiers from the 27th Indiana spotted a small bundle of cigars, what they might consider a treasure trove. But the cigars were wrapped in paper, something official-looking, which turned out to be orders from General Lee, Order #191, laying out an attack on the Union forces at Harper's Ferry, one of several outposts, which could be targeted by overwhelming force. If McClellan didn't pull his units back, or reinforce them before the attacks, more Confederate victories were near certainties. Lee learned of the intelligence coup, that his orders had fallen into Union hands, and he rushed his units forward to blunt McClellan.

Two days later, Confederate artillery fired on the Union garrison at Harper's Ferry, which returned the barrage, until they ran out of ammunition and were forced to surrender; 13,000 total, while the Confederates tallied 400 casualties. It would be one of the most lopsided Confederate victories of the war. Following closely after Second Bull Run, the Rebels were flush with enthusiasm that just maybe they had a miniscule chance of securing ultimate victory.

The battle of South Mountain, also known as the battle of Boonsboro Gap in Maryland and the skirmishes there in mid-September, would be pivotal for both sides. South Mountain is part of the Blue Ridge range and separates eastern Maryland from the rest of the state. Whichever side controlled the over watch approaches into Cumberland Valley and Hagerstown Valley could blunt anything thrown at them. Lee's forces retreated then attempted to block the Union soldiers pursuing them. Once General Lee realized he was outnumbered, he withdrew though not before enduring numerous casualties—325 killed, another 1560 wounded and 800 missing (probably taken as prisoners). *The New York World* would report in September of 1862 that the battle of South Mountain "turned back the tide of Rebel successes." More importantly, it stated that "the strength of the Rebels is hopelessly broken."

For Custer, on September 15, he was with General Alfred Pleasonton, leading a division of cavalry, when they spotted the rear guard of departing Rebel soldiers on

The battle along the Chickahominy was just another in the string of skirmishes in mid-1862. (July 1862 issue of *Harper's Weekly*)

the edge of Boonsboro. The Union horsemen took off in hot pursuit and, afterward, Custer wrote a hasty account of it, "We captured between two and three hundred prisoners in Boonsboro. Our cavalry has made several dashing charges. The Rebels are scattering all over the country … Everything is, as we wish."

If McClellan had continued the pursuit, Union forces not only could have been victorious in the Maryland Campaign, but also secured a Confederate surrender, in the fall of 1862 (two and a years before Lee finally called it quits, in April of 1865). Instead, McClellan allowed the Confederates time to regroup around Sharpsburg. This led to the most devastating one-day battle in American history at Antietam on September 17.

After his role in the battle of South Mountain, Captain Custer wrote the following account and sent it to McClellan, noting the Rebels' position around the next battle, at Sharpsburg: "The enemy is drawn up in line of battle on a ridge about two miles beyond [Keedysville]. They are in full view. Their line is a perfect one about a mile and a half long … Longstreet is in command and has forty cannon that we know of."

On the morning of September 17, the battle of Antietam commenced, with three separate engagements, in open field, the woods, and dirt roads around Sharpsburg. The National Public Radio, on the 150th anniversary, reported:

It is called simply the Cornfield, and it was here, in the first light of dawn that Union troops—more than 1,000—crept toward the Confederate lines. The stalks were at head level and shielded their movements. Cannon fire opened the battle with puffs of white smoke rising from the tree line. Just 200 yards in front of the Union forces, Confederate troops from Georgia were flat on their stomachs. They leveled their guns and waited, and when the Union troops broke out of the corn, the Georgians all rose up and fired. It was complete chaos in and around the cornfield, with people screaming and bodies everywhere. In that first phase of the battle, 10,000 soldiers were killed and wounded.

The cornfield quickly became a stalemate, so the Union forces veered to the south, thinking the old Sunken Road, later known as Bloody Lane for all the carnage, would be a safer route. But more than 2,000 Rebel troops were lying in wait and rose up unexpectedly when the Union soldiers walked within range.

The third phase unfolded along the banks of Antietam Creek. But once again the Rebels were waiting. All told, during 12 hours of battle, more than 23,000 casualties were inflicted and it would be known as "the bloodiest single day in American military history ..." Ted Bollard wrote for the Center of Military History report in 2008:

In the annals of American military history, the battle at Antietam became the bloodiest ever, with both sides claiming minor victories. It was not the overwhelming victory he'd hoped for, but President Lincoln used Antietam to announce his Emancipation Proclamation. (October 1864 issue of *Harper's Weekly*)

Although Antietam was not the decisive Union victory for which Lincoln had hoped, it did give the president an opportunity to strike at the Confederacy politically, psychologically, and economically. On 22 September Lincoln issued the preliminary Emancipation Proclamation, declaring that the Federal government would after 1 January 1863 consider slaves in any state in rebellion against the Federal government to be free. The proclamation had no immediate effect behind Confederate lines, nor did it free any slaves in states still in the Union. Nevertheless, Lincoln's proclamation would be the Federal government's first official step toward the abolition of human slavery.

After Antietam, both armies needed time to lick their wounds, regroup and reassess their next move. The Confederates abandoned the Maryland Campaign, while the Union forces remained in and around Sharpsburg for a month. On September 26, Custer carried a flag of truce as he escorted some Rebel prisoners back to their lines. He took the opportunity to inquire about former classmates. In a letter to Mrs. Reed, he wrote: "Yesterday I accompanied a Rebel colonel, a lieutenant and several prisoners, under a flag of truce inside Rebel lines. I found several who were acquainted with my classmates and friends … and we had an hour's social chat, discussing the war in a friendly way. And we exchanged cards."

Without any sense of what was about to take place, totally upending his career, young Custer lamented in a letter to his sister, "After I get back to Monroe, I do not intend to eat hard bread, salt pork, nor drink coffee without milk," his almost daily fare. Maybe he was thinking of a winter interlude, when many officers were granted leave, hoping he could return home for a few weeks of much-needed rest.

In early October, President Lincoln visited his Army in the field, and met with General McClellan. The president was anxious to continue the fight while the Rebels were on the run, but Little Mac knew his troops needed rest, the logistics pipeline was broken and he wasn't about to rush, no matter what the commander in chief had to say about it. A review of the troops was staged for the president, who sarcastically referred to them as McClellan's bodyguard. The same day, Custer wrote a letter to his cousin, Augusta Frary, recapping the day, and his personal feelings about the war:

> The president has paid us a visit and today accompanied by Gen McClellan and staff he reviewed that portion of the Army which is encamped in this vicinity. This occupied nearly the entire day. Yesterday the same party visited the late battle ground. The president will probably return to Washington tomorrow.
>
> You ask me if I will not be glad when the last battle is fought? So far as my country is concerned I, of course, must wish for peace, and will be glad when the war is ended … when I think of the pain and misery produced to individuals as well as the universal sorrow caused throughout the land, I cannot but earnestly hope for peace, and at an early date.

After his visit and disagreements with his field commander, the president had seen enough. In early November he relieved McClellan. Four days later, after a final review and farewell comments to the troops, the general boarded a train to Washington, with orders to wait in Trenton, New Jersey, for further assignment. Custer too was left without an assignment.

After President Lincoln announced the emancipation of enslaved African Americans in September of 1862, he hoped it would inspire citizens to support the cause. But many in the north were either indifferent or quietly supported the continuation of slavery in the southern states. (January 1863 issue of *Harper's Weekly*)

Both Custer and McClellan were Democrats, critical of Lincoln and his Republican administration in Washington. They didn't support Lincoln's war aims, nor felt his declaration to emancipate the slaves should be tied to the war itself. And both felt it was this political difference of opinion which led to the general's dismissal. Both refused to believe it was his excessive delays in executing the war, in following Lincoln's demands to confront and put down the southern rebellion. Custer's admiration and devotion to General McClellan would never waver, much to the detriment of his own military ambitions.

Uncertainty During a Winter Homecoming

General McClellan advised young Custer to go home to Monroe and wait for a new assignment. He reluctantly agreed, though he would have preferred to remain with his comrades. It was quite common for officers to return home during the winter months, when the weather curtailed military operations. Frederick Whittaker wrote that "while his military life was so bitter during this winter, he yet enjoyed plenty of opportunity for fun in a civil capacity. Partly to drive away care, and partly from the natural physical buoyancy of youth, that would not be denied, he plunged into all the mild little dissipations of Monroe society with great zest that winter, sleigh riding, flirting, dancing, enjoying all the pleasures of a holiday, during November and December, 1862, and part of January, 1863."

It was during these dalliances and social outings that Captain Custer spotted his latest conquest, in the form of a precocious teenage beauty, who enjoyed the attention but rebuffed his every advance.

That precocious young lady, properly educated and appropriately refined, was the coquettish Elizabeth "Libbie" Bacon, only daughter of Judge Daniel Bacon, and neither of them were much impressed with Custer and his cavalier attitude, especially regarding the many young ladies of Monroe who swooned over his every move, and his exaggerated stories of glory in battle. His friend and former roommate at West Point would say, "He is a handsome fellow, and a very successful ladies' man. Nor does he care an iota how many of the fair ones break their hearts for him." That reputation was well known around town.

They first met at a Thanksgiving Day party in 1862, when Custer was back in town and had been seen staggering down the street, obviously inebriated. Neither Libbie nor her father were impressed, even though he vowed to never touch alcohol again. When they were formally introduced, she was polite, but uninterested in his braggadocio. But, even a year later, Captain Custer was smitten, and the more Libbie Bacon rebuffed him, the more he focused his attention on her. But there was one major obstacle blocking his every attempt to woe her.

The judge had seen this brash cavalier dancing and socializing with anyone of the fairer sex, and he was not about to allow his only daughter to fall prey to his phony enticements. But Custer was willing to retreat for the time being, though he had no intention of abandoning the mission, which was to woo, and some day marry, Elizabeth Bacon.

With dogged persistence, and surreptitious communications, the irrepressible Custer won her over, though she refused to admit his advances had been successful. But in her diary, she confessed: "I love him still. I know it is love from fancy with no foundation, but I love him still and theory vanishes when practice comes in to play. There is no similarity of tastes between us and I will never think of it, but I love him. His career is dear to me." But Libbie was also aware that her father was not a fan of Custer, had even told her not to see him again, and so she flirted with other eligible young men in Monroe, partly to keep her options open, but also to show Custer that she wasn't just his for the taking whenever he wanted. She was also quite aware that eventually he would be headed back to the army, a very dangerous occupation, and maybe, out of sight and out of mind, she could find another suitor who would be more to her father's liking.

In mid-January McClellan requested that Custer join him in New Jersey to assist with the laborious task of making a final report of the Army of the Potomac during the Peninsular Campaign. After that, in April, Custer was ordered to link up with the 5th Cavalry, situated near Falmouth, VA. His promotion to captain had still not been approved, so when he joined General Hooker's army preparing for the battle of Fredericksburg, he reverted back to lieutenant.

Custer Returns to the War

"Under McClellan and [Ambrose] Burnside, the Union cavalry had been scattered about at different headquarters, assigned to the command of infantry generals, used in small forces for outpost duty and scouting, and seldom or never employed on the field of battle," wrote Whittaker. "The few exceptions to the rule had been signally disastrous. At Gaines' Mills a single regiment of cavalry, the Sixth Pennsylvania, then acting as McClellan's bodyguard, had been sent to charge a whole hostile army, and had of course effected nothing. One or two mounted charges, with equally poor results, had taken place in [John] Pope's campaign, but as a rule the Federal cavalry was too green to be usefully employed. The only portion kept in mass was a brigade under Pleasonton, and this small force had been worked to death. [General Joseph] Hooker gathered together all the regiments, organized them into three divisions under Pleasonton, Gregg and Averill, and kept them together, where they remained ever after as the Cavalry Corps, Army of the Potomac."

There were some, mostly among the infantry leadership, who doubted a massed cavalry division could have any more success on the battlefield than foot soldiers supported with artillery. But Pleasonton had already proven himself when he commanded a cavalry brigade in July and August 1862, followed a month later by taking charge of a cavalry division.

At the end of April 1863, the Army of the Potomac was on the move, ready to take the fight to the Rebels. Unfortunately Union forces were carved up into three separate commands, making it much easier for Robert E. Lee to focus on one of the three and overwhelm it, then move on to the next and then the next, which is exactly what he did. The only one of the three commands that didn't endure massive casualties and carnage, was the Cavalry Corps, which is where Lieutenant Custer was attached.

The Union infantry had been mauled at Chancellorsville in April and May, until a cavalry brigade came to the rescue. After that, the Cavalry Corps took the lead, leaving the infantry regiments watching from the periphery.

Lieutenant Custer returned to active duty in April, and he learned he would take over a cavalry company in the 5th Cavalry Division, at Fredericksburg. He quickly met General Pleasonton and they reaffirmed their undying loyalty to General McClellan. Custer had first come to Pleasonton's attention during the Maryland Campaign, and it would prove a fortuitous friendship for the junior officer. But he arrived too late for the next battle at Chancellorsville. Pleasonton was not involved, and held Custer back, along with a cavalry brigade.

Union Army Major General George McClellan was not known for making quick decisions, much to the aggravation of President Lincoln. Some of Lincoln's Republican advisers felt McClellan, a known Democrat, was simply opposing him at every opportunity. Mac would eventually get the axe, much to the disappointment of Custer. (September 1864 issue of *Harper's Weekly*)

On April 29, following the battle strategy of General Joseph Hooker, Union cavalry rode out, intent on striking behind Confederate lines, with disastrous results. A week later, Custer wrote a letter to General McClellan:

> My dear General, I know you must be anxious to know how your army is, and has been doing. We are defeated, driven back on the left bank of the Rappahannock with a loss which I suppose will exceed our entire loss during the seven days' battle. To say that everything is gloomy and discouraging does not express the state of affairs here. You will not be surprised when I inform you that the universal cry is "Give us McClellan." If I am not mistaken there will be such a howl go up from the conservative press and people of the North which will leave but one course open for the Administration to pursue.

Custer Gains a Patron

Lincoln never considered bringing McClellan back, in any capacity. Instead, Pleasonton was elevated to command the Cavalry Corps and he quickly moved to make Custer his aide-de-camp. He would soon be dubbed "Pleasonton's Pet."

"The cavalry had shown in their first general fight, that they were capable of holding their own against the much dreaded 'Stuart's Cavalry,' that caused the Army of the Potomac so much alarm, from the Peninsular to Maryland," wrote Whittaker. "They had met and parted fairly, 'broken a lance' as it were, found that all they needed was to put a bold face on matters; and so learned that their first lesson under Pleasonton's command. The time was coming and very near at hand, though [Custer] knew it not, for him to win his star, and emerge from the inconspicuous position of a staff officer to one in which he could command public attention."

Robert E. Lee was pushing north again, up through the Shenandoah Valley, and on to the west of the Blue Ridge Mountains. He was bypassing the Union's capitol, to probe Maryland, cross the Potomac and, unless he was stopped, would take the fight into Pennsylvania. General J. E. B. Stuart led the Rebel cavalry as a blocking force, to protect the infantry as it marched through the Shenandoah. Unsure of where exactly the Confederates were, or where they were headed, several Union cavalry brigades fanned out from DC to find them.

General Pleasonton tasked his new aide, Lieutenant Custer, to get word to his subordinate commanders, to mount up and locate the Rebels. Union scouts spotted J. E. B. Stuart's forces along the Rappahannock River and were concerned the Rebels might attempt an attack on Washington.

General J. E. B. Stuart oversees Confederate cavalry troops during a probe into Pennsylvania. (*Harper's Weekly*)

Skirmishing at Beverly Ford on June 9 revealed the Rebel cavalry massing near Culpepper, staging there for a push into Maryland and Pennsylvania. The cavalry clash at Brandy Station was especially telling, victorious for the Union cavalry against fearful odds, and Custer played a key role in the outcome, explained by J. Allen Bigelow from Detroit of the 5th Michigan and published in the *Detroit Evening News*:

> At Brandy Station, Va., during Meade's fall back, Custer and the cavalry brought up the rear, and all soldiers know it is the worst place on God's footstool to cover a retreat. To allow the infantry ample time to cross the Rappahannock the cavalry kept fooling around with an average of 10,000 Rebs on all sides of them. Once when a lull had seemed to come with an ominous stillness ... about 5,000 Rebs were suddenly soon to be massed in our front and right in the path we must travel if we ever saw "the girls we left behind us." Custer was sitting on his horse at the head of our regiment, the Fifth Cavalry. He took one look of about ten seconds, then snatched off his hat, raised up in his stirrups and yelled out, "Boys of Michigan, there are some people between us and home; I'm going home. Who else goes?" Suffice it to say we all went. General Alger, then colonel of our regiment, can vouch for our flying movements as we followed Custer, with his bare head and golden locks, and long straight sabre, putting the very devil into the old Fifth Cavalry, until a clear track was before us.

A week later, for his actions at Aldie in Virginia, Custer would earn his first star. Whittaker wrote in his Custer biography:

> Coming into action as a reserve to check the tide of defeat, is always the hardest task for young soldiers, and ... this was the first serious action in which many of the Union regiments had been engaged. Confusion began to spread, horses were plunging and fighting, men turning pale, and shrinking back from the moral effect of the yelling line of Confederate cavalry coming on, wrapped in clouds of dust. Add to this, the shrieking of the enemy's shells, and the sharp crash of their explosions, the dead and wounded horses and men lying about...and it is not surprising that the green northern men wavered, nor that their officers were yelling confusedly, instead of commanding coolly.
>
> So great was the turmoil ... when forth from the crowd rode ... a young captain, wearing a broad plantation straw hat, from under which long bright curls flowed over his shoulders. His uniform was careless and shabby, but his bright curls attracted attention wherever he went. Out he rode ... waved his long blade in the air, and pointed to the enemy, then turned his horse and galloped alone towards them. An electric shock seemed to silence the line. He looked back and beckoned with his sword. "Come on, boys," he shouted.
>
> An involuntary yell burst from the men, and away they went. All fear and hesitation had vanished, and the long line, broken by its own impetuosity, little clumps of horsemen, went racing down to charge the enemy. They were met by a tremendous fire. In the foremost of the triumphant group was the young captain with the bright curls, and in all the confusion the men followed him as a guiding star. Kilpatrick went down, his horse shot from under him, Douty was stricken dead, but the young captain with the floating curls seemed to bear a charmed life.
>
> Far ahead of the Northern riders was the young captain with the floating curls. He rode his favorite black 'Harry,' named after the innocent child at home. In his hand gleamed the long straight blade he had captured from the Confederate, one year before, when he shot him and took his horse, down in front of Richmond. Custer wore that sword all through the war, a long straight Toledo blade, with the Spanish inscription, *"No mi tires sin razon, no mi envaines sin honora"* (Draw me not without cause, sheathe me not without honor). Years after, men said that hardly an arm in the service could be found strong enough to wield that blade, save Custer's alone.

Union Colonel Hugh Kilpatrick—nicknamed "Kill Cavalry"—too often led his horse soldiers into ill-advised skirmishes and more than too often paid a heavy price. (May 1863 issue of *Harper's Weekly*)

Often Custer found himself in hot pursuit of an enemy rider, completely oblivious to what was transpiring around him. In this instance, after dispatching a Rebel officer to the hereafter, he suddenly realized he was far from friendly lines, with enemy cavalry in close proximity. He wrote about this, in a letter to his sister. "I was surrounded by Rebels, and cut off from my own men, but I made my way out safely, all owing to my hat, which is a large broad brim, exactly like that worn by the Rebels. Everyone tells me that I look like a Rebel more than our own men. The Rebels at first thought I was one of their own men, and did not attack me, except one, who rushed at me with his sabre, but I struck him across the face with my sabre, knocking him off his horse. I then put spurs to Harry and made my escape."

Custer Earns a Star

Captain Custer's actions at Aldie Station not only attracted attention from the field reporters covering the battles, but General Pleasonton noted it and recommended him for promotion. But rather than climb the ranks incrementally, from major, then lieutenant colonel and full colonel, Custer leapfrogged thousands of his fellow officers, and was recommended for brigadier general. Pleasonton also recommended Colonel Kilpatrick, and captains Farnsworth and Merritt for promotion. For Kilpatrick, it was the next step up, but for the three captains, they were leapfrogging many hundreds of majors, lieutenant colonels, and colonels, and elicited sarcasm and ridicule, especially directed toward the fair-haired, baby-faced Autie Custer. It didn't help that the latter often boasted that he was destined to become a general officer, which was met with caustic bantering and harassment.

"One evening, eleven days after Aldie, when Custer returned to headquarters, after a long ride, in which he had been posting the pickets of the entire corps for the night, he was greeted in the large tent, where the staff was wont to gather at night, by the salutations, 'Hallo, general.' 'How are you, general?' 'Gentlemen, General Custer.' 'Why, general, I congratulate you.' 'You're looking well, general,'" recapped Whittaker. "The greetings came from all quarters of the tent, where staff officers were lounging, smoking, chatting, laughing, telling stories. They impressed Custer as being merely a continuation of the usual ill-natured banter on the subject of his aspirations and, further, as being carried a little too far. He answered, 'You may laugh, boys. Laugh as long as you please, but I WILL be a general yet, for all your chaff. You see if I don't that's all.' He was greeted by a universal shout of laughter in answer. It seemed as if his tormentors were determined to irritate him into an explosion; and they nearly succeeded; for his blue eyes began to flash, and he looked round as if seeking someone on whom to fix a quarrel."

Finally one of them suggested he look on the table in his tent. There was an envelope addressed to "Brigadier General George A. Custer, U.S. Vols." He nearly fainted, not sure what to say, and sat down before he collapsed. His fellow officers surrounded him with congratulations.

Custer was the premier cavalry officer, always preferring the close-quarters sabre, while many of his Rebel counterparts relied on the pistol or single-shot rifles. Though he had many close shaves, Custer never lost a battle during the Civil War. (May 1863 issue of *Harper's Weekly*)

Custer would be given command of the 1st, 5th, 6th and 7th Michigan cavalry regiments and Battery M of the 2nd U.S. Artillery, as the Michigan Brigade, the Wolverines, part of the recently formed Cavalry Corps. He wasted little time tracking down Joseph Fought, the soldier he had met in DC while searching desperately for a horse, who was now his orderly, and near-constant shadow. Now he gave Fought another task, to find a pair of stars for his uniform. The trooper checked local houses, with little luck. Eventually he found a pair of stars, then looked for needle and thread to sew them on the new general's collars.

"The next morning he was a full-fledged brigadier general," Fought remembered, in *The Custer Story*, published in 1880. "All the other officers were exceedingly jealous of him. Not one of them but would have thrown a stone in his way to make him lose his prestige. He was way ahead of them as a soldier, and that made them angry."

"Exceedingly jealous" may not have accurately described how many of Custer's fellow officers felt about his advanced promotion. "… it seemed almost incredible that at the age of twenty-four he should be appointed general. He was probably the youngest man who ever held that rank," wrote W. Sanford Ramey, in *Kings of the Battle-Field*. "There was considerable ill feeling shown at his sudden elevation. Men who had been colonels and brigadiers while he was still a cadet did not relish this rapid advancement of one who was so much their junior. A certain dandyism in dress which Custer practiced called out a good deal of sarcastic comment. The young general was quite aware of this state of feeling, but trusted that the first battle would show his seniors that he was not a mere military coxcomb."

Never one to wear a regulation Army officer's uniform, Custer set out to distinguish his, almost to the point of ridiculousness. Fought explained it: "He wore a velveteen jacket with five gold loops on each sleeve, and a sailor shirt with a very large collar that he got from a gunboat on the James [River]. The shirt was dark blue, and with it he wore a conspicuous red tie—top boots, a soft hat, Confederate, that he had picked up on the field, and his hair was long and in curls almost to his shoulders." Such a garrulous outfit would certainly attract attention, but for Custer, who chose to lead his soldiers into battle, he also attracted more than his share of enemy gunfire, and had several stallions shot from under him. It was simply a clear expression of who Custer as a leader wanted to be, and how best to communicate it to everyone around him. The impression was not lost on those who observed him.

Colonel J. H. Kidd, with the 6th Michigan Cavalry and a former brevet brigadier general of volunteers, wrote about Custer in *Personal Recollections of a Cavalryman with Custer's Michigan Cavalry Brigade in the Civil War*: "Custer with flashing eye and flowing hair, charging at the head of his men, was a grand and picturesque figure, the more so by reason of his fantastic uniform, which made him a conspicuous mark for the enemy's bullets, but a coward in Custer's uniform would have become the laughing stock of the Army." Whittaker, in his Custer biography, wrote:

[Custer] was distinctly conscious all the time, that his subordinates disliked, suspected, and distrusted him. Grey-headed colonels came in to salute him with outward respect, but the stiff dignity of their manners convinced him that they were inwardly boiling over with disgust and anger at having this "boy," this "popinjay," this "affected dandy," with his girl's hair, his swagger, and West Point conceit put "over men, sir, men who had left their farms and business, men who could make their own living, sir, and asked no government a penny for their support, men old enough to be his father, and who knew as much about real fighting, sir, as any epauletted government pensioner and West Point popinjay who was ever seen—too lazy to work for their living, and depending on government for support—hired mercenaries, by heavens, good for nothing alongside of the noble volunteers."

On June 17, the two forces clashed, at Aldie, in Loudon County, Virginia, then Middleburg and Upperville over the next few days. The Rebel cavalry had experienced devastating losses in recent skirmishes, preferring to use the pistol in close quarters clashes, while Union troopers used the sabre. Captain James Stevenson, of the 1st Cavalry, published years later in *The Philadelphia Weekly Times* in 1870, recalled:

The two columns drew nearer and nearer, the Confederates outnumbering their opponents (at) three or four to one. The gait increased—first the trot, then the gallop. The orders of the Confederate officers could be heard by those in the woods on their left "Keep to your sabres, men, keep to your sabres!" for the lessons they had learned at Brandy Station and at Aldie had been severe. There the cry had been: "Put up your sabres! Draw your pistols and fight like gentlemen!" But the sabre was never a favorite weapon with the Confederate cavalry, and now, in spite of the lessons of the past, the warnings of the present were not heeded by all.

Union artillery was firing at the advancing Rebel cavalry, who struggled to maintain order as their mounts panicked, some crippled by canister shot and shrapnel. Stevenson continued:

Staggered by the fearful execution from the two batteries, the men in the front line of the Confederate column drew in their horses and wavered. Some turned, and the column fanned out to the right and left, but those behind came pressing on. Custer, seeing the front men hesitate, waved his sabre and shouted, "Come on, you Wolverines!" and with a fearful yell the First Michigan rushed on, Custer four lengths ahead.

The two forces clashed, hand to hand, neither giving ground, though eventually the fringes of the Rebel troopers peeled away and withdrew, many of them with horrible gashes about the head and upper torso. Despite the numbers advantage prior to the skirmish, Confederate losses were heavy. Custer and his Michigan Wolverines continued to be the vanguard of all mounted soldiers. With his promotion to brigadier general, Custer continued the refinement of his ensemble, casting aside the regulation Union Army officer's uniform.

Colonel J. H. Kidd in *Personnel Recollections* recalled the first time he noticed Custer in the field:

Tall, lithe, active, muscular, straight as an Indian and as quick in his movements, he had the fair complexion of a school girl. His golden hair fell in graceful luxuriance nearly or quite to his shoulders, and his upper lip was garnished with a blonde mustache. A sword and belt, gilt spurs and top boots completed his unique outfit. A keen eye would have been slow to detect in that rider with the flowing locks and gaudy tie, in his dress of velvet and of gold, the master spirit that he proved to be. That garb, fantastic as at first sight it appeared to be, was to be the distinguishing mark which, during all the remaining years of that war, like the white plume of Henry of Navarre, was to show us where, in the thickest of the fight, we were to seek our leader for, where danger was, where swords were to cross, where Greek met Greek, there was he, always. Brave but not reckless; self-confident, yet modest; ambitious, but regulating his conduct at all times by a high sense of honor and duty; eager for laurels, but scorning to wear them unworthily; ready and willing to act, but regardful of human life; quick in emergencies, cool and self-possessed, his courage was of the highest moral type, his perceptions were intuitions. Showy like Murat, fiery like Farnsworth, yet calm and self-reliant like Sheridan, he was the most brilliant and successful cavalry officer of his time ... Stars of the first magnitude did not appear often in the galaxy of military heroes. Custer was one of the few.

Gettysburg, the Pivotal Confrontation

While still getting to know his men, many of them Michigan Wolverines, and assessing their battle readiness, Custer was getting his marching orders for the next confrontation, somewhere near a small village in western Pennsylvania. More than any other battle during the Civil War, Gettysburg has been written about and studied, replayed, and reenacted every year in early July, with each of its major players etched in history, though many overlook the crucial role the cavalry forces played in the outcome.

"Little has been written of the operations of the cavalry during the battle of Gettysburg. So fierce was the main engagement, of which the infantry bore the brunt, that the 'affairs' of the cavalry have almost passed unnoticed, yet on the right flank there occurred one of the most beautiful cavalry fights of the war, and one most important in its results," wrote Colonel William Brooke-Rawle in *The Annals of the Civil War, written by Leading Participants, North and South.* "It may be confidently asserted that, had it not been for [the Union cavalry], on July 3d, 1863, that day would have resulted differently, and, instead of a glorious victory, the name of Gettysburg would suggest a state of affairs which it is not agreeable to contemplate."

Soon after 1:00 p.m. on July 3, the Confederate battery opened up near Hanover Road. Custer's pickets were positioned in a stand of trees near Low Dutch Road, listening to distant gunfire when the enemy big guns unloaded hell fire, as a prelude to Rebel General George Pickett's charge, more than 4,000 strong, on the Union forces at Cemetery Hill. Soon they were engaged as Rebel infantry advanced, threatening to overrun them. Custer's brigade was ordered to reinforce the beleaguered Union troops, who were running out of ammunition. Colonel Brooke-Rawle recalled:

> The Seventh Michigan ... was just then coming upon the field ... in column of fours. Custer who was near, saw the emergency, ordered close column of squadrons to be formed at the gallop and advanced with it to meet the attack. In close columns of squadrons, advancing as if in review, with sabers drawn and glistening like silver in the bright sunlight—the spectacle called forth a murmur of admiration. It was, indeed a memorable one. Canister and shell were poured into the steadily approaching column as fast as the guns could fire. The dismounted men fell

A rare sighting—Brigadier General George Custer dressed in something resembling a Union Army uniform! Normally his "look" would be considered flamboyant, outrageous, ostentatious—but rarely regulation. (National Archives)

back to the right and left, and such as could got to their horses. The mounted skirmishers rallied and fell into line.

The two columns drew nearer and nearer, the Confederates outnumbering their opponents three or four to one. The gait increased—first the trot, then the gallop. As the charge was ordered the speed increased, every horse on the jump, every man yelling like a demon. Meanwhile the heads of the two columns had met—the one led by Hampton and Fitz Lee, and the other by Custer—and were fighting hand to hand.

The successful result of this magnificent cavalry charge was attributed by the victors to the steadiness and efficiency with which they used the sabre, en masse, against greatly superior numbers of the enemy, many of whom had exchanged that weapon for the revolver. It should be a strong point, in favor of the retention of the sabre as a cavalryman's weapon. To borrow the language of Custer in his report of it: "I challenge the annals of warfare to produce a more brilliant or successful charge of cavalry than the one just recounted."

"Justice had not been done to the cavalry in the campaign of Gettysburg," Major General Alfred Pleasonton continued in *The Annals of the Civil War*. "… the renown for all that is great and glorious in cavalry warfare they established for themselves in that campaign, made them the peers of the famous troopers of the Great Frederick, and the splendid horsemen who swept over the plains of Europe led by the white plume of the dashing Murat."

As a young cavalry officer at Gettysburg, William Brooke-Rawle was proud of what they had done. Three decades later, in an article in *Cavalry Journal* in 1891, he wrote, "We cavalrymen have always held that we saved the day at the most critical moment of the battle of Gettysburg—the greatest battle and the turning point of the War of the Rebellion."

Four months after the battle, President Lincoln visited Gettysburg, specifically Evergreen Cemetery on Cemetery Hill, where thousands of Union soldiers were buried. On November 19, 1863, the grounds were consecrated, and memorialized by the president:

Fourscore and seven years ago our fathers brought forth upon this continent a new nation, conceived in liberty, and dedicated to the proposition that all men are created equal. Now we are engaged in a great civil war, testing whether that nation, or any nation so conceived and so dedicated, can long endure. We are met on a great battle-field of that war. We are met to dedicate a portion of it as the final resting-place of those who here gave their lives that that nation might live. It is

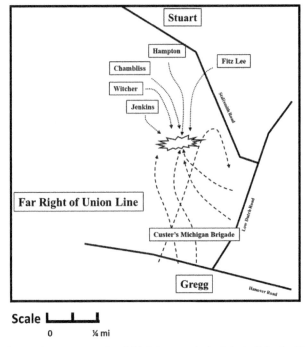

The battle of Gettysburg, east cavalry field, July 3, 1863 (3rd day). (Map by Ted Behncke)

altogether fitting and proper that we should do this. But in a larger sense we cannot dedicate, we cannot consecrate, we cannot hallow this ground. The brave men, living and dead, who struggled here, have consecrated it far above our power to add or detract … I here highly resolve that the dead shall not have died in vain; that the nation shall, under God, have a new birth of freedom; and governments of the people, by the people, and for the people, shall not perish from the earth.

Continuing the Pursuit from Gettysburg

E. A. Paul was a war reporter with the *New York Times*, who followed General Pleasonton, and quickly noticed the audacious Custer. Paul introduced voracious readers to this brash cavalry officer:

> The operations immediately after Gettysburg, in the case of Custer's brigade, first show clearly, in the handling of the command, a high order of military talent in the young general … as a brigade commander, he became indisputably the best in the Cavalry Corps, and his single brigade seemed to do more work and attract more notice than any other. This success was owing mainly to the same qualities conspicuous in the Urbana expedition—tact. What had been tact in the lieutenant became "coup d'oeil" in the general. It consists in doing (or saying) the right thing at the right time, the power of rapid decision.
>
> No man knew better than he that the sole aggressive strength of cavalry is found in the charge, while dismounted skirmishers are the best weapon for defensive battles. This truth was very seldom observed by other brigade commanders, who grew altogether too fond of dismounted work. Custer, at Gettysburg and after, always used both kinds of lines together, just

as Caesar did at Pharsalia, when opposing an enemy of superior force, but when his foes were equal or inferior, as invariably availed himself of the moral influence of the mounted charge, as the most efficacious of all.

Initially his soldiers and subordinate commanders may have been concerned that Custer may make irrational decisions with little concern for them, but in fact, they were uppermost on his mind. In a letter to a friend he wrote about his new responsibilities: "Often I think of the vast responsibility resting on me, in the many lives entrusted to my keeping, of the happiness of the so many households depending on my discretion and judgment and to think that I am just leaving my boyhood makes the responsibility appear greater. 'First be sure you're right, then go ahead!' I ask myself is it right? Satisfied that it is so, I let nothing swerve me from my purpose."

Colonel J. H. Kidd wrote:

> When the battle of Gettysburg was ended and the shadows of night began to gather upon the Rummel fields, the troopers of the Michigan cavalry brigade had a right to feel that they had acted well their parts, and contributed their full share to the glory and success of the Union arms. They had richly earned a rest, but were destined not to obtain it until after many days of such toil and hardship as to surpass even the previous experiences of the campaign. [Lee's forces were rapidly retreating south, with the Union cavalry hot on their heels, harassing the rear pickets at every opportunity.]
>
> My recollection is not clear as to the other battles, but I know that the day after Gettysburg the flood-gates of heaven were opened, and as the column of cavalry took its way towards Emmittsburg it was deluged. It seemed as if the firmament were an immense tank, the contents of which were spilled all at once. Such a drenching as we had! Even heavy gum coats and horsehide boots were hardly proof against it. It poured and poured, the water running in streams off the horses' backs, making of every rivulet a river and of every river and mountain stream a raging flood. But Lee was in retreat and, rain or shine, it was our duty to reach his rear, so all day long we plodded and splashed along the muddy roads towards the passes in the Catoctin and South mountains. It was a tedious ride for men already worn out with incessant marching and the fatigues of many days.

The Union cavalry troopers could hear vast trains of wagons and caissons in the distance, horses whinnying and mules braying under the strain, trying to avoid capture. The Confederate field forces could not afford to have rations, and ammunition fall into enemy hands, and so at choke points along the way, Rebel field guns and infantry pickets positioned themselves to harass and impede their Union Army pursuers.

Confederate General Lee managed to get his battered forces over South Mountain, through the Cumberland Valley and back across the Potomac into Virginia, before the Union Army could cut off his retreat, and capture his many wagons crammed with supplies and the wounded, his caissons and field guns. July had been a devastating month, and during the retreat, many stragglers, scavenging for anything to eat, fell by the wayside, or simply drifted away during the night. Brigadier General Custer had heard that an enemy wagon train was moving toward Monterey Springs, but as they closed the distance, a Rebel field gun—a 12-pounder Napoleon—blunted their approach temporarily, but then hustled back to rejoin the retreat. General Kilpatrick

Considered one of the Confederate army's most ferocious cavalry officer, J. E. B. Stuart saw his field guns captured by General Custer's cavalry brigade near Culpepper in September of 1863. (*Frank Leslie's Illustrated Monthly*)

ordered Custer to resume the attack, despite almost total darkness, treacherous terrain and near-impassable undergrowth. Always in the lead, Custer caught up to the vulnerable enemy wagons, and during the clash and the confusion, with cavalry from both sides engaged, he was thrown from his horse, and was nearly captured again.

In his own words, Custer filed the following report on the August raids on enemy forces along Opequon Creek and the battle of Winchester. "One continuous and heavy line of skirmishers covered the advance, using only the carbine, while the line of brigades, as they advanced across the open country, the bands playing the national airs, presented in the sunlight one moving mass of glistening sabres. This, combined with the various bright colored banners and battle-flags, intermingled here and there with the plain blue uniforms of the troops, furnished one of the most inspiring as well as imposing scenes of martial grandeur I ever witnessed on a battlefield." Frederick Whittaker, in his Custer biography, wrote:

> At Culpepper the enemy made a stand with all his artillery. General Stuart was there, getting ready to leave, fancying the whole of Meade's army was advancing. A locomotive and train of cars was ready, all steam up, when Custer's brigade came dashing on, only to find themselves stopped by a deep creek with a single ford. The enemy opened fire with three batteries, and Custer's guns tried to cripple the locomotive. In the hurry and confusion at the ford, however, the train got away. Custer himself was far ahead of his own skirmishers, who were bothered by the swamps at the border of the creek below, and he rode on with the skirmishers of the next brigade on the right, which happened to be the Second New York. With them and a few of his own men he galloped into Culpepper, cut off two of the enemy's guns, and captured them. Ten minutes later Culpepper was ours, and the enemy hastily retreating towards the Rapidan.

Monroe's War Hero Returns Home

It was during one of the many spirited close quarters battles Custer was engaged in that shrapnel cut through his thigh. Specifically, as Major General Pleasonton reported on September 13, "driving the enemy on the Cedar Mountain road slowly. General Custer was wounded in the charge, capturing the guns that were taken, and his horse was killed under him. His gallantry was distinguished." Not enough to permanently take him out of the fight, but enough to earn him a three-week convalescence back to Monroe.

The specific incident was retold by a member of the Army of the Potomac's headquarters staff. Colonel Theodore Lyman wrote on September 17:

> The whole Cavalry Corps (a good many thousand men) had been massed ... and orders to cross the Rappahannock. Then General Pleasonton ordered an advance, and, in a few moments, quite as if by magic, the open country was alive with horsemen; first came columns of skirmishers who immediately deployed and went forward, at a brisk trot, or canter, making a connected line, as far as the eye could reach, right and left. This was a really handsome charge and was led by General Custer, who had his horse shot under him. This officer is one of the funniest-looking beings you ever saw, and looked like a circus rider gone mad! His aspect, though highly amusing, is also pleasing, as he has a very merry blue eye, and a devil-may-care style. His first greeting to General Pleasonton, as he rode up, was: "How are you, fifteen-days'-leave-of-absence? They have spoiled my boots but they didn't gain much there, for I stole 'em from a Reb." And certainly, there was one boot torn by a piece of shell and the leg hurt also, so the warlike ringlets got not only fifteen, but twelve [additional] days' leave of absence, and have retreated to [his] native Michigan!

Local citizens followed Custer's meteoric rise through the ranks and his beyond-belief skirmishes, ever the victor, and so when he arrived back home, it was to a hero's welcome, the toast of the town everywhere he went. The *Monroe Monitor* reported on September 30, on one of these occasions, "Quite a number of young ladies and gentlemen of Monroe had a fancy dress ball at Humphrey House, on Monday evening last, in honor of Gen. Geo. A. Custer, who has been visiting his family and friends here for a few days past." He certainly basked in the adoration, but the one person he failed to sway previously—Libbie's father, Judge Daniel Bacon—was now duly impressed, and finally consented to his only daughter being courted by Monroe's national hero. By mid-September Custer returned to the saddle, with the Army of the Potomac, though a few months later, he would be back in Monroe, to marry Libbie on February 9, in the First Presbyterian Church. She would then follow him, as many officers' wives would do, following closely near the front, but first, before the wedding, he had to get back to his Wolverines for whatever awaited them. They didn't have to wait long.

In short order, he was again in the thick of the fighting, chasing the Rebels as they retreated back through Virginia. During a lull in the fighting, some two weeks after the fight at Brandy Station, Custer wrote about the 3rd Division's actions on October 10:

The heavy masses of the Rebel cavalry could be seen covering the heights in front of my advance, a heavy column was enveloping each flank, and my advance confronted by more than double my own number. The major-general commanding the Cavalry Corps at this moment rode to the advance. To him I proposed with my command to cut through the force in my front, and thus open a way for the entire command to the river. My proposition was approved, and I received orders to take my available force and push forward.

After ordering them to draw their sabers, I informed them that we were surrounded, and all we had to do was to open a way with our sabers. They showed their determination and purpose by giving three hearty cheers. At this moment the band struck up the inspiring air of "Yankee Doodle," which excited the enthusiasm of the entire command to the highest pitch and made each individual member feel as if he was a host in himself. Simultaneously both regiments moved forward to the attack. The enemy, without waiting to receive the onset, broke in disorder and fled … we succeeded in reaching the river, which we crossed in good order.

"Oh, could you but have seen some of the charges that we made!" wrote Custer, in a letter to Annette Humphrey, on October 12, further embellishing the battle. "I gave the command 'Forward!' And I never expect to see a prettier sight. I frequently turned in my saddle to see the glittering sabres advance in the sunlight. I was riding in front, and close behind me my new battle-flag so soon to receive its baptism in blood. Then came my orderlies, and behind them the regiments. After advancing a short distance I gave the word 'Charge!'—and away we went, whooping and yelling like so many demons."

Colonel J. H. Kidd with the 6th Michigan Cavalry reported:

Buckland Mills was, in some sort, a sequel to Brandy Station. The latter battle [October of 1863] was a brilliant passage at arms, in which neither side obtained a decisive advantage. [Confederate General J. E. B.] Stuart was at Buckland Mills with Hampton's division, and Fitzhugh Lee was at or near Auburn, but a few miles away. They had their heads together and devised a trap for [Union cavalry commander] Kilpatrick, into which he rode with his eyes shut.

Kilpatrick was to be attacked simultaneously by Stuart in front and by Lee in rear, and thoroughly whipped. It was a very pretty bit of strategy and came very near being successful. The plan was neatly frustrated by one of those apparent accidents of war which make or unmake men, according as they are favorable or unfavorable.

Custer was a fighting man, through and through, but wary and wily as brave. There was in him an indescribable something—call it caution, call it sagacity, call it the real military instinct—it may have been genius—by whatever name entitled, it nearly always impelled him to do intuitively the right thing. In this case it seemed obstinacy, if not insubordination. It was characteristic of him to care studiously for the comfort of his men. And he did not believe in wasting their lives. It is more than probable that there was in his mind a suspicion of the true state of things.

Opposed to Custer's five regiments and one battery, Fitzhugh Lee had twelve regiments of cavalry, three brigades … and as good a battery [of field guns] as was in the Confederate service.

Major H. B. McClellan, Stuart's adjutant general, commenting in his book on this battle, says that "Custer was a hard fighter, even on a retreat." He also says that "Fitzhugh Lee had come up from Auburn expecting to gain, unopposed, the rear of Kilpatrick's division, but he found Custer's brigade at Broad Run ready to oppose him. A fierce fight ensued."

During the battle at Chancellorsville, Union forces had a very tough fight, realizing the Rebels were far from defeated. (National Archives)

Whether by ignorance or Custer intuition, he held the 6th Michigan back, thus avoiding the trap, set by his former West Point instructor, Fitzhugh Lee.

Charles Morris in *Heroes of the Army in America* wrote:

> The most efficient work of the cavalry in the valley campaign was on October 19, during the notable fight at Cedar Creek in this critical state of affairs. [Generals] Custer and Merritt rendered the noblest service. While the Confederates, exhausted by sixteen hours of marching and fighting, stopped to rest and eat, and the broken lines made some effort to reform their ranks, these knights of the saddle, at the head of six or seven thousand gallant horsemen, rode into the open space between the two armies and served as a shield to the regiments forming behind them. When the Confederates again advanced, twenty thousand strong, they found their progress checked by these few thousands of mounted men, with a number of pieces of artillery. Charge after charge was made upon them, but they held firm, and were still acting as a stone wall of defence [sic] when Sheridan came riding up at headlong speed from Winchester and called his men to face the other way and win back the camp and cannon they had lost. Everyone is familiar with what followed, how defeat was turned into victory, and Early lost far more than he had gained. The cavalry took a leading part in the pursuit and helped to end Early's career in the valley. Custer's share in these operations brought him the brevet rank of major-general of volunteers.

Custer had more on his mind than pursuing Johnny Reb across northern Virginia, the Confederate field Army little more than a rag-tag scattering of reluctant secessionists wearing tattered uniforms, desperately hungry, despondently weary of battle. Back home, Libbie Bacon was waiting, anxiously planning her wedding to Michigan's most famous war hero. At least with winter fast approaching, he could ask for a leave of absence, while the enemy would hunker down, pray for provisions, and lick their wounds. Conversely, the Union Army was unstoppable, and its cavalry was finally being utilized as a combat multiplier, a fearsome weapon, led by Corps Commander Philip Sheridan, with Custer and his Michigan Wolverines, sporting the rapid-fire Spencer 7-shot rifles, always leading the assault. They couldn't wait for warmer weather to continue the pursuit and end this nonsense. But before winter weather set in, there was still fighting to be done.

At Morton's Ford on the Rapidan River, Custer's Michigan cavalry attacked Rebel infantry from November 27 to December 2, but fell back to the north banks of the river. By then winter weather was setting in, and both sides hunkered down as best they could. Senior commanders secured lodging in local houses, while the remainder of the troops lived in tents and make-shift huts.

Neither side pestered the other with harassing fire, even when officers on horseback were spotted traversing the far banks of the river, checking the lookout posts. It was quite common for the opposing pickets to freely converse and sometimes even cross over during daylight hours, to exchange various goods, such as tobacco for hardtack, or coffee for molasses. At night, strict rules of engagement were followed, including sentries challenging anyone approaching their position, asking for the password of the day.

For the Michigan cavalry, new recruits were arriving and needed to be trained before the coming spring offensive started. The 6th Michigan alone welcomed more than 200 recruits, all within a few days.

As the spring of 1864 approached, Union Army leaders were feeling confident. The first half of 1863 was devastating, with Confederate victories at Chancellorsville in Virginia and Chickamauga in Georgia. But their daring push into Pennsylvania was repulsed at Gettysburg, and they were chased back to Virginia. The only hope the Rebels were counting on was to fight a defensive war through the end of 1864 and hope the northern populace would become war-weary and oust President Lincoln in the November elections, then bring in someone more willing to make peace with the south.

"Some time after the beginning of the year 1864, there began to be rumors of some daring expedition that was afoot, to be led by the dashing general commanding the division," reported Colonel J. H. Kidd. "Hints were thrown out of an indefinite something that was going to happen. It is not known, as it was soon thereafter, that Kilpatrick had devised a daring scheme for the capture of Richmond, which had been received with so much favor by the authorities in Washington, that he was then awaiting only the necessary authority from the war department before setting out on what proved to be an ill-fated expedition."

Union General Kilpatrick, derisively dubbed "Kill Cavalry," wanted to seize Richmond, using Custer's 2,000 cavalry troops as a feint, with a raid on Gordonsville and Madison Court House, then on to Charlottesville, pulling the Rebel infantry and cavalry away from the real target, a direct assault on Richmond. Robert U. Johnson and Clarence C. Buell, in *Battles and Leaders of the Civil War*, Volume 4, wrote:

> Through the treachery of a guide the head of Custer's column was turned off to the right for the purpose, it was believed, of bringing it in upon the main body of Lee's infantry, where its capture would be certain. Custer discovered the attempt in time and retraced his steps to the main road which he had left. [Confederate General J. E. B.] Stuart meantime had learned of the departure of Custer from the direct route, and at once moved his command to intercept him. This cleared the way for Custer and enabled him to return within the lines of the Sixth Corps, with only an affair with a rear-guard. His movement had certainly had the desired effect as a diversion.

Colonel J. H. Kidd concluded that "Custer's part of the work was successfully accomplished. He created so much commotion in the direction of Charlottesville that Kilpatrick was across the Rapidan and well on his way before his purpose was either discovered or suspected. It was, however, a fatal mistake to leave Custer behind. With him the expedition as devised might well have been successful; without him it

Union commander Hugh Kilpatrick's final charge, at Waynesboro, in Virginia. (January 1865 issue of *Harper's Weekly*)

was foredoomed to failure." On December 4, Custer filed a report on skirmishing and a feint at Stevensburg, Virginia:

> At 6 o'clock on the morning of the 26th [of November] ultimo, this division left camp near Stevensburg and moved to the Rapidan River … My instructions were to make demonstrations at different points from Morton's Ford upward, as if to cross, the moment I heard cannonading at the lower fords. Our endeavors to mislead the enemy were entirely successful: it was evident that he supposed our intention was to effect a crossing.

Custer Weds

1864 promised to be a great year. The Union Army had the clear upper hand and it was only a matter of time before the Confederates called it quits. At least that was the thinking in DC, that the war would last only a few months more and then the healing process could begin. For George Autie Custer, he had a wedding to get to. Looking back over the past year, his conquests on the battlefield were much easier than convincing Judge Bacon that this brash Wolverine cavalry officer was a suitable husband for his only daughter. Possibly if the entire nation wasn't talking about the boy general with the golden locks the judge might be less inclined, but Brigadier General Custer was truly an undisputed hero of the Civil War.

Custer returned to Monroe and was married on February 9. They departed for Washington, for a little politicking while on their honeymoon. But their plans quickly changed. Libbie wrote in her book *Boots and Saddles*, in 1885:

> We had no sooner reached Washington on our wedding-journey than telegrams came, following one another in quick succession, asking him to give up the rest of his leave of absence, and hasten without an hour's delay to the front. I begged so hard not to be left behind that I finally prevailed. The result was that I found myself in a few hours on the extreme wing of the Army of the Potomac, in an isolated Virginia farm-house, finishing my honeymoon alone.
>
> After the raid was ended, we spent some delightful weeks together, and when the regular spring campaign began I returned to Washington, where I remained until the surrender and the close of the war.

In the final months of the war, Libbie would wait for Autie in Washington, though she considered it a dreadful city. She was quite the charmer though, and when she met President Lincoln, he said, "So you are the wife of the man who goes into the cavalry charges with a whoop and a yell!"

After accompanying her husband as he hobnobbed around DC, Libbie wrote to her parents, on March 28, 1864:

> I can't tell you what a place Autie has here in public opinion. It astonishes me to see the attention with which he is treated everywhere. One day at the House [of Representatives] he was invited to go on the floor, and the members came flocking round to be presented. One said, "So you are the youngest General in the Army, well, I wish there were more like you." And, when some old fogy objected to his confirmation on account of his youth, the rest said, "Pity there aren't more like him!"

During a brief visit home, local and national hero George Custer married Libbie Bacon, in February 1864. The lovebirds hoped to honeymoon and hobnob with politicians in Washington, DC, but it was cut short when he was called back to duty to continue the fight. (National Archives)

President Lincoln was still not happy with the conduct of the war in the East, and relieved General Pleasonton, replacing him with Philip Sheridan, as commander of the Cavalry Corps. Ulysses S. Grant, who had orchestrated a successful campaign with the Army of the West was now overall commander. Once again, Custer lost a superior he looked up to. First it was McClellan, and now Pleasonton. He'd heard about "Little Phil" but wasn't yet sure if they were compatible.

Libbie Custer had moved back to Washington, DC, and while dallying in social circles, heard plenty of gossip. In an April 1864 letter to her parents she provided a little insight into the Pleasonton dismissal: "Father, as an illustration of what you and Autie have cautioned me about holding my tongue on Army and political matters—I heard lately that General Pleasonton was removed, not on account of feeling between him and General Meade, but because his two sisters, maiden ladies living here, have talked so badly about the President and the Secretary of War, and it was supposed these were his views they were repeating."

"Little Phil" Sheridan takes the Lead

Frederick Whittaker would later write about the bonds Custer had with Pleasonton, McClellan and Sheridan, in his Custer biography:

> Custer wrote home about Pleasonton, "he has been more like a father to me than a general," and this was indeed the truth. There must, however, have been something peculiarly magnetic about Custer to have attracted to himself, as he did, the enthusiastic affection of three men of such very different characters as his three successive commanders. McClellan, the polished scientific soldier, kind-hearted to a fault, slow, methodical and cautious; Pleasonton, acrid, sarcastic, exacting, an excellent cavalry chief, but generally failing to attract any affection from his subordinates, a martinet in his discipline; Sheridan, fiery, impetuous, untiring, remorseless in the amount of work he exacted from his troops; all these three men loved, admired, and trusted Custer entirely; and it was nothing but the transcendent ability of his character that forced them to do so. When any work was to do which no one else could do, Pleasonton first, and Sheridan afterwards, always set Custer to do it.

Army surgeon C. J. Wood, in *Reminiscences of the War,* wrote that "during all of General Sheridan's brilliant successes in the Shenandoah Valley, Custer was among his favorite captains of the horse. Bold, dashing and daring, Custer was always chosen to head cavalry expeditions of unusual hazard or difficulty. His noble courage and impetuous charges always succeeded in confusing the enemy and winning success to the National cause. He always led his column in person, and never wanted a soldier to go with him who would hesitate a moment to ride right straight on to the Rebel army, if ordered."

Major General Philip Sheridan had proven himself a worthy cavalry commander during campaigns further west, and soon after joining Grant for the Virginia Campaign he insisted on independence. Cavalry troops would no longer be used in support operations, such as accompanying infantry, guarding rear elements, or held in reserve. Little Phil demanded a leading role for the cavalry, and he quickly realized Custer was the most capable field commander. But the Union cavalry's first priority was to track down and eliminate their ultimate opponent—Confederate General J. E. B. Stuart. It wouldn't be easy. In fact, on several occasions, Stuart had victory in his grasp, as his mission was to neutralize that pesky Union upstart with the golden locks, the boy general—George Custer.

Whenever there was a lull in the action, waiting for other units to catch up, giving his men much-needed rest and replenishment, General Custer filed his battle reports, with embellishments, which he'd learned from being a general's aide. After the raid into Albermarle County, Virginia, which took place from February 28 to March 1, 1864, Custer wrote, "While on this expedition [my command] marched upwards of 150 miles, destroyed the bridge over the Rivanna River, burned 3 large forges, with harness complete; captured 1 standard bearing the arms of Virginia, over 500 prisoners, and about 500 horses, besides bringing away over 100 contrabands. A large camp of the enemy was also captured and destroyed near Charlottesville."

Two months later, in early May, General Grant was leading the advance into Virginia. Dubbed the Wilderness Campaign, it was his first engagement in the eastern push toward Richmond. Custer was inspecting his pickets of the 1st Michigan, cautioning them to be alert. Colonel J. H. Kidd in *Personal Recollections* recalled:

> Suddenly, the signal came. A picket shot was heard, then another, and another. Thicker and faster the spattering tones were borne to our ears from the woods in front. Then, it was the "rebel yell" ... at first faint, but swelling in volume as it approached. A brigade of cavalry, led by the intrepid [Confederate General and Custer's former roommate Thomas] Rosser, was charging full tilt toward our position. He did not stop to skirmish with the pickets but, charging headlong, drove them pell-mell into the reserves, closely following, with intent to stampede the whole command. It was a bold and brilliant dash, but destined to fall short of complete success. Rosser had met his match.
>
> When the Confederate charge was sounded, Custer was near his picket line and, scenting the first note of danger, turned his horse's head toward the point where he had hidden his

Wolverines in ambush and, bursting into view from the woods beyond the field, we saw him riding furiously in our direction. When he neared the edge of the woods, circling to the front and curbing the course of his charger as he rode, he bade the band to play and, with saber arm extended, shouted to the command, already in the saddle: "Forward, by divisions!" Both commands kept on in full career, the Confederates surprised by the sudden appearance and audacity of the Michigan men and their gallant leader; Custer well content with checking Rosser's vicious advance. Some of the foremost of either side kept on and crossed sabers in the middle of the ravine.

Rebel artillery fired on the Wolverines but failed to dislodge them. Custer ordered one of his subordinate commanders to engage and silence the enemy battery. Soldiers of the 1st and 7th Michigan, supported by New York and Pennsylvania infantry, assaulted their front and dislodged the enemy, who fled the field. Disaster averted.

"The rapid firing of Sheridan's attack is good," General Grant wrote in his memoirs. "Sheridan is entitled to the credit of placing Custer where he was. But that is all. Sheridan was not on the ground to direct the attack in any way; nor was the division commander on the ground. It was Custer's attack and it was Custer's victory."

After successes in the Midwest, Ulysses S. Grant was called on by President Lincoln to take over the eastern campaign. One of his first moves was to task General Phil Sheridan to transform the Union cavalry from a support element of the infantry and turn it into a devastating fighting force. The Cavalry Corps quickly became near-unstoppable, with General Custer leading every battle he fought in. (May 1864 issue of *Harper's Weekly*)

In addition to writing embellished battle reports, Custer was an avid letter writer. He knew his new bride was worried, especially whenever she heard or read about his exploits, leading troops in battle, always leading. Trying to offer reassurance, he inadvertently caused her more worry when he wrote to her, on May 1, 1864. "On the eve of every battle in which I have been engaged, I have never omitted to pray inwardly, devoutly. Never have I failed to commend myself to God's keeping, asking Him to forgive my past sins, and to watch over me while in danger ... and to receive me if I fell, while caring for those near and dear to me. After having done so all anxiety for myself, here or hereafter, is dispelled. I feel that my destiny is in the hands of the Almighty. This belief, more than any other fact or reason, makes me brave and fearless as I am."

Major Louis Carpenter reported in the 1888 edition of *Cavalry Journal*:

> The crossing of the Rapidan May 4th, commenced the campaign of 1864 in Virginia. The cavalry was well equipped, and armed with the sabre and Colt's revolver, and the principal portion with the Sharp's carbine, a breech-loading weapon, using a paper cartridge with a cap or the Maynard primer. Custer's Michigan Brigade was supplied with the Spencer carbine, having a magazine carrying seven cartridges … and gave an immense advantage to the troops armed with it. The brigade could throw in a tremendous fire when necessary, with great effect upon the enemy, who was naturally very often deceived in his estimate of the force opposed to him, judging from the unintermitting, incessant rattle along the line that he was contending with at least a division.

First Sergeant L. E. Tripp, with the 5th Michigan, wrote:

> At Todd's Tavern [May 4] General Custer led his brigade with drawn sabers, driving the Rebel line and taking their position. Along in the afternoon we were cautioned against loud talking, and our coffee-pots had to be adjusted so that they would not rattle. Finally our brigade was ordered to the front, where we found a large field with a rail fence running east and west through the middle, with woods mostly on three sides. Our regiment and the 6th Michigan were moved down on the north side of the field in the woods, where we were formed and dismounted for a charge across the field. We had not advanced over twenty rods, I think, before a murderous cross-fire was opened upon us out of the woods on our left and rear. Words cannot picture the scene that followed out there in that level field, without any chance of cover. We were trying to return the fire, shooting in three different directions. Our brave and noble Custer rode up on his horse into that field among us—always cool—with the words: "Lie down, men—lie

In March 1864, *Harper's Weekly* did a montage of General Custer's raid on the Rapidan River. (*Harper's Weekly*)

down. We'll fix them! I have sent two regiments around on the flank." His words of cheer and sympathy to the wounded were deeply appreciated. All of this was of short duration, but it seemed like an age then. Right there in that field I think General Custer decided on taking that battery. The battery was taken. [Confederate General J. E. B.] Stuart received a death wound while endeavoring to rally his men.

Some reports say Stuart was killed during a cavalry charge, in close quarters with Union forces. Others say a Union sharpshooter nailed him from a distance.

"One thing is certain. Stuart's death befell in front of Custer's Michigan Brigade and it was a Michigan man who fired the fatal shot," wrote Colonel J. H. Kidd. "Stuart was taken to Richmond, where he died, leaving behind him a record in which those who wore the blue and those who wore the gray take equal pride. He was a typical American cavalryman—one of the very foremost of American cavaliers and it is a privilege for one of those who stood in the line in front of which he fell in his last fight to pay a sincere tribute to his memory as a soldier and a man."

The Wilderness campaign was ill-suited to Custer's style of war fighting. With dense woods and underbrush, it was near impossible to mount any semblance of a cavalry charge, and he reluctantly ordered his horsemen to dismount as skirmishers and slug it out on foot. Enemy troops lay in wait, hiding behind felled timbers and hasty defensive breastworks, opening up with volleys of deadly fire when the Union troops entered the killing field.

Once they were back in the saddle, Custer's troopers were ready to carry out the mission recently established by General Sheridan when he reconstituted the Union's horse soldiers into the independent Cavalry Corps.

Frederick Whittaker wrote about General Sheridan's vision of mounted warfare:

> Sheridan's idea was that it should operate as an independent body, raid around the enemy's rear, and fight [against Rebel] cavalry only, till that should be destroyed. Grant consented, and it succeeded so well that it was constantly repeated thereafter.
>
> On May 9, 1864, accordingly, the whole Cavalry Corps, nearly 12,000 strong, started out on its road to Richmond, and was soon well on its way, Custer's brigade in the extreme advance. Before the evening, Custer reached the North Anna River, at Beaver Dam Station, where the Richmond and Gordonsville railroad crosses the river. He at once charged right into the station, which was directly in the rear of Lee's centre, captured three long trains and two engines, and released four hundred Union prisoners, going to Richmond. The cars were full of rations for Lee's army, and were burned, and the railroad destroyed for miles.

The pursuit continued with what became known as the Yellow Tavern Campaign on May 11. Colonel J. H. Kidd, with the 6th Michigan Cavalry, wrote about the action in his *Personal Recollections*:

> After crossing the [North Anna River], Custer was ordered to proceed with his brigade to Beaver Dam Station. Here the First Michigan was given the advance. The Sixth followed the First. A mile or so before reaching Beaver Dam, Brewer came upon several hundred Union prisoners who were being hurried under the escort of Confederate infantry to the station, where trains were waiting to convey them to Richmond.

May 12th, found the entire corps concentrated south of the Meadow bridges, on the broad table-land between Richmond and the Chickahominy River. Sheridan still kept his forces well together. The next stage in the march of his ten thousand was Haxall's Landing, on the James River, where supplies would be awaiting him. The only gateway out, either to advance or retreat, was by the Meadow Bridge, over the Chickahominy, unless fords could be found. The river had to be crossed and, owing to the recent rains it was swollen. Sheridan sent for Custer and ordered him to take his brigade and open the way across the Chickahominy at the Meadow bridges. Where work was to be done that had to be done, and done quickly and surely, Custer was apt to be called upon.

When Custer reached the river he found that the bridge was gone. The enemy had destroyed it. The railroad bridge alone remained. A line of skirmishers firing from the edge of the woods kept the pioneers from proceeding with the work. But Custer could not be balked. His orders were imperative. He was to make a crossing and secure a way for the entire corps to pass at all hazards. He ordered the Fifth and Sixth Michigan to dismount, cross by the railroad bridge on foot and engage the enemy. The enemy's artillery swept the bridge, and as soon as it was seen that the Michigan men were climbing the railroad embankment to make the crossing, they trained their pieces upon it.

One man, or at most two or three, at a time, they tiptoed from tie to tie, watching the chance to make it in the intervals between the shells. It looked perilous, and it was not devoid of danger, but I do not remember that a single man was killed or wounded while crossing. It may have been a case of poor ammunition or poor marksmanship or both.

Soon after, it was reported in the *Pioneer and Democrat*, St. Paul's weekly newspaper, based on the writings of correspondents with the *New York Herald*:

Gen. Custer in the Advance—The Affair at Beaver Dam: While these exciting events were transpiring in the rear, our advance composed of General Custer's brigade of the First Division, was doing glorious work in the front. They forded the North Anna River, charged into Beaver Dam Station, recaptured 378 Union prisoners, including colonels, majors, captains and lieutenants, belonging to the Fifth Corps, and taken prisoners while charging the Rebel breastworks at Todd's Tavern. Their joy when they saw the flashing blades of the Union cavalry approaching, knew no bounds. They set up a deafening cheer, while the Rebel guard, composed of a lieutenant and twenty-five men, skedaddled into the woods.

… General [Sheridan] ordered General Custer to take his gallant brigade and carry the position. Gen. Custer placed himself at the head of his command, and with drawn sabres and deafening cheers, charged directly in the face of withering fire, captured two pieces of artillery, upwards of a hundred prisoners, together with caissons, ammunition and horses, which he brought off in safety. It was, without exception, the most gallant charge of the raid, and when it became known among the corps, cheer after cheer rent the air.

It was a victorious night as the troopers bedded down on Crump's Creek, but everyone knew there was more fighting to be done. General Grant, who was unsure of what his opponent was planning next, needed to know. Colonel J. H. Kidd wrote:

This led to what was one of the most sanguinary and courageously contested cavalry engagements of the entire war—the battle of Haw's Shop—in which Gregg and Custer with the Second Division and the Michigan Brigade, unassisted, defeated most signally, two divisions under the command of Wade Hampton … As soon as Custer made his appearance on the flank, the enemy, abandoned the earthworks [at Haw's Shop] and fled. The charge of the Fifth and Seventh Michigan … led by General Custer in person, was most brilliant and successful, the Seventh continuing the pursuit for about three miles. Indeed it is not certain that it was not even a more notable victory than that over Confederate General J. E. B. Stuart on the right flank at Gettysburg. It was won at a greater sacrifice of life than either Brandy Station or Yellow Tavern.

With the Confederate soldiers hunkered down behind piles of discarded rails and logs, Gregg's cavalry troopers advanced early morning of May 28 and it was in this killing field that the First New Jersey suffered numerous casualties. Seeing the carnage unfolding, General Sheridan ordered Custer to mount up and reinforce the beleaguered Gregg. Colonel J. H. Kidd wrote about what transpired next:

> The Michigan men ... were instantly in the saddle and en route. Custer lost no time. Massing the brigade ... he dismounted it to fight on foot. Every fourth man remained with the horses which were sent back out of danger. Custer, accompanied by a single aide, rode along the line from left to right, encouraging the men by his example and his words. Passing the road, he dashed out in front of the Sixth and taking his hat in his hand, waved it around his head and called for three cheers. The cheers were given and then the line rushed forward. Custer quickly changed to the flank but, though thus rashly exposing himself, with his usual luck, he escaped without a scratch.
>
> In a moment the Wolverines and the Palmetto men were face to face and the lines very close. Michigan had Spencers, South Carolina, [had] Enfields. Spencers were repeaters, Enfields were not. The din of the battle was deafening. The Spencers were used with deadly effect. The South Carolinians, the most stubborn foe Michigan ever had met in battle, refused to yield and filled the air with lead from the muzzles of their long range guns as fast as they could load and fire. The sound of their bullets sweeping the undergrowth was like that of hot flames crackling through dry timber. The trees were riddled. Men began to fall.

Cold Harbor was the next flash point. The Confederate cavalry under Hampton and Fitzhugh Lee, along with a brigade of infantry would be assaulting a hasty defense made of logs and steel rails. Union General Sheridan was ordered to hold it until infantry reinforcements could be brought forward.

"Ammunition boxes were distributed on the ground by the side of the men so they could load and fire with great rapidity," wrote Colonel J. H. Kidd. "This was a strong line in single rank deployed thick along the barricade of rails. Behind the line only a few yards away were twelve pieces of artillery equally supplied with ammunition. The brigade was thus in readiness to make a desperate resistance to any attack that might be made. The only mounted man on the line was General Custer, who rode back and forth giving his orders. The Sixth was lying down behind the rails and directly in front of the artillery, the pieces being so disposed as to fire over our heads. As soon as the enemy emerged from the woods General Custer ordered all the twelve pieces of artillery to fire with shell and canister, which they did most effectively. So furious was the fire that the Confederate infantry did not dare to come out of the woods in front of Custer's left where the Sixth was, the artillery and the fire from the Spencers from behind the rails keeping them back. An attempt was made to charge the part of the line where the First Michigan was posted but each time it was repulsed."

The New York Herald, in its June 2 issue, reported:

> As the fight waxed hottest, Custer's brigade of Michiganders was ordered to assist Davies' and Gregg's brigade, who already had the enemy weakening in putting him to rout. This command is completely armed with Spencer rifles (seven-shooters), and the enemy would rather see the devil coming at them than these. General Custer exhibited his usual daring and impetuosity. His horse was shot—being the seventh he has had hit during the war—but he escaped unhurt. This was unquestionably the sharpest cavalry fight of the war—the hottest fire of musketry and shell. The enemy had long Tower musket against our carbines. Their guns were admirably served, and the shells flew over among our reserves …

A week later, Major General Sheridan had his cavalry forces on the march, leaving Old Church Tavern and relocating at Newcastle's Ferry, on the Pamunky River. *The Nashville Daily Union* detailed the action in its June 25 issue:

> June 11, was an eventful one. Custer had not proceeded far from his camp before he struck the enemy's advance. He at once charged them, and drove them back on to what appeared to him to be their main body. There had been a constant din and roar of cannon and musketry and of bursting shells from six in the morning till noon, and no one could tell Custer's guns from those of the enemy.
>
> It seems that when Custer had driven the force which he found opposing to a point near the station, he ordered a charge by the Fifth Michigan, which managed to get in between the enemy and their horses. The result was the capture of eight hundred horses and about five hundred men. Custer's command also had ninety of their wagons, four or five caissons and fifteen ambulances [but] before all could be removed everything was retaken, except 200 prisoners, and with it a portion of Gen. Custer's pack train, his headquarters wagon and a large number of the Fifth Michigan. The "Boy General" now began to rave some and look about for reprisals, when Pennington rode up to him and said: "General, they have taken one of my guns."
>
> "No! Damned if they have, come on," and off he dashed. General Custer's color-bearer was shot, and the flag was so near falling into the hands of the enemy that it was only saved by being torn from the pole by the General, who stuffed it into the bosom of his shirt. Custer's colored cook and laundress, Elisa, was captured with the train; but she escaped with the General's valise, which she succeeded in bringing to the outer picket, where they took it from her, but she came safely to camp. When Custer again joined Torbert, short work was made of routing the Rebels out of Trevilian Station.
>
> The station was destroyed, two locomotives, three trains, consisting of 100 cars, ninety wagons, several hundred stands of arms, a large number of hospital tents, 200,000 pounds of bacon, flour, meal, sugar and molasses, making about 1,500,000 rations, and a great portion of the medical supplies for Lee's army. In addition, eight or ten miles of railroad track was thoroughly broken and the culverts destroyed. The loss must have been a serious blow to the Confederates as it was estimated at $10,000,000 by the *Richmond Dispatch*, in a copy which afterwards fell into our possession.

Among the wagons seized by the Confederates was Custer's personal effects, including love letters from Libbie. These were soon passed around in the camps and secessionist social circles, and some were even published in newspapers. Custer promptly cautioned his young wife to be careful what she wrote in subsequent letters. Colonel J. H. Kidd in *Personal Recollections* recalled:

When Custer approached the [Trevilian] station he found [Confederate General and former West Point classmate Thomas] Rosser in his way on his front and right flank. Fitzhugh Lee, coming from Louisa Courthouse, also attacked his left flank. For a time there was a melee which had no parallel in the annals of cavalry fighting in the Civil War, unless it may have been at Brandy Station in Buckland Mills. Custer's line was in the form of a circle and he was fighting an enterprising foe on either flank, and both front and rear. Fragments of all the regiments in the brigade rallied around Custer for the mounted fighting, of which then was plenty, while the First and Sixth dismounted took care of the rear. Custer was everywhere present, giving directions to his subordinate commanders, and more than one mounted charge was participated in by him in person. In the final stages of the battle, Gregg concentrated against Fitzhugh Lee, Torbert effected his junction with Custer, and the latter was extricated from his difficult and dangerous predicament.

War correspondents at Trevilian Station were convinced Custer would not escape the encirclement and they rushed off a hasty news report via telegraph, announcing his demise. Soon the presses in every city along the Eastern Seaboard were printing the startling news. In Washington, DC, the news was met with skepticism. Ohio Congressman John Bingham, who had nominated the young Autie Custer for an appointment to West Point, refused to believe it. He recalled it in his reminiscences, reprinted in *The Custer Story* in 1880:

> George killed. In one of the battles of the Wilderness? I rushed to the War Department, into [Secretary] Stanton's office, asked if this terrible news were true.
> "Killed? No," thundered Stanton. "He was hemmed in on all sides by the enemy—cut his way through with his sword—and covered himself with glory!"
> Ah, how like my brave boy! I went at once to see Mrs. Custer. I found her pale and trembling. She had heard the newsboys under her windows crying, "Custer killed. All shout Custer being killed." She was waiting for some word, and, seeing me, feared the worst. But when I told her, she broke down completely from relief and joy."

Later, historians would refer to the near debacle at Trevilian Station as "Custer's First Last Stand." Custer wrote from his headquarters:

> At daylight on the morning of the 9th [of July] the corps started on the Richmond raid, this brigade being in the advance. Just before reaching the North Anna River the advance guard reported a train of the enemy's ambulances to be in sight. Before reaching the station the advance encountered a considerable force of the enemy, conducting upward of 400 Union prisoners to Richmond. Among the recaptured men of our Army was 1 colonel, 2 lieutenant colonels, and a considerable number of captains and lieutenants, all belonging to infantry regiments, and had been captured during the battles of the Wilderness. Pressing on, we obtained possession of Beaver Dam Station, where we captured three trains, heavily laden with supplies for this army. In addition, we captured an immense amount of army supplies, consisting of bacon, flour, meal, sugar, molasses, liquors, and medical stores, also several hundred stand of arms, a large number of hospital tents, the whole amounting to several millions of dollars' worth. After supplying my command with all the rations they could transport, I caused the remainder to be burnt. I also caused the railroad track to be destroyed for a considerable distance. The enemy made frequent attempts during the night to drive me from the station, but were unsuccessful.

Supply wagons and caissons carrying artillery shells and other vital ammunition were often targets of opportunity for both sides. Even as the Army of the Potomac was pursuing fleeing Rebel forces, southern guerillas such as Mosby's Rangers, were threatening the supply trains, which were typically undermanned by sufficient guards. (*The Illustrated London News*, April 1862)

Less than a month later, Sheridan and his cavalry troopers were on the move again. The drive into the Shenandoah Valley included one corps of infantry (the 6th) and two divisions of cavalry (the 1st and 3rd) from the Army of the Potomac. Colonel J. H. Kidd in his *Personal Recollections* reported:

> Custer crossed and marched through Front Royal but no enemy was found. He then recrossed and took position on commanding ground half a mile or so back from the river, and ordered the horses to be unsaddled and fed and the men to cook their dinner. Headquarters wagons were brought up, mess chests taken out, and we were just gathering around them to partake of a hastily prepared meal, when [Rebel General] Fitzhugh Lee's cavalry, which had stealthily approached the ford, charged across and made a dash at our pickets … of the Sixth Michigan [which] met Lee's attack and checked it. That dinner was never eaten. Custer's bugler sounded "to horse." As if by magic, the men were in the saddle. Custer dashed out with his staff and ordered the Fifth Michigan forward, to be followed by the other regiments. I supposed he would charge in the direction of the ford, where Fitzhugh Lee's cavalry was still contending with the Sixth Michigan. He did nothing of the kind. Moving diagonally to the left, he reached the crest overlooking the river just in time to surprise [General Joseph] Kershaw in the act of crossing. The Fifth Michigan deployed into line in fine style and opened such a hot fire with their Spencers, that the head of Kershaw's column was completely crushed. Every Confederate who was across was either killed or captured.

THE CIVIL WAR'S BOY GENERAL • 79

This encounter at Front Royal was one of the most brilliant affairs of the war and it illustrated well the marvelous intuition with which General Custer often grasped the situation, in an instant of time. He did not anticipate Kershaw's movement or he would not have given the order to unsaddle. It was a surprise but he was alert, and equal to the emergency. Custer divined that the dash of Lee's advance was a mask for the infantry, and by a movement that would have done credit to Murat or Ney, caught Kershaw astride the river and trapped him completely. The behavior of the Fifth Michigan was never more superb. I do not believe that a single regiment, on either side, at any time, during the entire war, performed a more brilliant deed."

Custer wrote about the battle at Front Royal in a letter to Libbie, on August 21, while camped at Berryville, Virginia. "Imagine my surprise as I watched the retreating enemy [near Front Royal] to see every man, every officer, take off cap and give 'Three Cheers for General Custer!' It is the first time I ever knew of such a demonstration except in the case of General McClellan. I certainly felt highly flattered. The commander is a graduate of West Point long before my time, and yet as enthusiastic over your boy as if he were a youth of eighteen. After the battle I heard 'By God damn Custer is a brick!' 'Custer is the man for us!' And other expressions somewhat rough but hearty. The battle was called by many 'the handsomest fight of the war,' because [it was] fought on open ground, and successful."

The next confrontation was Shepherdstown and the Opequon Creek. Colonel J. H. Kidd recalled in his *Personal Recollections*:

Custer, coming to a piece of woods south of Shepherdstown, neither the enemy nor our own cavalry being in sight, halted and had his men dismount to rest, they having been in the saddle since early morning. We were all sitting or lying down with bridle reins in hand, taking our ease with more or less dignity, when a small body of Confederate horse made its appearance in the direction of Shepherdstown. The brigade mounted and started in pursuit but had hardly been put in motion when a line of infantry suddenly appeared in the woods we were vacating and opened fire upon us. The Confederate horsemen were driven away by the First and Seventh and, when General Custer rallied his brigade to confront the new danger, he found that Breckinridge had intercepted his retreat in the direction the rest of the cavalry had gone, and was closing in with a line that threatened to envelop the brigade. In a few moments, the enemy's right and left flanks began to swing in towards the river and he found himself face to face with two alternatives: To cut his way through, or fall back and take the risky chance of fording the river, with Breckinridge close at his heels. Of course there was no thought of surrender and Custer was not much given to showing his heels.

Custer, with surprising coolness, put his brigade into line, with backs to the river and faces to the enemy, and presented so bold a front that the infantry did not charge, but moved up slowly, maneuvering to get around and obtain possession of the ford in rear. Custer had the men cheer and dared them to come on. With characteristic audacity, he actually unlimbered his pieces and gave them a charge or two right in their teeth; then limbering to the rear he took successive new positions and repeated the performance. The greatest coolness was displayed by General Custer and his entire command. There was not a hint of weakness or fear in any quarter.

Presently, Custer finally withdrew ... and slipped away into Maryland before the enemy realized what he was doing ... as the Fifth and Sixth were marching up the Maryland bank, a line of Confederates came up on the other side, and so astounded were they to see how we had escaped from their grasp, that some of them actually cheered, so I have been informed. They had been deceived by the audacity of Custer and his men in the first place and by the cleverness with which they eluded capture in the second.

We neared [Locke's Ford on the Opequon Creek] about daylight. There was a faint hope that the enemy might be taken by surprise and the ford captured without resistance, as it was a difficult crossing when bravely defended. In this, however, we were doomed to disappointment, for an alert foe was found awaiting the attack. The regiment deployed forward into line under fire, and with General Custer by my side we charged across the field to the crest. Custer was the only mounted man in the field. All the regiments advanced to the attack simultaneously, and the crossing of the Opequon was won.

Occasionally Custer displayed literary flair in his battle reports, including one he wrote on September 28, for the battle of the Opequon: "One continuous and heavy fire of skirmishers covered the advance, using only the carbine, while the line of brigades as they advanced across the open country, the bands playing the national airs, presented in the sunlight one moving mass of glittering sabers. This, combined with the various and bright-colored banners and battle-flags, intermingled here and there with the plain blue uniforms of the troops, furnished one of the most inspiring as well as imposing scenes of martial grandeur ever witnessed upon a battle-field."

Both armies exchanged harassing fire, and, as Custer reported it, "at that moment it seemed as if no perceptible advantage could be claimed by either, but that the fortunes of the day might be decided by one of those incidents or accidents of the battlefield which, though insignificant in themselves, often go far toward deciding the fate of nations." Often the "insignificant factor" between Union and Confederate cavalry clashes was their choice of weaponry. "The enemy relied wholly upon the carbine and pistol, my men preferred the saber. A short but closely contested struggle ensued, which resulted in the repulse of the enemy. Many prisoners were taken, and quite a number on both sides left on the field."

After one of Custer's Wolverine sharpshooters was credited with killing Confederate cavalry hero J. E. B. Stuart, the Rebels set out to even the score, pursuing the boy general at every opportunity. In mid-September, a freak snowfall paralyzed military operations for both field armies. Still, the Confederates launched a clandestine mission and very nearly succeeded, while the Union troopers were bedded down in their tents covered with eight inches of snow and ice.

"The attack had been made on the wagon train," wrote Isaac Gause, in *Four Years with Five Armies* in 1908. "The enemy had evaded the pickets during the snow storm, crossed the woods and fields, and the first alarm was the volley fired into the train, killing some teamsters. Their command divided, part driving away some stock, and the others went to capture General Custer. He was not napping, and when they captured his sentinel he heard the demand, ran out the back way, mounted his horse, and by going out the back gate evaded them and was able to join his command. Having failed in their purpose they were endeavoring to escape up the pike."

A Second Star

Changes were in the wind for Brigadier General Custer in late September 1864. On the 26th he left his beloved Michigan brigade to take charge of the 2nd Division of the West Virginia Cavalry. A few days later, with General Sheridan steering the Cavalry Corps into a more active role as a fighting force, he relieved General Wilson as head of the 3rd Division and sent him out west to join General Sherman. Custer was back with the glorious 3rd Division, where he initially made a name for himself when General Torbert was the commander, who had given him free rein in every skirmish. Frederick Whittaker noted:

> Torbert, the division commander of Custer and Merritt, was lost to public view in a large measure, through the lustre of his subordinates, who engaged in a fierce rivalry with each other which resulted in splendid successes. Now Custer and Merritt were again to engage in the same rivalry, but as division commanders, the latter having the additional advantage of retaining the brigade which Custer had made so famous. Custer was to take up the division which had so far, under Wilson's lead, only held its own with respectability, and was to transform it into the most brilliant single division in the whole Army of the Potomac, with more trophies to show than any, and so much impressed with the stamp of his individuality, that every officer in the command was soon to be aping his eccentricities of dress, ready to adore his every motion and word.

Sheridan, with Grant's blessing, intended to cripple the south, by destroying bridgeworks, dismantling railways, and burning grain fields, and storage barns, often in clear view of their Rebel pursuers. For Custer and the 3rd Division, his primary pursuer was his old friend and West Point roommate, Thomas Rosser, who attempted on several occasions to even the score.

The rebel soldiers were incensed as they followed fast on the heels of their opponents, who were demolishing and setting fire to barns and silos, warehouses, and even haystacks in an attempt to cripple the Virginia populace. But while Merritt's Union troopers were shadowed by rebel cavalrymen at a safe distance, Custer's rear guard was continually harassed by his friend and nemesis, Rosser. While he preferred to take the lead, Custer could hear the sporadic gunfire behind him and finally had enough. Whittaker explained what unfolded next:

> Not far from the Union rear-guard could be seen a brilliant group of cavaliers, headed by the same bright debonair figure at Aldie and Brandy Station. Whenever any trouble is anticipated, when Rosser becomes too bold, the flaming scarlet neckties of Custer and his staff are seen coming, and the bright-haired warrior comes trotting leisurely along the skirmish line, whistling a tune, and tapping his boots with his riding whip, his blue eyes glancing keenly about, his short curls, just growing again, flung from side to side, as he jerks his head in his peculiar nervous manner … and when he knew, as he soon did, that it was his old classmate Rosser, who was following him so persistently, he was doubly disgusted. All that long day of the 7th October, he was compelled by his orders to retreat from the face of a foe he was only too anxious to fight, and even till dark his pickets were annoyed.
>
> At daybreak (on the 9th) the movement commenced, soon to become famous under the name of Woodstock Races. Now Custer was to avenge himself for his long suffering. His

experience, it must be confessed, since he had taken command of the Third Division, was peculiarly mortifying. For the first time … he had been obliged to retrograde in face of the enemy, and to suffer severe punishment while doing it. Out swept, as at Winchester, side by side, Custer and Merritt to attack Rosser and Lomax; and to Custer's share fell the greater part of the force of his old classmate Rosser.

Rosser's position … occupied a low but abrupt range of hills on the south bank of Tom's Run, and had posted his dismounted men behind stone fences at the base of the ridge. A second line of barricades crowned the ridge, also defended by dismounted men. On the summit he had six guns in position strongly supported, and he had the great advantage of being able to see all of Custer's movements. And now occurred one of those little incidents that stamp the innate romance of Custer's character on his biography, "Let's have a fair fight, boys." Here it was, fair and square and no favor, perhaps the first in the war. No infantry to bother the horse, numbers about equal, his first fight as a division commander, and Rosser in sight. Out rode Custer from his staff, far in advance of the line, his glittering figure in plain view of both armies. Sweeping off his broad sombrero, he threw it down to his knee in a profound salute to his honorable foe.

Rosser had but just come to the valley and was already hailed as its savior. He saw Custer and turned to his staff, pointing him out, "You see that officer down there," said he. "That's General Custer, the Yanks are so proud of, and I intend to give him the best whipping to-day that he ever got. See if I don't." And he smiled triumphantly as he looked round at his gallant Southern cavaliers.

If only declaring it could make it so for Rosser. He watched as the flamboyant Custer motioned with his sabre and led his troopers at a trot, despite Confederate field

At what would become known as the "Woodstock Races," General Custer spotted his old friend and West Point roommate Thomas Rosser on the opposing side, so he rode out in front, snatched his wide-brimmed hat from his head, and respectfully bowed, then promptly led his troopers in an overwhelming victory, chasing after the fleeing Rebels, thus the "race" was on. (Public Domain)

guns opening up on them, followed by volleys of rifle fire. Men and horses fell, but the pursuit continued at full gallop, and before he could respond, Rosser's troopers were overrun. Whittaker wrote about the chaos of the fight:

> The pattering of bullets becomes heavier, a wild savage yell breaks from every throat in that long wave of cavalry, and away they go, the lines lost in confused clumps of horsemen, with waving sabres, the horses crazy with excitement, leaping half out of their skins as they race for the Confederate batteries and lines of cavalry.
>
> Custer's attack, arranged in full sight of Rosser, yet proved triumphantly successful. One brigade in front, another to the right, the third to the left, they swept on at a charge, not heeding the fire, curled round Rosser's flanks in a moment, and before he could tell what had happened, had him enclosed in a semi-circle of charging horses. Vain all his efforts when his flanks were threatened. Had the attack been made on foot he might have had time to think, but the sudden and impetuous rush of a whole mounted division completely demoralized the Confederates.

Rosser and his Rebel horsemen scattered in confusion, despite his appeals for them to turn and fight. He was able to halt some of his men and blunt Custer's pursuit, but only temporarily. Custer unleashed his field artillery and seized the upper hand again, and the Confederate cavalry beat a hasty retreat, for 26 miles, back to Mount Jackson. Whittaker concluded:

> Thus ended "Woodstock Races," the first pitched battle in which the Third Division took part under Custer's command. Completeness of the victory was owing to two things—the open ground, and the vicious cavalry school in which Rosser and his command had been reared. All through the Virginia campaign, the Confederate cavalry displayed the same taste for firearms, and the same distaste and contempt for the sabre as a weapon. Out in the woods, this method of warfare is possible, but on a plain, suicidal. The only place in Virginia besides the Valley, where open fields exist, adapted for mounted cavalry fighting, is around Brandy Station, where the sabre had always proved triumphant, Rosser, in common with most of the Confederate officers, distrusted the sabre, which was rarely used by the Confederate cavalry after Stuart's death, and not enough during his life. Custer, on the other hand, was never more in his element than in a sabre charge, and the same thing was true of the whole of the First and Third divisions, especially the former. Custer's influence soon gave the same taste to the latter, and they became excessively fond of rapid mounted work, wherein pistol, carbine and sabre were used, one with the other, with the happiest effect. The moral impetus of that day of charges never left the Third Division. Henceforth they became imbued with a certain contempt for the Confederate cavalry. They had found the certain way to drive it in confusion. It never afterwards gave them serious trouble.

The *Army and Navy Journal*, in its July 1876 issue, reported:

> At the ever-memorable battle of Cedar Creek, his division was on the right, and when Sheridan arrived on the field, after the twenty-mile ride, he found the cavalry under Merritt and Custer [was] ready for service. His immediate order to them was "Go in." The brave young generals only waited for the word; they went in and never came out until the enemy was driven several miles beyond the battlefield. Nearly one thousand prisoners were captured, among them a Major-General. Forty-five pieces of artillery were also taken. For this service Custer was made a Brevet Major-General of Volunteers. Sheridan, as a further mark of approbation, detailed him to carry the news of the victory and the captured battle-flag to Washington. From this time he

continued steadily to advance in the esteem of his superiors and of the American people. Custer had the advance of Sheridan's command, and his share in the action is well described in the entertaining volume entitled, *With Sheridan in Lee's Last Campaign*, by Colonel Newhall [then of Sheridan's staff], who says: "When the sun was an hour high in the west, energetic Custer in advance spied four heavy trains of freight cars; he quickly ordered his regiments to circle out to the left through the woods, and as they gained the railroad beyond the station, he led the rest of his division pell-mell down the road and enveloped the train as quick as winking. Custer might not well conduct a siege of regular approaches; but for a sudden dash, Custer against the world."

In the middle of August, the armies of Sheridan and Early confronted each other in the valley north of Winchester. Then ensued that brilliant campaign of the Shenandoah which, through a score of minor engagements, resulted in the thorough defeat of Early's army in the battle of Winchester, or the Opequon, on September 19, followed on the 22nd by its disastrous rout at Fishers Hill, and its confused retreat beyond Staunton, where the pursuit was discontinued. At this time Sheridan and his whole victorious Army considered the enemy in the Shenandoah Valley as thoroughly and permanently broken, dispirited and disposed of.

General A. B. Nettleton recalled the Shenandoah Valley campaign and what happened after they thought the Rebels were "thoroughly and permanently broken, dispirited and disposed of." He wrote, in *The Annals of the Civil War*:

During our return march, the rear of our several columns was persistently harassed by a large force of surprisingly active cavalry, under General T. L. Rosser. Among many memories of hard service, those who were among Custer's troopers in the Valley will not soon forget their arduous task of protecting the rear of a victorious Army against the onslaughts of the crushed enemy's horsemen! Rosser's saucy cavalry numbered about three thousand effectives, and was supported by some fifteen hundred infantry and two batteries.

As evening closed above the Valley [on the 18th of October] the soft pleadings of some homesick soldier's flute floated out through the quiet camp, while around a blazing camp-fire an impromptu glee club of Ohio boys lightened the hour and their own hearts by singing the songs of home.

Taps had sounded, lights were out in the tents, cook-fires flickered low, the mists of the autumn night gathered gray and chill, the sentinels paced back and forth in front of the various headquarters, the camp was still that many-headed monster, a great Army, was asleep. Midnight came, and with it no sound but the tramp of the relief guard as the sergeant replaced the tired sentinels ... all was tranquil as a peace convention; two, three o'clock, and yet the soldiers slept. At four the silence was broken by sharp firing in the direction of our cavalry pickets, toward the western side of the Valley. The firing increased in volume, suggesting an attack in force by cavalry. General Custer quietly dispatched a regiment to support our outposts and awaited developments, which speedily came. Fifteen minutes later heavy skirmish firing was heard on the left of the infantry, two miles from where our cavalry division was encamped. The firing on our extreme right gradually died away and that in front of the infantry line rapidly increased, showing that the movement on our right had been a feint, while the real attack had now begun against the centre and left.

"Boots and saddles!" was blown from division, brigade, and regimental headquarters. The darkness rang with the blare of bugles and the shouts of officers hurrying the troopers from their dreams to their horses. The rattle of musketry in front of the infantry increased to heavy volleys, the volleys thickened into a continuous roar, and now, as day began to dawn, the deep bass of the artillery came in to complete the grand but terrible chorus of battle.

As we came into full view of the field, the whole sickening truth flashed upon us. The infantry had been surprised in their beds by Early's reinforced army; our best artillery was already in the hands of the Confederates and turned against us; thousands of our men had been killed, wounded, or captured before they could even offer resistance; Sheridan's victorious and hitherto invincible Army was routed and in disorderly retreat before a confident, yelling, and pursuing enemy. At nine o'clock a portion of the enemy's troops occupied, and were plainly seen plundering the camps where the Sixth Corps had slept the night before …

The attack was repulsed at every point. Panic seized every part of the Rebel force; infantry vied with artillery, and both with the wagon trains, in a harum-scarum race for the Cedar Creek ford, and, as the sun went down, the army, which at daybreak had gained one of the most dramatic and overwhelming victories of the war, was a frantic rabble, decimated in numbers, and flying before the same army it had, twelve hours before, so completely surprised and routed.

The pike was blockaded for miles with cannon, caissons, ambulances, and baggage wagons, which our troopers easily captured, and turned backward toward our lines. The chase continued, with constant captures of prisoners and war material, until, near the foot of Fisher's Hill, the dense darkness enforced a truce between pursuers and pursued. Both infantry and cavalry returned to sleep in their camps of the night before, hungry and half dead with fatigue, but happy, and having about them, as trophies of the day s work, forty-five pieces of captured and recaptured artillery, and a field full of wagons, ambulances, and prisoners of war.

The New York Times reported on Custer's feats at Cedar Creek, a few days after the skirmishing concluded:

Custer who, since the arrival of General Sheridan, was authorized to act according to his own judgment in an emergency, by a single dash opened the way for the final success attained [at Cedar Creek, on October 19th]. It was a critical moment … Rosser was forced to retire precipitately across the Creek … and here Custer, young as he is, displayed the judgment of a Napoleon. He considered a moment, then, quick as thought, saw that the time for a dash had arrived … with a small command pushed through a rocky ravine, striking the Creek at a blind ford, one fourth of a mile from the pike … The rebel artillery could be heard rumbling over the pike, a prize too great to be lost …" Charge! Charge!" Custer fairly screeched … and the small but gallant band did charge.

Custer was understandably proud of the 3rd Cavalry Division, and how they handled themselves at Cedar Creek. On October 21, he sent the following to the entire division:

With pride and gratification your commanding general congratulates you upon your brilliant and glorious achievements of the past few days. On the 9th of the present month you attacked a vastly superior force of the enemy's cavalry, strongly posted, with artillery in position, and commanded by that famous "Savior of the Valley," Rosser. Notwithstanding the enemy's superiority in numbers and position, you drove him twenty miles from the battlefield, capturing his artillery, six pieces in all; also his entire train of wagons and ambulances and a large number of prisoners. Again, during the memorable engagement of the 19th instant, your conduct throughout was sublimely heroic, and without a parallel in the annals of warfare. Among the substantial fruits of this great victory you can boast of having captured five battle-flags, a large number of prisoners, including Major-General Ramseur, and forty-five of the forty-eight pieces of artillery taken from the enemy on that day, thus making fifty-one pieces of artillery captured within the short space of ten days. This is a record of which you may well be proud—a record won and established by your gallantry and perseverance. You have surrounded the name of the Third Cavalry Division with a halo of glory as enduring as time. The history of this war, when truthfully written, will contain no brighter page than that upon which is recorded the chivalrous deeds, the glorious triumphs, of the soldiers of this division.

After the battle at Cedar Creek, General Custer and several of his soldiers were ordered back to DC for special recognition. Their exploits and the general's accomplishments were written about in the October 26 issue of *The New York Herald*:

> Brigadier General George A. Custer, commanding the three divisions of cavalry in General Sheridan's Army, was in this city [Newark] yesterday. General Custer visited Washington, having in charge ten battle flags captured from the Rebels in the battle of Wednesday last, and subsequently came to this city to spend a few hours with his wife, who has been staying here for several days past. He left again for Washington last evening, and will return to his command today. General Custer represents that the victory ... was the most complete and decisive which has yet been achieved in the Shenandoah. Before the charges of our cavalry, the Rebel forces were scattered in utter confusion, throwing off everything that could impede their flight. Custer's division pursued the enemy, driving them into the fields and mountains, capturing whole companies at a time, and putting hundreds of the fugitives "hors de combat." Our men fought as they never had fought before, feeling that the annihilation of the enemy depended upon their blows.
>
> General Custer states that the cannon captured by our forces numbered over fifty. He counted forty-nine at Sheridan's headquarters on Friday night, and several pieces had not yet been brought from the field. General Custer's division captured forty-one pieces and several battle flags, including the headquarters flag of General Ramseur, which bore the inscription, "On to Victory, presented by Mr. W. T. Sutherlin." General Custer also captured a large number of wagons, with many horses, mules, & c. It is a curious coincidence that the Rebel General Ramseur who was killed was a classmate of General Custer at West Point. Before his death Ramseur sent for the latter, and the two, thus strangely brought together, reviewed, in the presence of death, the reminiscences of their cadet life. General Custer, who at the outbreak of the war ranked as first lieutenant in the Fifth Regular Cavalry, and has now probably the stars of a major general within his reach, is only twenty-four years of age, and a splendid specimen of the finished soldier. He speaks in the highest terms of our New Jersey soldiers in the valley, and especially commends the Third Cavalry, which he says have achieved a better reputation, considering the time they have been in service, than any regiment in that department.

For his stunning leadership during the Shenandoah Campaign, Brigadier General Custer was promoted to the rank of Brevet Major General, by Secretary of War Stanton. Custer, more than any other warfighter, had captured the interest of the American populous. More than Ulysses S. Grant, or Robert E. Lee, the war correspondents and even reporters who remained closer to home, wrote about the boy general, with the golden locks. Often a feature in one newspaper would be repeated and embellished by another. As an example, an unnamed reporter in St. Paul, Minnesota, who claims to have been a boyhood classmate of Autie Custer, lifted a story from the *Cincinnati Gazette,* added his personal remembrances, and it was later published in the *Gate City* daily newspaper in Keokuk, Iowa, in its November 15 issue:

I see by the late papers that Brigadier General Custer, of Ohio, has been promoted to a Major General. This is a promotion eminently fit to be made. I have the honor of an intimate acquaintance with General Custer, as we were school boys together, and I have watched his course since the war began with more than ordinary interest. His whole military career, from the Peninsular Campaign down to Sheridan's last great victory, has been one of daring feats, crowned with the most brilliant successes. General Custer is a native of New Rumley, Harrison County, Ohio, and is but a little over twenty-four years of age. He has risen to his present exalted position by his own genius and daring alone. He had no friends in high places to secure him position, but was compelled to fight his way up, and nobly has he done it. Among all the noble men which Ohio has sent to the field of battle she can boast of no more gallant spirit than her youthful hero—Maj. Gen. Armstrong Custer.

While General Custer enjoyed the attention—craved it and couldn't get enough of it—he still had a mission to complete. Many thought Jefferson Davis and Robert E. Lee would call it quits by the end of 1864, but they stubbornly held out hope, not that the Confederacy could defeat the Union, but that the northern electorate would tire of war, choose someone else for president—General McClellan was running against him—and then seek a peaceful solution. During the two previous winters, skirmishing was kept to a minimum and an unofficial ceasefire was maintained, at least in the eastern campaign, where bitter weather made it treacherous and miserable to conduct field operations. But the winter of 1864, still just as bitter as

General Custer never feared plunging head-long into the Confederate armies opposing him, relying on the sabre as his primary weapon. (Public Domain)

the previous two, proved to be quite different. The *History of the Ninth Regiment, New York Volunteer Cavalry,* published in 1901, reported:

> The wintry weather was now severe, snow falling frequently to the depth of several inches, and the mercury often sinking below zero. The rigor of the season was very much against the success of any mounted operation, but General Grant, being desirous to have the railroads broken up about Gordonsville and Charlottesville, on December 19, Sheridan started the cavalry out for that purpose. Hoping to hold the enemy's troops in the valley, Custer was surprised by Rosser and Payne near Lacy's Springs [also known as Lacey's Springs in some reports and newspaper accounts] before reveille and had to abandon his bivouac and retreat down the valley with the loss of a number of prisoners, a few horses and a good many horse equipments, for the suddenness of the attack gave many of the men no time to saddle up.

A reporter with the *New York Tribune* provided an account of the confusion and chaos created by a deceptive Confederate raid, in the early hours of December 23, published a week later in *The Daily Dispatch,* on the 30th:

> The Third Cavalry Division of General Custer returned from a reconnaissance up the Valley as far as Lacey's Spring, nine miles from Harrisonburg. The division, had a cold march, but met with no enemy until they reached Lacey's Spring, where they encamped.
>
> There was no alarm during the night. But about 6 o'clock in the morning word came … that the Rebels were advancing on the flank … At this juncture, a yell and a simultaneous volley, and the flash of Rebel carbines and rifles, gave warning that the enemy was already in their camp in large force. The two regiments which received the first shock of the charge replied with their carbines and revolvers. It was very dark. The enemy had on our own overcoats, which rendered it impossible to discriminate between friend and foe. All firing was made at random. The Rebels came in with drawn sabres and a hand to hand encounter commenced.
>
> It was a free fight, and no one knew who stood next [to] him. The only way to distinguish friend from foe was by the sound of the voice. Indiscriminate robbing and plunder took place. The Rebels seemed to be quite sure of capturing all the horses. A Rebel would capture, strip and rob one of our men, and then take him right into one of our regiments as a prisoner. By the time they had exhibited the trophies, they found themselves in the wrong camp, and in turn yielded themselves prisoners. The same laughable mistakes were, in some cases, committed by our own men. One Rebel marched into General Custer's headquarters, and asked what regiment that was. General Custer ordered him to "take off that blue overcoat," and handed him over a prisoner.

In mid-December, Custer led a raid on Harrisonburg, but soon the cold weather took its toll on the horses and soldiers. Little skirmishing of any significance was done in January 1865, when new cavalry troops arrived, and the horses were allowed to rest. In early February, Sheridan began planning a spring offensive, against a Confederate force much depleted, starving, barely hanging on, hoping beyond hope for some miracle. On February 27, Sheridan led what would become the last operation for the Union cavalry. Among his subordinate commanders was Major General Custer, leading the 4,600-strong 3rd Division. The combined strength, including supporting artillery, was nearly 9,500 men. As they traversed up the Shenandoah Valley, small groups of Rebel cavalry could be seen off in the distance, tracking their every move throughout the day. Occasionally, a few Union horsemen might gallop off toward their Confederate shadows, only to lose chase, not wishing to be led into a trap. It was later learned the Rebel troopers were part of the notorious Mosby's guerrillas. General Sheridan advised leaving them alone, but Custer sought to destroy them at any opportunity.

In late February it was time to break camp and resume the fight via the Shenandoah Valley. Soon a long line of cavalry, infantry, artillery and the supporting caissons and wagon trains extended through the Valley Pike, struggling in the mud.

Captain Moses Harris of the 1st Cavalry, recalled the advance on Winchester in *Cavalry Journal* in 1891:

> The rain had been pouring down incessantly for several days, and the road way was a sea of liquid mud, marked only by the forces on either side. We were already well splashed, but as we dashed through this pasty mess, with heads down to save our eyes, we were pelted and plastered with the sacred soil beyond all recognition. As we galloped through the town the firing had almost ceased, and we heard off to the right and rear, the victorious shouts of Custer's men. The completeness of this victory was only marred by the escape of Early and Rosser, who wisely made prompt and effective use of their horse-flesh. [The Union troops pulled back toward Dinwiddie, but the remaining Rebels re-grouped and continued the pursuit.]
>
> On the enemy came, with lines well extended to the right and left, two divisions of infantry, the equals in efficiency of any to be found in the Confederate armies. As they came within closer range their opening fire was answered by a tempest of lead from the repeating carbines of Custer's division, which, with the quick discharges of the artillery, made in the evening twilight a veritable line of fire. The fire of the enemy soon died away into scattering shots, then spluttered and went out, like an expiring candle. The attack had failed, and night, the welcome friend of weary and hard-pressed soldiers, soon claimed full possession and dropped her sable mantle over the field.
>
> Finally, about noon, the First Cavalry found its progress checked by a particularly vicious nest of sharpshooters, snugly ensconced behind a line of fallen logs surrounded by thick brush, on the farther side of a cleared field. After considerable firing our men managed to occupy some out-buildings within about two hundred yards of the annoying position, when the parties amiably pegged away at each other with no very definite results on either side. Everything being in readiness, and sudden cheers to the left indicating a movement of Custer's line, the squadrons burst out from behind the sheltering buildings, and with cheers—trumpets sounding—rode straight for the barricades in its front. The attack was unexpected; the nerves of the hostile marksmen lost their steadiness, their fire was delivered in a straggling and ineffective manner, and before they could reload we were upon them.

As night descended on the battlefield it become near impossible to carry on the fight, to tell friend from foe, so both armies wheeled about and settled down for the night at a safe distance. Trumpet calls and shouted pronouncements continued for a good hour as stragglers fell back into camp, looking for their units. Union forces braced for more skirmishing and were surprised to learn Lee's army was in full retreat, even abandoning Richmond. All along the pursuit, small groups of enemy stragglers were waiting without resistance to be taken prisoner. Weapons were cast aside, wagons broken down, still laden with supplies and ammunition, the carcasses of emaciated horses and mules littering the road.

Custer's troops and the Army of the Potomac were at Jettersville, anticipating a fight at Amelia Court House, but General Lee marched on to Rice's Station on the South Side and Lynchburg Railroad. Captain Moses Harris continued:

> As we approached Sailor's Creek, beyond Deatonsville, the Confederate columns, with wagons and artillery, could be seen across the intervening valley and through openings in the timber, marching on higher ground on the opposite side of the stream. Orders were given for the two divisions in rear to pass … along the enemy's line of march, and seek a point of attack which might promise a chance of success. The First Division proceeded to follow these instructions, but what was our disgust on seeing Custer's division trot along the flank of our column … and dashing across the creek, without looking for a ford, charge into the midst of the enemy's trains and marching columns, almost before a formation could be made to receive its attack.
>
> Meanwhile, the noise of battle away off to our right and front has been steadily increasing, and we are informed that we have only to hold our position to insure the capture of a large portion of the Confederate army. That troublesome Custer, however, cannot be persuaded to keep quiet and wait to be attacked, but must needs go to yelling and charging again. The combined captures of the Sixth Corps and the cavalry in this battle amounted to some six or eight thousand prisoners (including six general officers), fourteen pieces of artillery, and a large number of wagons.

In early March, Custer's division was in the lead and came upon a bridge being burned by a detachment of Rosser's, who was attempting to blunt their advance. A Union detachment of 300 was sent forward to chase off the Rebels, then save the bridge so the supply wagons and caisson of the combined force could cross safely, while the cavalry troops forded the river, all on their journey to Waynesboro. Whittaker noted in his Custer biography:

> Now it was that a man of rapid decision and fiery energy like Custer was worth his weight in gold. A slower and more methodical man would have utterly failed in the task set him next day. It was to reach Waynesboro' seventeen miles off, in the midst of a driving rainstorm, on a dirt road, mud up to the horses' knees everywhere, and up to their bellies in the mud holes, to cross a river of unknown depth, and to attack and whip [Confederate General] Early who had an unknown force.
>
> He did it with the triumphant success that always marked his independent efforts. He had three brigades, each about 1,500 strong. Custer pushed on after Early's trains, and did not halt until he got to the Blue Ridge. The results of this capture, made by Custer, single-handed (with no other brigade or division), were eleven guns, complete with caissons, teams, etc., two hundred wagons, sixteen hundred prisoners, and seventeen battle-flags. That night he crossed the Blue Ridge and encamped on the other side. Thanks to Custer, it was now open to our forces in every direction, with not an enemy nearer than Petersburg, and the end was coming fast.

Next on the map was Charlottesville, with Custer always in the lead. He was greeted there by the mayor, who gave up the keys to every building, hoping to save his town from destruction. The Union troops took advantage of the hospitality to rest their horses, which were on the verge of breaking down after plodding through the unforgiving mud, and eating corn instead of hay. On March 4 the pursuit was resumed, on a mission to destroy anything the Rebels could use, including public property, flour mills and factories, bridges and canal works. Their next mission was the railway from Richmond to Gordonsville, which could be used by the Rebels to rush a strong force of infantry and threaten Sheridan's advance. In fact, two Confederate divisions—one of infantry, the other cavalry—were waiting to ambush Sheridan along the Southside Railroad.

"When Custer struck the Gordonsville Railroad at Frederickshall, he came on some very agreeable intelligence in the telegraph office," noted Whittaker. "It informed him that the irrepressible Early was not either dead or sleeping. The telegram was from Early to Lee, stating that he was following Sheridan with two hundred cavalry, and intended to strike him in rear about daylight. The news tickled Custer immensely. He at once dispatched a regiment after the unfortunate Early, caught and destroyed his party, and nearly took Early himself, the latter swimming the South Anna to escape, accompanied by a single orderly, after a campaign in which he lost all his army, every piece of artillery, and all his trains."

General Custer's battle report on the early March raid detailed what they seized from the Rebels:

> So sudden was our attack and so great was the enemy's surprise that but little time was offered for resistance. The artillery, however, continued to fire till the last moment and till our troops had almost reached the muzzles of their guns. One piece was captured with the sponge-staff still inserted in the bore and the charge rammed half way home. The rout of the enemy could not have been more complete; no order or organization was preserved. The pursuit was taken up by my entire command, and continued through Rockfish Gap ... and thereby saved us from several days' delay and marching. In the battle of Waynesborough, in which the loss of the enemy in killed, wounded, and captured was upward of 2,000, my loss was but 9 in all.

A few weeks later, several soldiers from Custer's division were in Washington, DC, for a special ceremony, reported in the *Evening Star*, on March 21:

> This morning Major Compson, 8th New York Cavalry, and others of the officers and men of Custer's Division appeared at the War Department with seventeen Rebel flags captured by them at Waynesboro' and Charlottesville in Sheridan's late victory over Early. Each officer and soldier in this party captured, with his own hand, a battle flag, which is now inscribed with the name of the captor. These men were of the 3rd Division, under command of General Custer, and were mostly of the 2nd Brigade ... On arriving at the War Department, the flag bearers were ushered into the Secretary's room, filled with interested spectators. Among those present were ... Mrs. Custer, the beautiful young bride of the gallant Custer, and who naturally took a deep interest in the proceedings. On Secretary Stanton's entering the room, Major Compson handed him a letter from General Sheridan, in which, after concisely narrating the deeds of the brave men who captured the flags, he asked for them a furlough of 30 days.

In Pursuit of a Surrender

Custer had a mission to complete—the total defeat of Confederate forces—but he held no animosity toward his Rebel counterparts. On several occasions, he even took the time to chat with captured officers. One of these occasions occurred in March of 1865, when Confederate General Joseph Kershaw surrendered to a lone Union soldier from Custer's 3rd Division, who was guarding a small group of Rebel soldiers, leading them back to his encampment. At first the Confederate general hadn't noticed any other Union soldiers nearby, until one of the prisoners motioned toward a group of infantry in a tree line close by. Kershaw elected to surrender rather than flee or take on the Union soldiers. He had only one request, to surrender his sword to the commanding officer. He was taken to Custer's headquarters camp and waited for his return from skirmishing. Kershaw—who was senior to several other Rebel officers taken prisoner—recalled his interaction with meeting the boy general, in *The Custer Story*, published in 1880:

> The sun had gone down, peaceful evening settled on the scene of recently contending armies, when a cavalcade rode up briskly, A spare, lithe, sinewy figure bright, dark, quick-moving blue eyes; florid complexion, light, wavy curls, high cheek-bones, firm-set teeth—a jaunty close-fitting cavalry jacket, large top-boots, Spanish spurs, golden aiguillettes, a serviceable sabre … a quick nervous movement, an air telling of the habit of command—announced the redoubtable Custer whose name was as familiar to his foes as to his friends.
>
> [After an exchange of pleasantries, Custer invited Kershaw to stay for a while.] This made us quite at home, and the conversation became free, general, and kindly. With soldierly hospitality our host made us feel welcome. And, despite our misfortune, we enjoyed not a little the camp luxuries of coffee, sugar, condensed milk, hard tack, broiled ham, spread on a tent-fly converted into a table-cloth, around which we sat on the ground, Custer and his Rebel guests.
>
> After supper we smoked and talked of subjects of common interest, dwelling on the past. Our host, with true delicacy, avoided the future, which to us was not an inviting topic. We slept beneath the stars, Custer sharing his blankets with me. We lay in the midst of Custer's squadrons. Thousands of men with their horses lay about us within easy call. As the last bugle call sounded "Tattoo" and "Taps" silence reigned, broken only by the neighing or snorting of a horse, the cough of some wakeful soldier. Custer was soon asleep. As I lay there, watching the glittering hosts of Heaven, I buried my dreams of Southern independence. The God of Battles had deserted our banners. I bowed my spirit in submission. Mine, thenceforth, the task to help bind my bleeding country's wounds.
>
> The sun was shining bright when I awoke. All was bustle and activity. My host gave me cheery greeting as I joined him standing by the fire. He wore an air of thought, receiving and sending many communications. While we breakfasted some thirty troopers rode up, one after another … each carried a Confederate battle-flag—all except my captor, and he carried two. I counted. Thirty-one banners—thirty-one of our regiments killed, captured, or dispersed, the day before. It was not a comforting thought.
>
> Custer's whole Division was now drawn up in columns of squadrons in full view, a spectacle to a soldier of keenest interest. Finally he turned to me. "You will remain here a few minutes when horses will be brought for you and your companions, and you will be conducted to Burkesville where you will find General Grant. Good-bye!" He shook my hand, mounted a magnificent charger, and rode proudly away, followed at a round gallop by his splendid escort bearing the fallen flags. As he neared his conquering legions, cheer after cheer greeted his approach. Bugles sounded. Sabres flashed as they saluted. And the proud cavalcade filed through the open ranks, and moved to the front, leading that magnificent column in splendid array. Me thoughts no Roman victor had ever a more noble triumph.

The respect Custer had for the Confederate army, was reciprocated by "the enemy." The following was written by Basil W. Duke, a Rebel soldier, and published in *The Southern Bivouac*, in the June 1885 to May 1886 annual issue:

The night of the 2d of April, 1865, was a memorable one in the annals of the [Confederate] Army of Northern Virginia. All along the line strict silence was commanded, but the scene was touching in the extreme. The hearts of the brave fellows who had so long like a wall of fire stood around Richmond sank within them. They saw the hand-writing on the wall, and knew this move was preliminary to the evacuation of the capital of the Confederacy, and many gave vent to their feelings in tears, albeit before unused to the melting mood. But no time was to be lost. At midnight all was in readiness, and without so much as a drum-tap we fell into line, leaving our tents standing in grim and solitary loneliness, with no occupant save the piles of manufactured tobacco, with which the Confederate Government, in lieu of provisions, had supplied us bountifully. During the third, fourth, and fifth days of our retreat no enemy was visible, but rumors of his near approach floated everywhere. Meanwhile, hunger, an enemy which had not been absent from the Confederate camp for nearly a year, was becoming now not only bold and aggressive, but ferocious. We had exhausted our meager supply of meat and bread and parched corn, and it began to be quite trying to one's patriotism. What we dreaded the day before we now began to crave—the appearance of the enemy. Imprisonment or death in battle was better than starvation, while victory would mean an abundance of food. We did not wait long. A Federal battery was seen unlimbering to our left, about a half mile away. A minute after a shell came whizzing over us; another, nearer and deadlier than before, exploded in the midst of us ...

We were ordered to lie down—and it is amazing how flat even a two-hundred-pounder can make himself under such circumstances, and yet how mountainous he imagines himself to be. Soon we hear the notes of a cavalry bugle. How merrily it sings, how defiant its tones! How martial the strains as the gentle south wind brings its cadence to our ears! It is no stranger to us, for its strains we have heard before, and we know their meaning. It is Custer's trumpeter rallying his dashing squadrons to the headlong charge. We fall back to the foot of the hill to receive it. A Georgia brigade reinforces us. On, on they come, as though on pleasure bent. The sharp clang of sabers is heard as they fly from the scabbards. A moment more they flash in the sunlight magnificently. The enemy ascends the summit of the hill and dash on us. We pour in a deadly and appalling volley, and thirty brave fellows fall from their saddles. The conflict is short, sharp, and decisive, and the gallant Custer and his squadron fall back before overwhelming numbers as gaily and gallantly as they came. But the lines are closing around us, and the Confederacy was in its death throes. We saw surrendered eighteen battle-flags which bore upon their tattered folds the historic names of Manassas, Cold Harbor, the Wilderness, and Spottsylvania Court-house.

Wait! Every cloud has its silver lining. The next morning, after a refreshing slumber on the sweetest of all beds—the bare ground—we are again marshalled in line. Down that line came General Custer. By his yellow hair and boyish face he is known to all of us. Near the center of the line he turns to his band and orders it to play "Dixie." As the marvelous strains of the Confederate war-song floated in liquid sweetness around us and over us, we break into tumultuous cheering. General Custer waves his hat, and a thousand gallant soldiers in blue dash their caps in the air. Such was General Custer in the presence of a conquered foe. A Confederate Soldier.

On April 6, the battle of Sailors' Creek unfolded, covered by a reporter for the *Boston Journal*, known simply as Carleton. His story was published two weeks later in the *Burlington Free Press*, April 21, 1865:

This illustration shows General Custer accepting the flag of truce from his Confederate opponent, near Appomattox Court House, but in fact it was nothing more than a white rag. Finally, the guns were silent. (National Archives)

The part which the cavalry had in this engagement was most brilliant. They operated on both flanks. Ewell, with the troops which had been withdrawn from Richmond, received the full force of the attack. There has been no cavalry charge during the war which has surpassed that of Custer's in this attack, in energy and power. It was terrible to the foe. With sabres drawn, with horses upon the run, goaded by spur and quickened by shouts till they caught the wild enthusiasm of their riders; till horses and men became fiery centaurs, the hue swept on. The earth trembled beneath the tread of thousands of hoofs; the air rang with bugle blasts and soul-thrilling cheers. There was the roar of the cannonade, the fiery streams of grape and canister, the flashes of thousands of muskets. Riders and horses went down, but on, still on, with louder shouts, wildly, madly, without fear of death, bent only upon breaking the enemy's line—of crushing it by one ponderous blow—they drove—leaped the intrenchments, shooting and sabreing all who resisted—gathering up thousands of prisoners, who stood seemingly without power to run away—amazed, astonished, stupefied by the audacity of the irresistible charge which swept all before it.

General Lee realized he was running out of options to sustain the fight. Union General Grant saw the futility also and sent a letter to Lee on April 7. "The result of last week must convince you of the hopelessness of further resistance on the part of the Army of Northern Virginia in this struggle," Grant wrote. "I feel that it is so, and regard it as my duty to shift from myself any further effusion of blood, by asking of you the surrender of that portion of the C.S. [Confederate States] Army known as the Army of Northern Virginia."

On the same day, while waiting for Lee's response to surrender terms, General Sheridan's scouts got word back to him that four Rebel trains filled with rations, supplies, weapons and ammunition were positioned at Appomattox Station, waiting to be off-loaded. Sheridan had planned to move his forces along the Cumberland Turnpike to Richmond, but he elected to divert to the Station to capture those trains.

Captain Moses Harris wrote in *The Cavalry Journal* in 1891:

> Along in the afternoon [of April 8] Custer went ahead at a trot, and as we neared the station, towards evening, the sound of artillery intimated to us that he might be glad of some assistance. So urging our tired horses forward, we were soon crossing the railroad a few hundred yards east of the station, and as we came out into some open fields to take in flank and rear the force which had assailed Custer's troopers with so much noise and assurances. While we were groping through the woods in the darkness, which had now fallen, the artillery fire suddenly ceased; Custer, having discovered that the force opposing him was simply an escort to some wagons and reserve artillery, which had been pushed on in advance of Lee's army, settling the matter by charging with his usual impetuosity, capturing guns, trains and escort. Meanwhile, the news which had passed around, that Custer's advance had surprised and captured a number of trains of cars loaded with supplies for the Confederates, was confirmed by ear splitting screeches from the captured locomotives, with which the Wolverines were amusing themselves on the railroad. Again in the saddle, the cavalry stretches away in a long column to the right and front, and Custer's troopers, following headquarters, with its forest of captured battle-flags go galloping past.

After four long years, Confederate General Robert E. Lee, left, surrendered to Union General Ulysses S. Grant at Appomattox Court House, in April 1865. (National Archives)

With his beleaguered forces getting squeezed by Union infantry and cavalry at Appomattox Court House and closing in from the rear at New Hope Church, General Lee realized it was impossible to break through the cordon, or rush reinforcements in to clear a path to retreat. He sent word to Grant, requesting a suspension of hostilities until the two could have a face to face meeting to discuss the terms of surrender. Grant agreed and allowed General Lee to select the meeting place.

Lee dispatched two of his subordinates to search the area for a suitable meeting site. They approached local homeowner Wilmer McLean, who offered up a dilapidated and unfurnished house, but this was quickly rejected. They needed something more suitable for such an historic event, so then McLean offered his own home, and it was deemed appropriate.

News of the tentative surrender spread through the Union camps, but the Rebel soldiers kept hanging on, maybe sensing the end was near, but refusing to believe their sacrifices over the past several years had been in vain. Then, unexpectedly, a Union cavalry officer approached Confederate lines near the Appomattox Road. It was Custer and he was carrying a flag of truce. Edmund Hatcher, one of those Confederate soldiers, wrote about Custer that day, in *The Last Four Weeks of the War*, in 1892:

> Whether his appearance was in response to a request from General Lee, or he was the bearer of a formal demand for the surrender initiated by General Grant, we are not informed. At this time, our army was in line of battle ... the skirmishers thrown out, while two hundred and fifty yards from those, on an eminence, was a large body of Federal cavalry.

Moses Harris remembered that day, writing in 1981:

> There is a sudden halt; the cheering up in front grows louder; a knot of horsemen can be seen off to the left, surrounding something which looks like a white flag, and the word is passed back from the front—Lee has surrendered ... we realize that the long chase is ended, that the great rebellion has received its death blow, and that our work is finished.

To continue on would be foolish, with Union forces positioned to obliterate the rag tag remnants of the war-weary rebel troops. Charles Morris in *Heroes of the Army in America*, in the chapter "George A. Custer, A Knight of the Spur and the Sabre," wrote:

> Custer was "in at the death" of the Confederate army. When the exhausted Confederates, finding themselves opposed by a strong body of cavalry backed up by infantry, gave up the struggle in despair and sent out a flag of truce, it was Custer's fortune to receive it—a white towel on a pole.

Shortly after noon, General Lee arrived at the McLean house in Appomattox, and waited in the parlor for General Grant. Thirty minutes later, Grant, Phil Sheridan, Edward Ord and Custer arrived. There was little need for introductions, or hostility. Though at present they were enemies, during the Mexican War they had served together, and they recalled the occasion, before Grant got down to more serious affairs. Trevor Plante, for the *National Archives Prologue* magazine, spring 2015, wrote:

> Grant proposed that the Confederates, with the exception of officers, lay down their arms, and after signing paroles, return to their homes. Lee agreed with the terms, and Grant began writing them out.
>
> One issue that Lee brought up before the terms were finalized and signed was the issue of horses. He pointed out that unlike the Federals, Confederate cavalrymen and artillerymen in his army owned their own horses. Grant stated that he would not add it to the agreement but would instruct his officers receiving the paroles to let the men take their animals home. Lee also brought up the subject of rations since his men had gone without rations for several days. Grant agreed to supply 25,000 rations to the hungry Confederate soldiers. [Most of the rations were provided from Confederate supplies captured by Sheridan when he seized Rebel supply trains at Appomattox Station the previous day.]

Though there was verbal agreement of the surrender, formalities would take place the following day. Still, General Custer took the opportunity to address his troops of the 3rd Cavalry Division:

> With profound gratitude toward the God of battle, by whose blessings our enemies have been humbled and our arms rendered triumphant, your Commanding General avails himself of this his first opportunity to express to you his admiration of the heroic manner in which you have passed through the series of battles which today resulted in the surrender of the enemy's entire army. The record established by your indomitable courage is unparalleled in the annals of war. Your prowess has won for you even the respect and admiration of your enemies.
>
> During the past six months, although in most instances confronted by superior numbers, you have captured from the enemy, in open battle, one hundred and eleven pieces of field artillery, sixty-five battle flags, and upwards of ten thousand prisoners of war, including seven general officers. Within the past ten days … you have captured forty-six pieces of field artillery and thirty-seven battle-flags. You have never lost a gun, never lost a color, and have never been defeated; and notwithstanding the numerous engagements in which you have borne a prominent part, including those memorable battles of the Shenandoah, you have captured every piece of artillery which the enemy has dared to open upon you.
>
> Let us hope that our work is done, and that, blessed with the comforts of peace, we may be permitted to enjoy the pleasures of home and friends. For our comrades who have fallen, let us ever cherish a grateful remembrance. To the wounded, and to those who languish in Southern prisons, let our heartfelt sympathy be tendered. And now, speaking for myself alone, when the war is ended and the task of the historian begins—when those deeds of daring, which have rendered the name and fame of the Third Cavalry Division imperishable, are inscribed upon the bright pages of our country's history, I only ask that my name be written as that of the Commander of the Third Cavalry Division. G. A. Custer, Brevet Major General Commanding.

On April 12, the formal surrender of arms took place. The Confederate soldiers could now head home. Printing presses churned out paroles for them, granting them free passage without threat of being detained. General Robert E. Lee departed Appomattox, bade farewell to his staff, then returned to Richmond, where his wife awaited him. But General Lee was not acting on behalf of the entire Confederacy, only the Army of Northern Virginia. In other campaigns, Rebel forces continued the fight, including North Carolina, Tennessee, Alabama, Mississippi, a portion of Louisiana, territories west of the Mississippi River, and the far west, including Texas.

But for George Armstrong Custer, his participation in the eastern campaign was done. Frederick Whittaker, in his biography of Custer, explained what separated him from other cavalry officers:

> Everything he did succeeded, failure seemed unknown to him, and the surrender at Appomattox left him with the highest individual fame as a cavalry commander of any man except Sheridan. His name and figure, when only a division commander, were better known all through the Union, and attracted more compliments from Confederates, than those of any corps commander then in the Army of the Potomac ...
>
> A cool and candid examination of the evidence ... shows that Custer's luck was peculiar to Custer himself, and, coming to other men, would have been lost. It consisted mainly in the quickness with which he seized every opportunity as soon as it occurred, and this quickness was entirely owing to the difference of his method of directing a battle from that adopted by most general officers.

Many battlefield commanders prefer to direct their forces from an over-watch position, safely in the rear, where they can see the battle unfold or receive feedback from messengers and redirect as necessary. But communicating orders requires time, whether by signal flags, or couriers, and often the lag of a few minutes can spell defeat or victory. Custer preferred to be in the thick of the fighting, exposing himself to constant peril, but where he could immediately see a shift in the direction of the fight, and respond viva voce and his troopers can follow his lead. The only time he relied on messengers was to bring forth reserves waiting to join the fight.

While he was an easy target for Confederate marksmen, his presence in the thick of the fight proved to be invaluable to his own cavalrymen. Whittaker wrote:

Just after the Civil War ended, President Abraham Lincoln was killed by a southern loyalist at Ford's Theatre in DC. Mourners view his body at New York's City Hall. (May 1865 issue of *Harper's Weekly*)

His constant presence is a great encouragement to the soldiers, who value kind words exactly in proportion to the rank of the person from whom they come. The general who shares their dangers they are ready to adore, after one or two battles, as Custer always found.

The objections to this position for a general are two. First, it is fatiguing, and uses up horses very fast. Second, the general may get shot. These risks Custer always took, along with Sheridan, Phil Kearny, and one or two others in the Army who followed the same plan. To be "always in the advance, and always in rapid motion," was their secret. It showed them the opportunities, the moment they occurred. This was the secret, the real secret, of Custer's wonderful success in Sheridan's last campaign, and the difference between him and Devin. While the latter was watching his own line, Custer was watching that of the enemy. Who shall deny that his laurels were fairly won?

It was a fine sight to see Custer and his staff on the field, during that last campaign. There were more shocks of long, shaggy, unkempt hair in the Third Division than anywhere else in the Army. As for neckties, Custer's division could be recognized a mile off, by its fluttering, scarlet handkerchiefs, and they were to be met with all over the country.

During the draw down after the surrender, General Sheridan paid 20 dollars for the table Grant and Lee used to sign the surrender documents. Little Phil then gave that table to Libbie Custer, with a short message—"I respectfully present to you the small writing table on which the conditions for the surrender of the Army of Northern Virginia were written by Lt. General Grant—and permit me to say, Madam, that there is scarcely an individual in our service who has contributed more to bring about this desirable result than your gallant husband."

The relief and jubilation sweeping across the northern states took an abrupt plunge into immense sorrow days later, with the news that President Abraham Lincoln had been assassinated by a southern loyalist.

"A conspiracy had been in progress for a long time among a few half-crazy secessionists in and about the capital," wrote Rossiter Johnson, in *From Campfire and Battlefield*, in 1894. "It culminated on the night of Good Friday, April 14, 1865. One of the conspirators forced his way into Secretary Seward's house and attacked the Secretary with a knife, but did not succeed in killing him. Mr. Seward had been thrown from a carriage a few days before, and was lying in bed with his jaws encased in a metallic frame-work, which probably saved his life. The chief conspirator, an obscure actor, made his way into the box at Ford's Theatre where the President and his wife were sitting, witnessing the comedy of 'Our American Cousin,' shot Mr. Lincoln in the back of the head, jumped from the box to the stage with a flourish of bravado shouting '*Sic semper tyrannis!*' and escaped behind the scenes and out at the stage door. The dying President was carried to a house across the street, where he expired the next morning."

The assassin, John Wilkes Booth, himself a well-known actor, fled to southern Maryland on horseback, then was tracked down 12 days later to a farmhouse in northern Virginia. It was soon discovered he hadn't acted alone, but was part of a conspiracy group that had initially planned to kidnap the president, Vice President Andrew Jackson (a southerner), and Secretary of State William Seward.

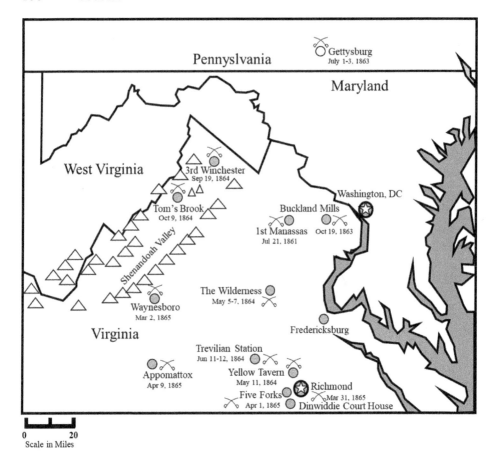

Custer's battles of the Civil War, 1861–65. (Map by Ted Behncke)

The country was still in mourning a month later, when a military parade was planned in Washington, DC. It was much needed to begin the healing process, and reunite the country.

In typical manner, General Custer had to lead his cavalry troopers, though his entrance took an unexpected turn along the way. Edmund Hatcher, in *The Last Four Weeks of the War*, in 1892, wrote:

Every available space where human feet could stand or hands could cling, was appropriated long before the prancing steeds of Sheridan's cavalry led the advance up Pennsylvania Avenue. Stands, staging, boxes, tables, chairs, vehicles, lamp-posts, indeed everything that promised a lookout, was crowded to suffocation with eager people. Windows, balconies and housetops were even more densely packed. Indeed, the mass of civilians pressing their eager homage upon these soldiers coming home from the war, was a sight long to be remembered and attaining to the grandly sublime, as an independent pageant; but when the fiery cavalry steeds, prancing to their well-known bugle notes; the long lines of infantry with burnished arms flashing in the sunlight; the thundering rattle of artillery wheels in an unceasing surging mass, swept along

Some considered him the greatest of America's cavalry officers. Others compared Custer to the world's greatest ever. Had he retired after the Civil War, he could have had his pick of numerous prestigious positions. Instead, he chose to remain in the Army, and so his Civil War legacy is often lost in heated discussions about who this complex soldier really was. (March 1864 issue of *Harper's Weekly*)

through the day, how shall words be found to express the fervent, sacred emotions stirred within every heart?

The troops as they moved along Pennsylvania Avenue presented a grand appearance, all arms of the service being represented in full force. The dark and light blue uniforms gave a fine effect to the spectacle. Looking up the broad Pennsylvania Avenue, there was a continuous moving line as far as the eye could reach of National, State, division, brigade, regiment and other flags. Some of them were new, the stars of gold leaf glittering in the sun, and these contrasted strongly with flags borne in the procession tattered in battle or mere shreds. Other flags were thickly covered with names and dates of battlefields where victories were won by these proud veterans.

General Custer rode a powerful horse; at times he became restive and ungovernable; when near the Treasury Department the animal madly dashed forward to the head of the line. The General vainly attempted to check his courser, at the same time endeavoring to retain the weight of flowers which had previously been placed upon him. In the flight the General lost his hat. He finally conquered his horse and rejoined his column. Passing the President's stand, he made a low bow and was applauded by the multitude.

Further explanation of Custer's "mad dash" were revealed in *The Custer Story*. "Among the spectators were groups of schoolchildren trained to sing patriotic ditties. One young girl … later told Mrs. Custer, 'We were massed along the sidewalk waving flags, throwing flowers as we sang. Custer had always been my hero, so as he rode by I tried to throw a wreath of flowers about his horse's neck.' Others too, were paying his tribute. But the beautiful horse, which had never quailed under fire, shied at this floral bombardment and attempted flight." Colonel Horace Porter's account recalls Custer's mad dash along the parade route: "Conspicuous among the division leaders was Custer, his long golden curls floating in the wind, his low-cut collar, crimson neck-tie, buckskin breeches—half General, half scout, dare-devil in appearance. Within 100 yards of the President's stand his spirited horse took the bit in its teeth, and made a dash past the troops like a tornado. But Custer was more than a match for him. When the Cavalry-man, covered with flowers, afterwards rode by the officials, the people screamed with delight."

Custer's Civil War legacy was perhaps summed up best by Horace Greeley, when this famed *New York Tribune* correspondent wrote:

> Future writers of fiction will find in Brig. Gen. Custer most of the qualities which go to make up a first-class hero, and stories of his daring will be told around many a hearth stone long after the old flag again kisses the breeze from Maine to the Gulf. Gen. Custer is as gallant a cavalier as one would wish to see. Always circumspect, never rash, and viewing the circumstances under which he is placed as coolly as a chess player observes his game, Gen. Custer always sees "the vantage of the ground" at a glance, and, like the eagle watching his prey from some mountain crag, sweeps down upon his adversary, and seldom fails in achieving a signal success. Frank and independent in his demeanor, Gen. Custer unites the qualities of the true gentleman with that of the accomplished and fearless soldier.

CHAPTER 3

Indian Wars

> We all agreed that the nomad Indians should be removed from the vicinity of the two great railroads then in rapid construction, and be localized on one or other of the two great reservations south of Kansas and north of Nebraska; that agreements not treaties, should be made for their liberal maintenance as to food, clothing, schools, and farming implements for ten years, during which time we believed that these Indians should become self-supporting. To the north we proposed to remove the various bands of Sioux, with such others as could be induced to locate near them; and to the south, on the Indian Territory already established, we proposed to remove the Cheyennes, Arapahoes, Kiowas, Comanches, and such others as we could prevail on to move thither.
>
> LIEUTENANT GENERAL WILLIAM T. SHERMAN, COMMANDER OF THE ARMY,
> *MEMOIRS OF GENERAL W. T. SHERMAN*, 1875

When the Indians first saw those ribbons of steel encroaching on their cherished hunting grounds, they never realized how disastrous it would be to the sacred buffalo, to their own way of life. From distant bluffs, they could see the railroad crews laying down tracks, they could hear the clanging of sledgehammers on steel pikes, each one punctuating the serenity of life on the Great Plains. And as the massive engines snorting steam chugged their way across the prairies, they brought the white man with his thunder sticks, who hunted the buffalo for sport, leaving their carcasses behind by the hundreds. After, came the arrival of every imaginable enterprise of the white man, which promised a permanence impossible for the Indian to overcome. For an expanding nation with a bloody Civil War behind it, this was progress. For the Indians, they fought for each inch of soil desperately attempting to hold onto their precious way of life. They moved only when they had to, but violence was inevitable. The region became the crucible and the battleground of learning for plains warfare for all of the combatants.

To Kansas

Major General George A. Custer mustered out of the Army in January 1866 with the expiration of his volunteer commission. At just 26 years old, he was being "put out to pasture," sadly packing his velveteen uniform of a major general and digging out his captain shoulder boards which he had worn briefly in 1862–63. Pinning them onto a new uniform (with far fewer buttons) he officially reverted to the permanent rank of captain. He reluctantly entered into the old army which existed prior to the Civil War, where rank progressed stubbornly slow, advancements occurring only when a more senior officer dies or retires. It was not uncommon to hold the same rank for decades and he hated it. For ambitious men like him who fast tracked on merit during the Civil War, it was as if stepping in the life-sucking mud he remembered during the Peninsular Campaign of Virginia. To ease his mind, Custer went on extended leave with Libbie in Monroe, Michigan, deliberating his future, both inside the Army and out. It was a special time for Autie and Libbie, visiting friends and attending social events around Monroe. They were newlyweds in every respect and for the first time for Libbie, able to spend time without fear about her hero and his personal safety. They were after all both still in their twenties, quite immature, and with their thoughts and emotions awash in

George and Libbie adored one another and tried to be with each other whenever possible even under field conditions. Libbie traveled great distances and endured hardships to be near her Autie. (Little Bighorn National Monument)

love for each other. For Libbie especially, her thoughts were consumed with the cherished arrival of children, wishes she confided in her closest friends. As spring stretched to summer, they lived in the Bacon home and Autie considered offers of employment and career, both in the Army and some in civilian life. Thanks to his fame earned in the Civil War, there was much to consider and many interesting offers. He was a national hero and loved the attention and potential offers of being propelled into wealth and more success. Some involved being a partner in new business enterprises in the east. He was urged to go into politics, but some early experience supporting President Andrew Johnson left him no stomach for it. An offer to serve in the Mexican Army came with a whopping annual salary of 10,000 dollars (Custer made 8,000 dollars as a major general of volunteers) but would involve resigning his commission in the U.S. Army. But, he was a soldier, and recent expansions of the frontier army could provide a good stepping stone to serve at the general officer level again.

In June 1866, four new regiments of cavalry, the 7th through the 10th were approved by Congress. The 7th and 8th were all "white regiments," while the 9th and 10th were to be "black regiments," the latter regiments being filled with black enlisted troopers led by white officers. The coveted position George wanted was a colonelcy in either the 7th or 8th Regiment, making him their commander. It was one step away from brigadier general, the real prize, and a promotion which would surely come with the kind of combat service on the frontier he was known for. To his surprise and disappointment, he was instead offered the colonelcy of one of the black regiments. Despite his profound service in freeing enslaved blacks during the Civil War, there was a stigma leading a black regiment, and he did not want it. His own views about the recently freed men were not progressive enough to accept the position. The colonelcy of the white regiments were already full with more senior officers. The only remaining possibility was to serve as the second in command as a lieutenant colonel in the 7th Regiment. When he learned the new commander of the 7th, Colonel Andrew Jackson Smith was to be away on detached duty in Arkansas, and would place him in operational command of the 7th, he accepted.

Lieutenant General William T. Sherman, who was second in command of the Army to General Ulysses S. Grant at the time, held Custer in some esteem. From the book, *The Sherman Letters*, published in 1894, General Sherman's confidence in Custer can clearly be seen in an 1867 letter to his brother, United States Senator John Sherman:

> G. W Custer, Lieutenant-Colonel Seventh Cavalry, is young, VERY brave, even to rashness, a good trait for a cavalry officer. He came to duty immediately on being appointed, and is ready and willing now to fight the Indians. He is in my command, and I am bound to befriend him. I think he merits confirmation for military service already rendered, and military qualities still needed—youth, health. Energy, and extreme willingness to act and fight.

Clearly, great things were expected of Custer on the plains of Kansas and Nebraska.

The "lucky" 7th was considered a premier unit from the time of its organization, a place where the best and brightest wanted to serve. And with the Civil War ending, it was soon filled with exemplary officers who had performed distinguished service in the conflict. Early arrivals included Major Wycliffe Cooper, and captains Albert Barnitz, Myles Keogh, Robert West, Frederick Benteen, and Louis Hamilton. Barnitz had known Custer while assigned under him in the 3rd Cavalry Division in the Civil War. He was an initial fan of Custer, but his opinion would change quickly. Both Barnitz and Robert West would grow to hate Custer inside of a year. Myles Keogh was a hard-drinking, but likeable Irishman, who came to America via the papal wars in Italy. He had performed good service in the Civil War, being brevetted to lieutenant colonel before the war's end. He was a Custer friend and supporter from the beginning. Louis Hamilton was the grandson of the famed Alexander Hamilton. Bright and gifted, young Hamilton was only 22 years old, the youngest captain in the Army. Frederick Benteen was a Virginia native who had chosen to serve in the Union Army during the war. He was actually five years older than Custer, but had a boyish,

General William T. Sherman, the designer of total war in Georgia and his "March to the Sea." Originally a fan of Custer, he brought him to Kansas to bring Sherman's brand of war to the Plains Indians. Sherman would sour on Custer over time, but he would intervene to allow Custer to accompany the Dakota column on the Little Bighorn campaign. (Public Domain)

feminine face and smile, along with gray hair which hid an ornery disposition. He was however a courageous and very capable officer. Yet, if he took a disliking to anyone, he had a passive aggressive nature which sought an opportunity to manifest itself. He hated Custer from their first meeting. Benteen's bitterness for Custer would not diminish with time, and many critics over the years believe this bitterness played a pivotal role in Custer's demise at the battle of the Little Bighorn.

The lieutenants were to become loyal and trustworthy Custer supporters. Among them was George Custer's younger brother Tom, recently transferred from the 2nd U.S. Infantry with ample help from George. Also included was Algernon "Fresh" Smith, Myles Moylan, Thomas Weir, and a Canadian, William W. Cooke. All had interesting past lives. Of course Tom Custer's courage preceded him. Twice decorated with the Congressional Medal of Honor for two separate events during the Civil War, he was fearless. Myles Moylan had been promoted to brevet major during the Civil War, but then enlisted in the 7th and served first as a sergeant major before being promoted to lieutenant. Algernon Smith had a significant handicap, losing the effective use of one of his arms from a severe wound received at the battle of Fort Fischer, South Carolina. Smith was called "Fresh" to avoid confusion as there was already a "Salt" Smith serving in the regiment when he arrived. Lieutenant Cooke would eventually become one of Custer's most trusted officers. Born in Canada, Cooke had gone south to serve in the Union Army during the Civil War. He came from a well-to-do family, but reportedly fled home among rumors of a questionable paternity. He was very loyal to Custer, who would appoint him adjutant just prior to the Little Bighorn fight. Thomas Weir had served in a Michigan regiment during the Civil War and was a dependable and capable officer. A bachelor and handsome, Weir was a ladies' favorite but, like many officers of his time, he liked to drink too much.

Fort Riley, Kansas Territory, was designated as the organizational site of the 7th Cavalry Regiment in the summer of 1866. It was just ten miles from the end of the Union Pacific Railroad line, most recently terminated at nearby Manhattan, Kansas. From Fort Riley, a scattering of other forts—Hays, Harker, Dodge, Larned, and Wallace—loosely tied the railroad with stage stations which extended to the Colorado gold fields. Fort Riley was relatively newly constructed in the late 1850s. It was not a picketed fort (a stockade enclosure with vertically driven logs sharpened at the top), but rather an open post constructed of sandstone and limestone buildings, spread stoically across a wide plain elevated above the Kansas River. Visibility extended for miles due to the vast prairie and the harvesting of most of the available timber for construction and fuel. It was as beautiful as it was stark.

Throughout the autumn of 1866, the 7th Cavalry Regiment organized, gained over 900 officers and men, and was then formed into companies. As violence increased between whites and the Indians in Kansas, these companies were sprinkled in ineffective quantities to the new frontier forts so they could quell the violence. By the time George and Libbie would make their way west, only the regimental headquarters and four companies remained at Fort Riley. George and Libbie, along with two of her close friends, arrived at Fort Riley on October 16, 1866. It was not exactly what they expected. The endless landscape was a dreary brown carpet of prairie grass dancing in nearly constant wind. There were few buildings, all constructed for purpose not beauty, and none to impress the observer. The trooper barracks at Fort Riley were built on the south side of an open parade ground where worn paths gave ample evidence of the drilling being conducted there. On the north side, officer houses (side-by-side duplexes) constructed of native flat faced sandstone ran neatly east to west. They were modest, a parlor and kitchen on the first floor, and two bedrooms on a half story above. A large and inviting porch ran across the entire front of the home. Relatively small in comparison to Libbie Custer's family

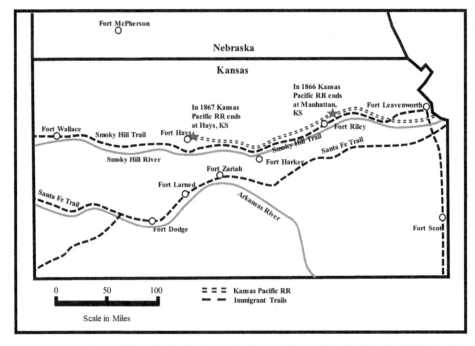

Frontier Army forts in Kansas/Nebraska during the Indian Wars, 1867–69. (Map by Ted Behncke)

home in Monroe, she both loved and hated their cozy, first real home they shared together. She shared with a cousin in 1866, writing, "Our house is comfortable and cheery," and later in a letter to her friend Rebecca Richmond, "It does not seem life in the army for you know I have had mostly a rough time." Of course she was referring to the contrast with the camp life of traveling with the Army, as she had during the last year of the Civil War with Custer. While conditions were rough in the field, she preferred them to separation, which brought great worry. She was terrified and hated being alone. She would later write in her book *Tenting on the Plains*, "I am tormented with anxieties that I cannot overcome. I look out so startled, if a mounted man passes our house, fearing he is the bearer of bad tidings." She feared Autie would die, recalling his devil-may-care cavalry exploits during the Civil War, knowing he had cheated death many times. She was young and terrified he would be killed. She had lost everyone in her life who mattered, was an only child, and Autie was the joy in her life.

Custer assumed formal command of the regiment on November 1, 1866. He and Libbie would enjoy just a few weeks together before he had to report to Washington, DC, for examination boards necessary for competency confirmation of his new rank. He would not return to Fort Riley until December 16. During Custer's absence, the highly social Libbie learned all about the regular army and the life of those assigned at the fort. Then as now, army units have divisions of personalities which form over time, and the remote frontier forts were particularly so. Being an extrovert and socially adept herself, Libbie was quick to recognize the subtle social divisions and associations within the regiment. She was very apparent and savvy of the cliques which formed, who she could trust, and those to distance herself from. Custer was a strong personality, larger than life to many, and she worried about the negative rumors brought to her. As Libbie would remember in her book, she was worried and Custer cautioned her, she "must neither look for fidelity or friendship, in its best sense, until the whole of them have been in a fight together." Of course he was right in the larger sense. The stress of combat always served to draw men together, enduring the same fears and hardships. However, this was not the Civil War, where regiments would serve together in large battles. Over the next nine years, the regiment would rarely serve together, except in the smaller scrapes spread across the plains of Kansas.

The 7th Cavalry's early work on the plains had to deal with policing thousands of square miles of endless, treeless prairie, extending to both ends of Kansas east and west, north to Nebraska and south into the Indian Territory. The opening of the Bozeman Trail, which struck north from the Oregon Trail in the vicinity of the North Platte River, just west of Fort Laramie in Wyoming Territory and extended north and west into Montana Territory (near Virginia City, Montana), particularly, and rightly, angered the Cheyenne and Sioux (the largest groups of the Plains Indians) because it upset their traditional hunting grounds of the buffalo. They resisted all forms of settlement and white permanency in the region with violence. The thin "blue" line of cavalry which dotted the region, was all the nation had to bring a new form of combat. The Plains Indians were formidable fighters and gifted horsemen. They were considered the finest light cavalry in the world, and the Army failed to recognize this or adequately respect their foe, and, as such, it was inevitable a disaster would happen. As the year 1866 came to a close, the Army would not have long to wait.

The Fetterman Massacre

The Bozeman Trail began serving emigrants and miners traveling through northern Wyoming to the gold fields and other ways of life in Montana and beyond. The region had been given to the Crow Indians as part of the Treaty of Fort Laramie in 1851. Over the ensuing dozen years, the area increasingly became the hunting grounds of the displaced Sioux, Cheyenne and Arapaho tribes, who lost their own hunting grounds to the ever-aggressive white opportunists. Together, the three tribes, often allies, moved increasingly further west on the Bozeman Trail in search of dwindling herds of buffalo. After the 1864 Sand Creek massacre by Colorado militia on a peaceful Cheyenne village, tribes began bloody and violent attacks on anyone using the trail. In response, and to protect emigrants on the trail, the U.S.

Army established three frontier forts along the route, including the larger Fort Phil Kearny in 1866, near present-day Buffalo, Wyoming. Sparsely sprinkled among the forts were 700 troops and 300 civilians, with the majority stationed at the newly established Fort Kearny under the command of Colonel Henry B. Carrington.

Indian attacks on Fort Fetterman and the surrounding area began almost immediately upon the arrival of the troopers and before its completion in the summer of 1864. They were small attacks at first, but generally with the Indians mounted and always testing the mettle and tactics of the troopers. The warriors, under the leadership of Chief Red Cloud, became increasingly emboldened to fight with groups growing to even 100 warriors at a time. The truth of the situation was the entire complement of the Army was significantly outnumbered by the Indians in the area. Both sides were aware of the Indian strength and the smaller number of troopers. Yet, Carrington's junior officers pressed him with expressions of bravado to tangle with the warriors and became impatient when he did not. When a company of cavalry under the command of Lieutenant Horatio S. Bingham arrived to reinforce the fort in early November 1866, the officers peppered the cautious Carrington, believing they had sufficient combat power to take on the aggressive Indians. About the same time, two infantry captains, James W. Powell and William J. Fetterman, also arrived at the fort. Both Powell and Fetterman had served during the Civil War with Fetterman's service quite distinguished. Fetterman though, had an arrogance and hubris about him which would soon lead to trouble.

The Indians took satisfaction by constantly harassing nearly every bit of movement necessary about the fort, including the cutting and gathering of wood from the nearby river. On an average day, the Indians watched a wood-cutting detail of government-contracted civilians leave the fort, and promptly attacked it. Colonel Carrington would predictably dispatch a rescue element to break off the engagement. Although Fetterman had not fought in a single Indian engagement, he criticized Carrington's lack of offensive spirit in taking the fight to the aggressive Indians. Pressed, on December 6, 1866, Carrington finally gave Fetterman permission to move against the warriors, once again harassing the wood cutters. Fetterman's detachment included 40 mounted troopers along with Lieutenant Bingham and Lieutenant George W. Grummond. Their orders were simple, relieve the wood cutting detail, then pursue the warriors in the direction of the nearby Peno Valley. There, Colonel Carrington's separate force would circle around the fleeing Indians, surprising them in ambush. The Indians gave way in front of Fetterman as predicted, but employing a common Cheyenne tactic, tried to lure Fetterman into an ambush. The wily Fetterman suspected as much, so he stopped his command on ground which supported a suitable fight. The Indian strength that day was later reported to Congress at over 100 warriors, and the Indians tested Fetterman's leadership. During the fighting Fetterman became separated from lieutenants Bingham and Grummond. Meanwhile, Carrington had arrived at his predetermined position

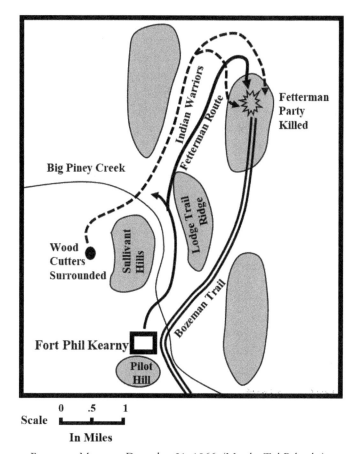

Fetterman Massacre, December 21, 1866. (Map by Ted Behncke)

only to hear the distant heavy firing, compelling him to respond by moving his column toward the firing, coming up and behind the mounted warriors. Pinched between the two Army commands, the Indians broke off the fight, dissolving into the surrounding terrain. The command was very fortunate, with only two dead, including Lieutenant Bingham, and five wounded.

The attacks on the wood-cutting party continued, occurring twice in December. In each case, Carrington instructed his leaders to not play into an ambush. It was a wise directive. The Plains Indians were excellent fighters and gifted on horseback. Custer, in his 1874 book *My Life on the Plains*, described his admiration for the mounted Indians. "The Indian warrior is capable of assuming positions on his pony, the latter at full speed, which no one but an Indian could maintain for a single moment without being thrown to the ground. The pony, of course, is perfectly trained, and seems possessed of the spirit of his rider." The Indians could emerge from seemingly nowhere, mass their combat power to place the troopers at disadvantage, and if they lost the upper hand, disappear with ease. Often, the Indians would bait an attack with a single mounted warrior trying to draw troopers into a fight. Up to late December, the Indians "baited attack" had not amounted to any real success.

On the morning of December 21, 1866, the history of plains warfare between the Army and the Indians would take a fateful turn at Fort Kearny which would affect Army tactics and leadership in significant ways. The wood-cutting detail left as scheduled to begin work, easily visible by Army lookouts on the nearby Sullivant Hills. Predictably, the detail was soon under attack. Captain Fetterman was given command of the 81-man relief force, consisting of 49 men of the 18th U.S. Infantry, including Captain Frederick Brown, and the remaining troopers being cavalry under command of Lieutenant Grummond. Two civilians armed with new Spencer repeating rifles accompanied the command. The Spencer rifle jokingly was referred by many as the rifle you "loaded on Sunday and fired all week." The Spencer rifles' amazing rapid-fire capability was new to the Indians at that time. One man equipped with a Spencer had the effect of seven in a fight, thus capable of tilting odds in the favor of those so equipped. Most of the army force were armed with muskets left over from the Civil War and had only 40 rounds of ammunition per man. Colonel Carrington personally inspected the group and knowing Captain Fetterman's contempt for Indian fighting ability, gave specific verbal orders to Fetterman. Francis Grummond Carrington remembered her husband's instructions in her 1910 memoirs *My Army Life and the Fort Phil Kearney Massacre*. Colonel Carrington said, "Relieve the wood train, drive back the Indians, but on no account pursue the Indians beyond the [nearby] Lodge Trail Ridge." Carrington repeated his directive from the gate as the last of the command departed.

Fetterman's movement initially followed Carrington's directive, but instead of approaching the wood-cutting detail from behind to perform the relief, he circled around the detail in a wide arc, dangerously placing his command between the Indians and the wood-cutting detail. To Fetterman's front was a small band of Sioux, no more than a dozen mounted warriors, led by a young, inspirational, warrior—the soon-to-be legendary Crazy Horse, who, along with his warriors, was the bait for the day. Disregarding orders, Fetterman followed them over Lodge Trail Ridge and disappeared out of sight. Firing was heard and Carrington, fearing the worst, put together a force of about 75 men and placed them under Captain Ten Eyck in an attempt to find out what was happening. Upon reaching Lodge Trail Ridge, Captain Eyck and his men saw a large force of Indians in the Peno Creek valley below. The Indians taunted the troopers, jeering them in their flamboyant warrior attire, wanting them to advance. Ten Eyck refused to advance, and after the warriors left, finally moved forward to discover horror. In what would become a staple of warfare with the Plains Indians, Fetterman's entire command of 81 troopers and civilians were found dead, stripped naked, and mutilated. Red

Cloud and his warriors had spoken loudly about their feelings on the invasion of the white man in their territory. The wiping out of Fetterman and his command had taken roughly an hour.

The December 27, 1866, edition of the *New York Times* aptly captured the reaction to the Fetterman Massacre, "Three Officers and Ninety Troopers Surrounded and Butchered." It went on: "A terrible massacre occurred on the 22d, near Fort Phil. Kearny. Brevet Col. Fetterman, Capt. Brown, and Lieut. Gammond [Grummond], of the Eighteenth Infantry, with 90 enlisted men of the Second Cavalry and Eighteenth Infantry, were surrounded by Indians, and every officer and man killed."

The news of the Fetterman massacre served to shock not only the public but also the Army. With the Civil War having so recently ended, both the public and the Army were conditioned to epic battles and large numbers of casualties. Both the North and South were like armies, with similar leaders and tactics. Outcomes then, could be expected. This new reality was quite different. There were 81 troopers killed in a single battle "surrounded by Indians," and "every officer and man killed." The Indians previously were never considered equals in warfare, but they were not only equals to the Army, they were superior. Fetterman's disdain and contempt for Indian tactical prowess was common among Army leaders, ignorant of the highly refined horse and warrior culture that was decidedly effective. Obviously there would have to be adjustments to thoughts and tactics when dealing with Indians. The Fetterman massacre gave ample evidence that the Plains Indians understood the strategic principle of "mass" and tactical timing. When they lacked advantage, they easily surrendered the field and dissolved away. Lieutenant Colonel George Custer, along with other Army leaders took notice, folding it into their thoughts and strategies with the Plains Indians and growing hostilities.

The Fetterman massacre had another effect on Army leadership—anger. Indeed, the official dispatch of December 28, 1866, sent by General Sherman to General Grant captured this sentiment, "We must act with vindictive earnestness against the Sioux, even to their extermination, men, women, and children." Though unsure of exactly how they would take the war to the Indians, when it came, it would resemble Sherman's "March to the Sea" during the Civil War. It would be "Total War."

Kansas 1867

> If I were an Indian, I often think that I would prefer to cast my lot among those … who adhere to the free open plains, rather than submit to the confined limits of a reservation, there to be a recipient of the blessed benefits of civilization, with its vices thrown in without stint or measure.
>
> —GEORGE A. CUSTER, *MY LIFE ON THE PLAINS*, 1874

With the advent of spring in 1867, the Army launched its initial campaign against the tribes of the central and southern Plains Indians. The plan proposed by the

Department Commander, General William T. Sherman to the Army Commander Ulysses S. Grant conceptually would move the Sioux north of the Platte River, and then move the Kiowa, Arapaho and the Southern Cheyenne south of the Arkansas River. The Indian resettlements would open a large tract of land, a portal through Kansas and Nebraska to support the expansion of the railroad westward. Grant liked and approved the plan, but the Sioux relocation plan drew opposition and additional inquiry from Indian advocates and peace advocates in the east. It was placed on temporary hold as a result, and only the southern campaign began as scheduled, in late March 1867. Sherman assigned overall command of the southern campaign to Major General Winfield Scott Hancock. Referred to as "Hancock the Superb," for his leadership as an Army corps commander at Gettysburg in 1863, he had an excellent reputation as an officer in the Civil War. However, he had no experience fighting Indians, and arrogantly assumed it couldn't be any worse than defeating the Confederates.

Hancock deployed with a sizeable force from Fort Riley designed to scare his new foe. Hancock reasoned the Indians, if nothing else, would respect the large numbers and impress them to surrender. Together, Hancock's force included seven companies of the 37th Infantry, 11 companies of the 7th Cavalry, and a supporting battery of artillery. With his support troops, the entire command numbered over 1400 troops. The command's destination was newly constructed Fort Larned, an impressive and comfortable fort located in east central Kansas just south of the Pawnee River. There, near the Santa Fe Trail, Hancock expected to meet with the tribal chiefs. By the time he arrived on April 7, 1867, he found a large village of Arapaho, Kiowa, Southern Brule and Oglala Sioux, along with tribes of Southern Cheyenne, wintered there, taking advantage of adjacent buffalo herds.

Hancock had been assured by local Indian agents that the chiefs sought peace, but they could not control their younger warriors. As a result, Hancock, along with Custer, met with just a few chiefs at Fort Larned. Hancock and Custer were about to be schooled on the practices of the Plains Indians. While Hancock dictated to the chiefs that the raiding of settlements and against railroad crews must stop, the large Indian camp was preparing to move. Hancock promised peace to them if they could halt their aggressions, otherwise he would bring war. To impress his point, he told them he would bring his troops to visit the village the following day for a larger council.

The chiefs departed, consenting to allow the troopers' safe passage. On the morning of April 13, 1867, the troops marched upstream to within ten miles of the Indian village before setting up their camp, while two chiefs—Pawnee Killer of the Sioux and White Horse of the Cheyenne—were visiting. The two chiefs agreed to return the following morning and bring the remainder of the chiefs with them. The Army officers viewed this as an enormous step toward a peaceful resolution. They never realized it was all a ruse.

When the morning broke on April 14, there were no Indians in sight. During the night they had moved out, and as the Hancock column moved out to find them, they discovered an Indian "rear guard" action in front of them. The Indians had tactically placed a line of mounted warriors across their own line of retreat. With the village on the move in the other direction, these warriors were protecting (or covering) their movement. Realizing what was happening, Hancock was furious. Custer, convexly and to himself, was privately impressed. Writing after the event, Custer shared the sight was "one of the finest and most imposing military displays, prepared according to the Indian art of war, which it has ever been my lot to behold. It was neither more nor less than an Indian line of battle drawn directly across our line of march; as if to say, thus far and no further. Most of the Indians were mounted; all were bedecked in their brightest colors, their heads crowned with the brilliant war bonnet, their lances bearing the crimson pennant, bows strung, and quivers full of barbed arrows." The drama and pageantry struck Custer at his core, he loved it innately. Further, the rear-guard action by the Indians to protect their slow moving village of women, children, and elders, demonstrated

Brigadier General Winfield Scott Hancock pictured in dress uniform during the Civil War. He had a favorable reputation mostly from his Civil War leadership. He was badly wounded at the battle of Gettysburg while defending the confederate attack on the third day of the fight. He was Custer's superior officer in 1867 during the Kansas Indian Wars. Hancock was not an Indian fighter and Custer would blame Hancock's poor leadership for his own problems and courts-martial later that year. (Library of Congress)

a sophistication he was not prepared for. He had new respect for the Indians and it was genuine.

Several Indians finally approached Hancock. They explained the women and children had fled upon the approach of the Army. It was the biggest group of troopers they had ever seen, and the Indians feared the worst. The group spoke until dark, when, through an interpreter, the chiefs promised the women and children would return to the camp. Hancock intended not to be fooled again. He gave orders to Custer to move clandestinely to surround the village and ensure they stayed put. The 7th Cavalry cordoned the village as ordered. While final preparations were being made, Custer advanced carefully toward the village, crawling toward the outer rings of lodges and campfires which were burning, but there was no milling about by the Indians. The entire village was empty except an old man and one child. It was a second tactical deception. They had anticipated the movement by the troopers and, by sacrificing their lodges, bought time to escape with their families. It had worked. Hancock ordered a chase, but it was too late. As the Indian column moved away, pieces splintered off with great discipline, eventually leaving nothing but a series of numerous, separate trails, too many to effectively follow. They had escaped. Custer had failed in his mission, but the embarrassment wasn't completely over. While on the march in pursuit of the Indians, he inexplicably rode away, alone from the column (in a pattern which would become all too familiar in the years ahead) pursuing a buffalo. Out of sight of his men, in full gallop, he accidentally shot his own horse in the head (Libbie's favorite) when a buffalo bull turned on him. It was a stupid move, one more consistent with a 20-something man, not the commander of a regiment of cavalry. With great self-deprecating humor Custer would later recount the incident in an article he wrote for *Turf, Field and Farm* in 1867. Custer wrote:

> In bringing pistol hand to the assistance of the bridle hand, I accidently pressed the trigger of my revolver, and discharged the bullet into my horse's neck, the ball entering about six inches in rear of the ears, and evidently penetrating the brain, and the noble animal fell dead from the leap he was then taking. It may now be asked what became of the rider, the late proprietor, in his own estimation, of the buffalo. I will answer. Describing something between a parabola and a circle, he reached mother earth by passing over the horse's head and striking ground fully ten feet from where the horse had fallen. Without attempting to analyze my thoughts at that moment, I will merely say the buffalo was uppermost in my mind. I expected the next moment to be gored and trampled to death. The buffalo was now within a pace or two of me; in fact in being thrown from the horse I had fallen directly in front of the buffalo.

Alone, on foot, and in unfamiliar territory full of hostile Indians, he was lucky when his men stumbled across him sometime later. Recovering his saddle and eventually being remounted, he returned to the command of his regiment.

Custer pushed his men on a night march on April 16 and into the early morning of the 17th in the attempt to find some of the Indian column. The Indians were ahead of him, attacking Lookout Station, a stage stop, killing the three men working for the stage line. Custer pushed both men and horses hard, not unlike in similar missions during the Civil War. He sent news back to Hancock of his location and his beliefs about what had transpired in the days before. "The hasty flight of the Indians, and their abandonment of, to them, valuable property convinces me that they are influenced by fear alone, and it is my impression that no council can be held with them in the presence of a large military force." Hancock had enough. He ordered the lodges of the abandoned village along with all of its contents to be burned. The move destroyed valuable food stores of the Indians along with many of their personal items. It may have given the embarrassed Hancock some satisfaction but it suitably served to ignite a war which would last well past summer and into the next year.

The 7th Cavalry continued west through cold rain in the early morning hours of April 18 finding the remnants of the stage station and the burned remains of the three men. Out of supplies, exhausted, and having lost the Indian trail, Custer had no choice but turn east to Fort Hays for resupply and rest. They would find little of either. Fort Hays had recently been established and was lacking adequate supplies for the garrison, let alone for a mobile command of 11 companies of cavalry. Both the officers and enlisted men grumbled about conditions and with good reason. They had covered some 150 miles between Fort Larned and Fort Hays in cold, wet weather, mostly at night. Both horse and rider were exhausted. Custer himself demonstrated the same vigor in the saddle which had impressed his men and officers during Civil War campaigns. Where his example had always brought admiration in the past, this time, surprisingly, it brought desertions among his men, a few at first, and then dozens. Despite the dangers deserters knew to be in the prairies ahead of them, the men clearly preferred the gamble in the wilderness instead of the miserable situation in camp. They took both mounts and weapons to improve their odds. As conditions worsened, more troopers fled. By the end of May 1867, a total equal to a company's strength (100 troopers) left the 7th Cavalry for a life somewhere else. Custer, unaccustomed to this behavior, used the only thing he knew to combat it—harsh discipline.

It was not hard to side with the departing troopers. Their pay was only 13 dollars a month, and when on campaign, they could expect little support. The frontier forts scattered across the region were poorly supported. Supply trains had to come from hundreds of miles away and through the same hostile and dangerous country the troopers were there to protect. Consequently, certain items were in short supply, especially fruits and vegetables. Malnutrition and afflictions such as scurvy were common and to say the troopers were starving was not an exaggeration. When Custer caught several men away from the camp attempting to buy canned fruit from a nearby settler, he added to their already existing misery. He had their heads shaved as an example. Even to many of his officers he had gone too far. Captain Albert Barnitz had served with Custer during the Civil War and greatly admired him during the time. Custer's lead-by-example bravery in the 3rd Cavalry Division impressed and inspired him. Barnitz expected the same would be found in the 7th Cavalry and was initially excited to serve under Custer again. But, in a letter penned to his wife and in his journal of May 1867, Barnitz wrote a considerably different description of Custer, accusing him of being mad and tyrannical in his conduct. "He is really quite obstreperous and that he would lose whatever little influence for good that he may have once possessed in the Regiment." Custer was coming unwound, and those around him were losing confidence.

There was no question Custer was in a depressed mood. His first attempt at dealing with Indians had failed. He failed to read their behaviors, predict their actions, and when they tactically deployed their forces to protect their families, he failed to track and stop them. Custer had always been a good reader of emotions, perhaps an expert in intuition. But in dealing with the Indians, his instincts left him puzzled. He also failed in his first field command of the 7th Cavalry. The art of command includes a comprehensive set of competencies including tactical employment, intelligence (discerning the unknown from the known), navigation, logistics, communication and maintaining the will of the command to fight and follow direction. Custer was being judged by all these facets now and he was not used to such critical dissection. The failure of the Army to adequately supply his force was not his fault. The insensitivity he displayed in dealing with the problem, he owned entirely. As far as gaining the edge on the Indians tactically, no one really in the Army knew enough to be an expert. The dynamics of predicting their movements, reactions, and behaviors, well, they were as diverse and confusing as the tribes themselves. Some knowledge would come with experience, though the judgement to know when to be humble was not in his character and would continue to plague him.

Custer badly needed Libbie. He had been separated from her for over two months and the circumstances of the recent campaign magnified the need for her emotional support. He fired off a couple of letters, sharing his loneliness and asking her to come to him. In her book *Tenting on the Plains*, Libbie remembered Custer's words, "The inaction to which I am subject to now, in our present halt is almost unendurable. It requires all my buoyancy of my sanguine disposition to resist being extremely homesick." She too was lonely and anxious. In successive letters to Custer, she poured out her heart saying, "Our separations grow more hopeless," and "I am tormented with anxieties I cannot overcome." Only reunion would provide a remedy. Just a week after Custer's second letter, Libbie, her friend Anna Darrah, and the housekeeper Eliza, arrived with an escort at the 7th Cavalry's camp near Fort Hays by Deep Creek. George could barely contain his excitement. He had prepared a crude home in the field courtesy of a large tent provided by his boss, Colonel Andrew Smith. There was plenty of room for everyone. Even though developing events and a pending mission imperiled the reunion for the present, all was well.

In the wake of Hancock's reflexive destruction of the Indian village, parties of warriors had taken the fight to the frontier. Small groups of Arapaho, Cheyenne and Sioux were killing any whites they came across, including settlers, railroad crews and stagecoach station attendants. General Hancock ordered Custer to send men to the stage stations and to patrol an area north of Fort Hays to offer a modicum of protection. On June 1, 1876, six companies of the 7th left Fort Hays to patrol the area south of the Platte River and along the Republican River. In *My Life on the Plains*, Custer explained Hancock's orders were to find and kill "the Cheyennes and that portion of the Sioux who are their allies between the Smoky Hill and the Platte [Rivers]." They were unsuccessful in finding or engaging the war parties who continued to kill without pause, but Custer's command remained in the field.

Libbie, friend Anna, and Eliza intended to leave the camp near Big Creek as soon as Custer departed on campaign, but the routes were deemed too dangerous to travel so they remained in camp. On June 6 and 7, the camp endured a series of tremendous thunderstorms. As is the case on the prairie, large amounts of rain fell, and Big Creek suddenly overflowed its banks. Several troopers drowned in the torrents and Libbie played a role in saving some of the men. On June 9 the way home was deemed safe enough, and the three women with an escort traveled first to Fort Harker and then home to Fort Riley. While Libbie was dealing with the severe weather in camp, Custer was having his own problems already, despite just leaving on campaign. Desertions in the field were at epidemic levels, speaking to the hardships of prolonged field duty and the quality of recruits. Custer wrote to Libbie on June 8, 1867:

> In the vicinity of the Platte River 35 of my men deserted in 24 hours. I was accordingly apprehensive for the whole command as I had before me a long march through a hostile country. When breaking camp, about 5 p.m. on the 7th, I caused Boots and Saddles to be sounded, when 13 of my men deliberately shouldered their arms and started off for the Platte, in the presence of the entire command, in open day. As I intended camping but about 10 miles from the place, and not knowing but that the remainder of the command, or a considerable portion of it, might leave during the night, I felt that severe and summary measures must be taken. The horses of only a few of the officers were saddled in addition to those of guard and picket. Major Elliott and lieutenants Custer, Cook and Jackson, with a few of the guard, [left] to pursue the deserters who were still visible, though more than a mile distant, and to bring the dead bodies of as many as could be taken back to camp.

The pressure of command on the plains was quite different than anything Custer was used to. Perhaps the most stressful was the potential loss of his command from desertion, to lose it from the inside and on the "hoof," while on the march. His only reaction was extreme discipline, a course that would propel desertion at an even higher rate. He could not share his thoughts to others and give the impression he had no plan. Without Libbie with him, he could only express his feelings in letters to her, and in between, let the pressure work on his emotions and well-being.

On June 10 Custer arrived at Fort McPherson, with his six companies, having crossed over 200 miles of prairie without incident. The command had observed over 100 warriors off in the distance some three days previous during their movement, but they had moved on without encouragement from the cavalry. The only casualty had been the believed suicide of Major Wyckliffe Cooper, a well-known alcoholic by the command, but his death still shook the regiment. At Fort McPherson, Custer found several small groups of Sioux Indians, including the Chief Pawnee Killer, had set up their lodges by the nearby Platte River. Custer met with the chiefs and invited them to move their lodges closer to the fort. The move would demonstrate their commitment for peace. Ultimately, no Indians took Custer up on his offer, but they reassured him they would remain peaceful.

General William Sherman arrived at Fort McPherson a couple of days later. He was disappointed in Hancock's progress in finding and engaging the "hostile Indians" throughout the past two months. He had real confidence in Custer's ability and directed him to return to the field. Sherman asked Custer to search for the Sioux

A trooper and his horse had an exceptionally hard life in the frontier army. The pay for a private was 13 dollars a month, which seemed insufficient in comparison to the dangers and difficult life while on campaign. Rations were rarely good even while in garrison at the isolated posts. Desertions were common. Cavalry horses had an even harder lot with the average horse lasting operationally just a few years. When no longer able to support a trooper in the field, horses were used to pull wagons or a field gun. (Library of Congress)

near the forks of the Republican and the South Platte rivers west of Fort Sedgwick in Colorado. If he ran into any hostiles, he was to engage and give chase, no matter where they moved to. To enhance Custer's effectiveness, he could keep the 7th Cavalry resupplied by "hugging" the Union Pacific Railroad, which now reached Fort Hays, and searching along the length of the Platte River. Libbie recalled in her book *Tenting on the Plains* that Custer liked this freedom of movement, and he wrote to her, "I am on a roving commission ... going nowhere in particular but where I please." Custer was also encouraged by General Sherman offering to obtain railroad passage for Libbie to join him when he reached Fort Sedgwick. Just knowing he had a possible visit from Libbie coming up at the end of the long march improved his spirits.

The 7th Cavalry departed Fort McPherson on June 17, averaging about 25 miles a day. They arrived at the assigned destination, the fork in the Republican River on June 21. There, they went into camp and launched a detachment to seek supplies. What happened next will always question the state of mind Custer had at the time. He had written to Libbie the day he left Fort McPherson. Rather than having her traveling by train to meet him, she should make her way to Fort Wallace and he would arrange to meet her there or have a representative from his command rendezvous with her. Custer's orders from General Sherman were quite explicit. He was to draw his supplies from Fort Sedgwick some 75 miles away from their camp on the Republican River. Yet, he decided to send a detachment to Fort Wallace, 75 miles in the other direction. There could be only one reason—a reunion with Libbie. So, without delay, on June 22, he directed a company-sized detachment under the command of Lieutenant Sam Robbins, along with 12 wagons to Fort Wallace. If Robbins found Libbie at Fort Wallace, he was instructed to bring her to Custer. Perhaps to cover his back, Custer sent the recently arrived Major Joel Elliott to Fort Sedgwick with a report for General Sherman and to gain new orders on how to proceed with the regiment. Of course Custer could have done it in person had he followed orders, but his desire to be with Libbie prevailed. Finally, to be complete, Custer sent a company under the command of Captain Robert West south to scout Beaver Creek for any Indian activity there.

Meanwhile, at the Republican River campsite, Sioux attacks suddenly found the 7th Cavalry on the defensive. With several companies out on their respective missions, the regiment was a far-depleted force. Custer met with Pawnee Killer who once again feigned peace, while at the same time having knowledge of (if not directing) a Sioux attack on the camp and an organized attempt to scatter and steal their cavalry's horses. Custer should have been most worried about the demonstrated Sioux threat to his immediate position, but his mind instead was clearly on Libbie. Worried about her safe transit to him, he launched Captain Edward Myers with yet another company to locate Captain West and his company, and then together, move east to find the supply train which was most certainly on its return trip to the

Republican camp. Captains Myers and West linked up and arrived on June 26 at just the right time to save the supply train. It had been under siege by 300 warriors led by Chief Roman Nose. The strength of three cavalry companies persuaded Roman Nose to break off the attack, and the supply train arrived at the Republican camp without further incident. Custer was in a poor emotional state by the time the train finally pulled into camp. There had been no report of any kind to him from any of his deployed companies. The aggressive actions by the Sioux against him in camp led him to believe they were operating in a similar way in the region elsewhere and his own actions, he believed, may have placed Libbie in danger or worse. Perhaps most unnerving to him, the innocent Libbie would not have been aware of the danger.

Custer was soon relieved to learn Libbie had not arrived at Fort Wallace, however the fort had been attacked on June 22, and Custer also learned Indian raiding parties were working the Smoky Hill Stage line and anything they came across in the vicinity. While determining the next steps for the 7th Cavalry, Major Elliott returned from Fort Sedgwick. There were no updated orders from generals Sherman or Hancock but Major Elliott had a recommendation from the commander at Fort Sedgwick, Colonel Christopher C. Augur, who thought the Smoky Hill stage line and the forts in the region were the targets of the raiding parties. Logically then, they were the best place to find and engage the hostile Indians. Without new orders, Custer was to use his judgement. Complying with Sherman's orders, he marched west and north, first along the South Fork of the Republican River before then turning north toward the Platte River.

While he rode, Custer wondered "where was Libbie, and was she safe?" He had told Libbie to travel to Fort Wallace on the supply train to meet him and he had taken some risk she would be safe doing so. General Hancock obviously believed she would not be safe and had instructed her not to travel with the supply train. Custer's overall desire was just to be with Libbie in any way possible. His mind was not right, bordering on hysteria, and it is not too hard to imagine his concern. A young newlywed on his required mission, riding across an empty landscape left with only fearful thoughts. The 7th Cavalry's march toward the Platte River was incredibly taxing for the men and the horses of the regiment. The terrain all around them was arid and broken, while the temperature was very hot. Leaders and men were increasingly discontented and word of potential desertions circulated among the ranks. Custer seemingly did not care. He was physically up to the grueling march and his men would have to follow his example. This was not the Shenandoah Valley of Virginia of 1864, nor was this the illustrious Michigan Brigade.

The 7th Cavalry intersected the Union Pacific Railroad line west of Fort Sedgwick on July 5, 1867. Almost immediately upon arrival, 30 men had had enough and deserted during the night. From a nearby rail station, Custer wired Fort Sedgwick for orders. His real purpose was to ease his mind about Libbie. His actions increasingly served only that purpose. As he explained in *My Life on the Plains*, "The mere thought of the danger to which she might be exposed spurred me to decisive action," the decisive action being erratic decisions with consequences for his men. From the time the 7th Cavalry had left the previous camp on the Republican Fork, he theorized Libbie may have gone on to Fort Sedgwick as General Sherman had offered. Custer then learned Libbie was not at Sedgwick. In fact, Libbie had actually been on quite a tour of Kansas forts in the interim. She had gone from Fort Riley to Fort Leavenworth, then on to Fort Harker and Fort Hays before finally returning to Fort Riley. General Sherman had told Libbie it was best she remain there, as Custer's movements on the campaign made it difficult to predict where or when she might find him.

In wiring Fort Sedgwick for orders, he learned Lieutenant Lyman S. Kidder of the 2nd Cavalry had departed Sedgwick with ten men and one scout just days before in the direction of the Republican River with orders for Custer. But Custer knew the 25-year-old Kidder was inexperienced and would be at some peril. Further, his small detachment would not be able to defend themselves with the larger Indian war parties known to be in the area. The commander at Fort Sedgwick repeated the orders carried by Kidder, which directed Custer to Fort Wallace. All along the Smokey Hill stage route Indians were raiding, even attacking Fort Wallace a second time on June 26. General Sherman needed the 7th Cavalry to give chase to the Indians in question, and to pressure and kill the warriors if necessary, to stop the attacks. Although the 7th Cavalry was tired from the grueling march from the previous week and short of supplies, they immediately started to Fort Wallace. Custer justified his urgency for movement on the concern for the Kidder detachment, but really it was for a possible reunion with Libbie. Consequently, the command assumed a forced march, stressing men and horses further. Around noon one day while on the march, Custer stopped to rest the horses and eat. In a brazen and rare event, 13 more men deserted with their mounts and weapons. Absolutely furious, Custer ordered Major Elliott and a small party to find them and bring them back, by force. Elliott found the deserters easily, but surprisingly one of the deserters took a shot at Elliott's detachment. Return fire by Elliott's men killed one and wounded several others. The detachment left the dead trooper, but returned with the two wounded and other surviving men. Custer, in a voice everyone present could hear, ordered the surgeon not to treat the wounded men. It was done on purpose, as he wanted to send a message to the rest of the command. Secretly, he had instructed the doctor to care for them.

On July 2 Custer and his troops were drawn to a point south of the Republican River where buzzards were circling. There, they found the remains of Lieutenant Kidder and his 11 men. They had been dead about ten days, and there was difficulty identifying one from another. They had all been scalped and their skulls smashed. Some of the men were partially burned, their noses cut off, and limbs slashed. After some work, Custer was able to identify Lieutenant Kidder from the other men. They carefully buried the detachment and in the morning headed south for Fort Wallace. They arrived at Fort Wallace exhausted, having traveled over 180 miles in just one week. Custer expected new orders and possibly some mail from Libbie at Wallace, but found none. He should have rested the entire command, given the circumstances. Fort Wallace was well supplied, and the horses of the command especially needed rest and attention. Instead, he gave instructions to each company commander to select a dozen of the most well-mounted troopers in each company for a detail (essentially the combined strength of one cavalry company). Leaving Major Elliott in command of the remainder of the regiment, Custer took command of the newly formed detail and left Fort Wallace and headed east. After all the crisscrossing of Kansas by Custer in the past months, this was the most bizarre and controversial.

Custer's destination was Fort Harker, 200 miles away. He would later explain his primary purpose was to draw supplies at Fort Harker, but there were sufficient supplies at Fort Wallace, a fact Captain Myles Keogh would later confirm during Custer's court-martial on September 18, 1867. Custer also said the mission was to bring badly needed medical supplies to treat an outbreak of cholera at Fort Wallace, but it was also another falsehood. Finally, Custer said he was after new horses for the command. None of it made any sense, and they were all excuses cultured weeks later when the entire affair blew up. There was no professional or military purpose in pushing men and horses who had already been used up. His real reason was to find and reunite with Libbie.

During the march to Fort Harker and near Downer's Station, six of Custer's men were attacked by a group of warriors, and two troopers were killed. The other four were able to break contact and return to the rest of the column. Custer inexplicably did not stop, even when the officer in charge of the station asked him to return, find the two men and bury them. Custer seemed unconcerned, ate his dinner and moved out. Interestingly, there was no apparent intent to engage the Indians either. Custer would later write in *My Life on the Plains,* the six men "had without authority halted some distance behind [the command]." The inference was they had drawn the attack by the nearby Indian party. The truth, according to the testimony of Sergeant James Connelly at Custer's court-martial, was Custer had dispatched the six troopers to recover his mare which had disappeared during the march. Before leaving the station, Captain Hamilton asked Custer if the detachment should wait and send a burial party to deal with the dead men. Custer refused, saying the commander of the station would take care of it. The station commander, Captain Arthur Carpenter, did go back and found the men. One was dead but the other only wounded. He had hidden and avoided being found by the Indians. He would recover from his wounds.

In the early morning of July 18, 1867, the exhausted detachment arrived at Fort Hays. They had covered an amazing 150 miles, just two-and-a-half days after leaving Fort Wallace. Handing off the detachment to Captain Hamilton, Custer instructed him to rest the detachment and move on to Fort Harker when ready. Meanwhile, Custer requisitioned two of the post's ambulances as they were more comfortable to travel in after riding horseback for so long (no one was sick or injured), livestock to pull them, and loaded an orderly, Lieutenant William Cooke, his brother Tom Custer and Theodore Davis, a reporter from Fort Hays, into them. They departed without delay. In the dark of late evening, they bumped into a supply train headed east which had orders for Custer. He was to stay at Fort Wallace and conduct operations between the Platte and Arkansas rivers. The orders further instructed, "The cavalry should be kept constantly employed." Custer was not near Fort Wallace and in any event was not returning there. He also had no intention of following any orders. His sole fixation was reaching Fort Harker and Libbie. He had gone completely mad.

The ambulances rolled into Fort Harker in the very early hours of July 19. Custer woke his commander, Colonel Smith at 2:30 a.m., requesting to leave by train for Fort Riley immediately. Colonel Smith, still in a bit of a daze, approved. Later that day, the train arrived at Fort Riley and Custer finally reunited with Libbie. All was right with Autie and Libbie. Nothing else for the moment mattered. But, back at Fort Harker, a storm was brewing. Colonel Smith, having learned the full nature of Custer's crazed movement from Fort Wallace, the forced march, the loss of the men at Downers Station, and the misappropriation of the ambulances, demanded Custer's return. Only orders from a superior would override them. Custer, thinking a bit clearer, and realizing the full extent of his malfeasance, tried to stall to spend more time with Libbie and to formulate his defense. Custer did not want to separate himself from Libbie. He could not endure a separation again, and he reasoned if he played his cards right, Libbie's charm could help him smooth things over. At least that was his hope. But Colonel Smith refused Custer's request to stay at Fort Riley and then ordered him to Fort Wallace instead of Fort Harker. Custer ultimately left Fort Riley without Libbie on July 21, and arrived at Fort Wallace later in the day. Custer was placed under arrest by Colonel Smith on his arrival. The charge—leaving his command without permission. There was more to follow as other leaders in Custer's chain of command learned of what had occurred. General Winfield Hancock wired Smith communication that Custer should have been arrested for acting "without warrant" and his behavior was "highly injurious to the service, especially under the circumstances." Custer, the boy general and national hero, had fallen, very, very, hard.

There had to be a reason for what had transpired. The past weeks could not have just been the unstable emotions of a 26-year-old newlywed. Or, could they have been exactly that? There are some who believed Custer was driven to do things out of jealousy. According to one theory, he learned from a letter or from another officer Libbie had taken a fancy to Lieutenant Thomas Weir, one of Custer's officers. Weir, a bachelor, had a reputation as a charming conversationalist and ladies' man. The problem with the theory is there is simply no evidence to support it. The letters between Libbie and Custer include zero references or mention of Weir or anyone else. Further, the dialogue between them genuinely suggests they were in love and desperately wanted to be together. It does not mean Libbie was not a flirt—she was. She was an attractive young woman and quite naturally drew attention from men young and old. General Grant ordered a general court-martial for Custer and it convened on September 17, at Fort Leavenworth. The weeks between Custer being placed under arrest and being court-martialed allowed him to be with Libbie and to get his emotions back in some balance. His charges were serious though. He was charged with absence without leave from his command, with one specification, or instance, and with conduct to the prejudice of good order and military discipline, with three specifications. The specifications on the latter charge, that he did seriously prejudice the public interest by over-marching and damaging the horses, using the ambulances without authority, and neglecting his duty by not trying to recover or bury the bodies of the two troopers, were the most damning. They were all true. To further add to the lot, an officer of his own regiment, Captain West, filed a charge accusing Custer of ordering deserters be shot down without trial. He further charged on the day the deserters were shot, Custer denied the wounded men medical treatment. Of course it was not true, but to all who were there at the time, Custer made it appear so.

Custer pleaded not guilty. For counsel, he gained the assistance of an academy classmate, Captain Parsons of the 4th Artillery in his defense. There was little to defend, but in the weeks leading up to the trial, Custer rationalized his actions, interpreting events and filling in some facts which were simply not there. Where the strategy didn't work, he blamed events on others. General Hancock's performance in directing the overall campaign during the summer became a target to support Custer's innocence. Custer and Libbie believed it was Hancock's poor leadership which should be on trial. In Libbie and Custer's collapsing world, a Hancock conspiracy provided a convenient excuse, and it should cover up the failure of the Indian expedition.

When it appeared things were not going Custer's way at trial, he reverted to techniques he had learned throughout his life. He would throw himself on the mercy of the authority. While it had been successful in the past, this time it did not work. Custer was found guilty of all three charges, but he was cleared of criminality in regard to the ambulances and the treatment of the deserters. The worst was the ruling about the sentence. He was suspended from rank and command for one year, and forfeited his pay during the time. General Grant, as head of the Army, approved the findings and the sentence but, given the circumstances, believed them lenient. General Grant, writing on November 20, 1867 about the outcome, emphasized, "awarding so lenient a sentence for the offences of which the accused is found guilty, must have taken into consideration his previous services." Custer had lost the confidence of the Army leadership, all the way to the top.

The Custers reacted predictably. To them, the court had been prejudicial and improperly constituted, the sentence unjust. They could not find defense inside the

Captain Thomas Weir was reportedly a great conversationalist and ladies' man. Unmarried, he was rumored to have had a relationship with Libbie Custer at Fort Leavenworth, compelling the crazed behavior of Custer that resulted in his court-martial in late 1867. At the Little Bighorn it was Weir who tried to reach Custer with his company only to see the closing moments of the demise. Sadly, Weir died at age 38 from the effects of alcoholism, just 5 months after the battle of the Little Bighorn. (National Park Service)

Army, so they went outside to the press. Certainly the press they believed, who had always been favorable to Custer, could help. In a letter to the Sandusky Register, which appeared on December 28, 1867, he attacked the court, its officers, and their competency. Custer challenged the courts findings of the abuses of men and horses during rapid forced marches across Kansas by describing them as "slow— the average being less than only three and a half miles an hour, which <u>every cavalryman</u> knows to be slow and deliberate rate of marching." The arrogance and action angered his superiors and leaders through the chain of command, up to General Grant. There were pleas to pursue other action against Custer for his petulant behavior. In the end, Grant let it go.

The Kansas and Nebraska frontier and the Indians had defeated Custer. Custer would later write of his great respect for the capabilities of the Indians in *Turf, Field, and Farm* in 1867, this time as Nomad, his pseudonym:

> No cavalry in the world, marching, even in the lightest manner possible, unencumbered with baggage or supply trains, can overtake or outmarch the Western Indians, when the latter is disposed to prevent it. The white man, in addition to his own weight, must add to the burden borne by his horse, several days' rations for himself, and not unfrequently for the latter also, unless the grazing is sufficient. Besides his clothing, blankets, and equipment far outweigh that

of the red man, who in case of flight travels in the lightest marching order. The Indian, born and bred to his prairie home, accustomed to look to it for his subsistence as well as his shelter, is never at a loss for either, let him by where he may. The buffalo supplies him with food; no bread is required; his pony, like himself, a stranger to the luxuries of civilization, seeks no better food than the wild prairie grass.

It was a different kind of war, one he was not ready for. In addition to his able Indian foe, Custer's opponents were supply problems, the tough terrain, and weather. His leadership directly and deliberately led to desertion and the deaths of men. Officers and men in the 7th Cavalry Regiment doubted his leadership and decision-making ability. He let his personal life affect his professional one. The official rebuke of his behavior, and the consequences following, hurt him deeply. He wanted and needed idolization, something his chosen profession had provided to him in the past. Without it now, he deluded himself into believing he had been unjustly accused and treated. Libbie then, and for the rest of her life, would not forget the lengths Custer had gone to for them to be together. Like the theater they both loved, it was a love story played out on the prairie stage of Kansas and Nebraska. After wintering over in General Sheridan's quarters, Libbie and Custer packed up and headed home to Monroe, Michigan. There, close to family, they could heal themselves and wait. More importantly, they would be together.

Return to Service

Custer and Libbie had enjoyed their time at home in Monroe. They settled back into the Bacon residence and into the community. Custer filled his time and made a living by writing for the magazine, *Turf, Field and Farm*. Meanwhile, a shake up in the Army was occurring out west. On March 2, 1868, Custer's old boss, Major General Philip Sheridan, assumed command of the Department of the Missouri. The department was large, comprising four districts with 27 forts and camps, and included control of 6,000 troops. The commander's billet had stood empty since his predecessor, General Winfield Scott Hancock, had been relieved for the failed campaign of the summer before. The debate over what to do with the "Indian question" was as strong as ever. In July 1867, Congress created a peace commission whose charter was to place Indians on designated lands, securing the region between the Platte and Arkansas rivers. The end state of the plan would place Indians in a place where they could be "reformed" and become farmers, while opening up the frontier safely to expansion and settlement.

In October 1867, the Commissioner of Indian Affairs, Nathaniel G. Taylor, led three Army generals and three U.S. senators to a location on Medicine Lodge Creek in Southern Kansas (present day Medicine Lodge, Kansas) to meet with representatives of four tribes—the Arapaho, Cheyenne, Kiowa, and the Sioux. When the meeting

Major General Phil Sheridan and his generals during the Civil War circa 1865. (L to R) Sheridan, Brigadier General James "Tony" Forsyth, Major General Wesley Merritt, Brigadier General Thomas Devin and Major General George Custer. By this point in the war Custer was Sheridan's go-to commander to accomplish the toughest missions. Sheridan would lobby President Grant for Custer's re-instatement to lead the 7th Cavalry on the Washita Campaign. Sheridan could think of no other officer with the right skills to be successful. (Little Bighorn National Monument)

was over, the four tribes ceded their traditional hunting grounds between the Platte and Arkansas rivers and in turn, would relocate to reservations in the Indian Territory. In addition, the tribes would receive annuities for 30 years. Captain Alfred Barnitz of the 7th Cavalry, who was present at the time of the treaty, wrote in his journal at the time, the tribes "have no idea what they have given up." Of course they did not know exactly what they had given up, nor did it matter. The Indians had little understanding of the concept of ownership of land. They came and went where they pleased in the region. No agreement with the white man would change it. Tensions would continue, with little trust on either side. In June 1868, the Cheyenne raided a Kaw Indian settlement. Raiding among rival tribes was common and the Indians gave no consideration to how attacking another tribe might be seen by whites. But as a consequence, when the Cheyenne reported to Fort Larned a month later, the Indian superintendent refused to provide them annuities. If they were going to use their annuities (which included arms and ammunition) to wage war, the government was not going to support it. The two sides stood at an impasse for a time, but there was little to do. If the superintendent did not give in, the treaty would be invalid, and there would be war. The superintendent eventually acquiesced and the Cheyenne left Fort Larned with their annuities. If the superintendent thought the issuing of annuities would keep the peace, he was wrong. Within a month, the Cheyenne would kill 15 men and rape five women at settlements on the Saline and Solomon Rivers in Kansas.

The people of Kansas responded predictably to the new violence. They demanded action from the Army present across the region. General Sheridan, in his new role and being responsible for preventing the violence, had no illusions about the work ahead of him. Only force would move the Indians onto the reservations set aside and only force could keep them there. He truly was in a no-win situation. If he acted with force against the Indians, he drew severe criticism from peace advocates. If he were too timid, the people of the frontier would howl, claiming he was not doing his job. With few troops to cover the expanse of the department, he simplified his approach, giving priority of protection first to the Union Pacific Railroad, and second, to the settlements. To better support the frontier, he transferred his headquarters to the "windy" Fort Hays and dispatched the 7th and 10th Cavalry regiments to police the area between settlements and the forts. Despite the well-meaning efforts, little was accomplished, and the violence continued.

Sheridan was dealing with the finest light cavalry in the world with an emphasis on "light." The Indians were gifted on horseback. Their ponies survived well on prairie grass. The Indian "commissary" existed all around them, they survived on buffalo and other game. They traveled without having to carry great amounts of stores with them. Finally, they knew the region they were operating in better than anyone. They had lived in and traveled over the ground for centuries. Picking up on these Indian strengths, one of Sheridan's officers, Major George "Sandy" Forsyth, wanted to innovate to match these strengths and use them to their advantage. Forsyth had a good reputation in the Army, having been brevetted to major general of volunteers during the Civil War, and he was trusted by Sheridan. Forsyth formed an all-volunteer force made up of tough frontiersmen who knew the region, field craft and survival skills equal to their potential quarry. To be speedy, they would travel light and take no pack wagons with them. They relied on mules with pack saddles to carry the limited supplies they needed—mostly ammunition. Army presence was limited to just three officers, Forsyth, Lieutenant Fredrick H. Beecher, 3rd U.S. Infantry Regiment, and Acting Assistant Surgeon J. H. Mooers, Medical Department. The force was well mounted and equipped with new repeating rifles.

The first test of Forsyth's scouts came in August 1868 when they took the field to help counter Cheyenne, Sioux, and Arapaho raids on the Kansas Pacific Railroad (whose railhead was then near Fort Wallace, Kansas), raids on settlements, and stage routes in western Kansas and southwestern Nebraska. On September 16, the group started to see Indian signs on the Arickaree fork of the Republican River, a few miles inside of the northeast present-day Colorado. The following day, they were attacked by a combined force of Arapaho, Cheyenne and Sioux Indians, estimated to be as many as 1,000 warriors. The group of scouts sought cover on the best ground available, an island in the nearby Arickaree, later to be known as Beecher's Island. There, for the next nine days, they withstood the continued assault of the Indians. Among them was a chief who several of the scouts knew from a distance. Given his size and impressive physique, he was not easy to miss. He was Roman Nose, a Cheyenne warrior who stood over six feet tall, the tallest Indian most had ever seen on the plains, and considered a great chief. Roman Nose played a direct role in continued assaults on the small defensive position, and he was believed by both sides to be untouchable. If it had not been for the effectiveness of the seven shot Spencer carbine, the Army scouts could not have held off the attacks.

Casualties mounted, including half of the scouts, Major Forsyth, Lieutenant Beecher, and Surgeon Mooers, the latter two dying from their wounds. At a climax, Roman Nose led a main body of mounted warriors right at the island. Roman Nose was killed and the attacking Indians sputtered without his leadership. The warriors broke off the attack, but the siege continued on the little island for a total of nine days. Two groups of two men left during successive evenings in attempts to reach help. Both made it 70 miles to Fort Wallace, an amazing feat on foot. On the morning of September 26, a relief column arrived, saving the survivors. The battle was a sensation in the press and Forsyth became a national hero.

From Monroe, Michigan, George Custer proclaimed it "the greatest battle on the plains." The engagement though was of little consequence in the overall war with the Plains Indians, with one exception. The seven-shot repeating Spencer carbine with adequate ammunition was the thin line between life and death for the survivors. Forsyth's scouts were badly outnumbered, perhaps twenty to one. Yet, the scouts were able to repulse well-executed Indian attacks, one after another, even when the fight was pressed extremely close. It was the ability of rapid fire which made the difference, breaking the Indian will despite the overwhelming numbers. It was a lesson-learned worth remembering and the Indians certainly remembered it. As the Indians traded for weapons in the years ahead they increasingly no longer wanted "needle guns," meaning single shot weapons. They wanted the repeaters or "magazine guns," and they knew how effective they could be. They would prove it at the Little Bighorn.

While the battle of Beecher's Island was being waged, nowhere in Kansas were settlers (or anyone else) safe. The Indians roamed the prairie at will, killing dozens and driving off their livestock. Sheridan regarded the "Cheyenne and Arapaho at war." But, it was impossible for the Army to distinguish "peaceful" from "hostile" Indians. Geography, it was reasoned, could logically make a difference. As a result, General Sheridan gave instructions for Colonel William Hazen, the commander at Fort Cobb, Indian Territory, to keep all peaceful bands of Indians at the post and use it as their agency. Any Indian not found there would be considered "hostile." That simple thinking aside, Sheridan still had a problem though. He lacked the talent to take the fight to the identified "hostiles." In his judgement, he did not have a field commander who could do it. Sheridan's thoughts continued to drift back to Custer when seeking a solution. Custer was Sheridan's go-to commander during the Civil War. No matter how tough the going got, no matter the courage needed, Custer never disappointed him. Even as the war closed toward Appomattox, Custer was relentless in pursuing the Rebel army, even to the point of ruined health. He was a physical mess at war's end, tired and gaunt from months in the saddle. Yet he went on. Sheridan was not the District Commander when Custer fell from grace. He had watched from a distance, not fully understanding what and why it had occurred. He *knew* Custer, and whatever happened the year previous, it was not the Custer he knew and understood. Sheridan had launched Colonel Alfred Sully in September 1868 with a force of cavalry and infantry on the Kansas frontier, hoping for some result. Sully returned less than a week later accomplishing nothing. Sheridan knew he had no one present in the command to lead the sort of campaign he had in mind. He was certain Custer was his man.

Sheridan had actually been working to return Custer to active duty since the spring. In June 1868, he had finally reached out to General Grant's chief of staff to lobby on his behalf, writing, "He [Custer] never failed me, and if his late misdeeds could be forgotten, or overlooked on account of his gallantry and faithfulness in the past, it would be gratifying to him and myself, and a benefit to the service." Grant would have nothing of it, Custer's parting shot letter to the press after his court-martial being the major obstacle. Grant was angry, and even if the Army's success on the plains went worse than expected, little would change it. He trusted and respected Sheridan, who had performed magnificently as the Cavalry Corps Commander the last year of the Civil War. Grant's respect though would never transfer easily from Sheridan to Custer. Nonetheless, by September the winds had changed. With two months remaining on his suspension, and with Grant's hesitant approval, Sheridan wrote to Custer in Monroe, Michigan:

> Headquarters Department of the Missouri
> In the Field, Fort Hays, Kansas, September 24, 1868
>
> General G. A. CUSTER, Monroe, Michigan
> General's Sherman, Sully and myself, and nearly all the officers of your regiment have asked for you, and I hope the application will be successful. Can you come at once? Eleven Companies of your regiment will move about the 1st of October against the hostile Indians, from Medicine Lodge creek towards the Wachita [sic] mountains.
> GENERAL P. H. SHERIDAN, Major General Commanding

The gratifying telegram was met with delight in the Custer household—at least by Custer himself. Noticeably absent was any mention of General Grant, and the reference to "nearly all of the members of your regiment," made it clear to Custer the command environment he would be entering into might lack some support. But the early re-instatement and the "need" for his particular skills were ego strokes for Custer. How could he refuse? The following day it was made official with the arrival of a telegraph from the War Department, "The remainder of your sentence has been remitted by the Secretary of War. Report without delay ... for duty." From pariah to a "report without delay," there seemed to be a great irony in communication.

Despite the enthusiasm, there was a life for Custer to disconnect from in Monroe. He had spent the past several months writing, both magazine articles, and Civil War memoir installments on a deal signed with publisher Harper and Brothers. Custer was developing into a good writer, probably a natural gift but enhanced during his time preparing correspondence for many purposes in the Civil War. He found it a particularly good tool for revisionist history, a procedure he was schooled with by a former commander during the Civil War, General Alfred Pleasonton, who was not a gifted cavalryman, but was much better at twisting the words to do what he could not do on the field of battle. One technique Pleasonton used expertly was to take a correct decision in a situation—even if it was not discerned until afterward—assign the origin of the insight to a subordinate, and then agree to the inspiration. Afterward, with assured success, Pleasonton could claim the victory (because it still required competence to achieve), and demonstrate how good of a commander he was by giving credit to a subordinate. Custer soon captured the ability to emulate the trait, probably first penning correspondence for Pleasonton, later for himself. He was an excellent student of the literary ruse, especially when it helped the cause, in this case, his own legacy.

Custer took a train out of Monroe immediately. Leaving Libbie was very hard, especially because of the depth and healing necessary to overcome the humiliation of his suspension. George and Libbie's time in Monroe served to heal many wounds and also allowed the development of a depth in their relationship which would serve them in the years ahead. Said another way—they had matured. Custer arrived at the Department Headquarters at Fort Leavenworth on September 30, 1868 before heading on to Fort Hays to meet General Sheridan, who was genuinely happy to see his subordinate. Upon meeting, Sheridan thought Custer looked different somehow. Maybe it was Custer's unfamiliar and closely cropped hair which gave him a look of maturity, but the rest and time in Monroe had clearly helped with his emotional balance. The 7th Cavalry was not at Hays, so Custer departed soon after his arrival there for the 7th's camp in the field (on Cavalry Creek), some 40 miles south of Fort Dodge, Kansas. His arrival at Cavalry Creek was great for his self-esteem. The officers of the Custer clique in the regiment each gave him a hearty welcome. The men of the rank and file also felt a change of energy in the camp. It seemed even the dissenters, which included about a third of the officers in the regiment, knew Custer was going to be the only officer capable of leading them to success. He was a good organizer, something he had learned serving under General George McClellan early in the Civil War. Men lined up willingly in preparation when they knew it had purpose. The 7th was leaving on an important campaign and everyone knew it. General Sheridan shared his trust: "Custer I rely on you in everything, and shall send you on this expedition without orders, leaving you to act entirely on your own judgement." The official guidance was tailor made for Custer. He could not be accused of *not* following orders, as he had none, while it gave him free latitude in the field. It was just the kind of operating environment he liked.

The upcoming campaign was to be conducted in the winter, a course of action never tried before in fighting Indians. Everyone agreed the Indians would be most vulnerable in winter camps (in fact General Sheridan and General Sherman thought it to be the decisive edge), though it was still thought by many to be ill advised. Legendary mountain man Jim Bridger, upon learning about the winter plains campaign, reportedly said to General Sheridan, "Blizzards don't respect man or beast." The overall campaign would utilize units from across the region, but primarily be formed of the 7th Cavalry under the command of Custer, and of infantry under the command of Colonel Alfred Sully. To survive the harsh conditions, the command would have to be well prepared. When they could not properly provision, the 7th moved north to Fort Dodge to lay in the necessities, including food and supplies and ammunition.

There was also reorganization in the regiment. A detachment of 40 sharpshooters was assembled under the command of Lieutenant William Cooke, an excellent shot himself. The practice of forming a group of sharpshooters was done to great effect during the Civil War. Custer also directed the "coloring" of the horses, a practice where all of the cavalry mounts in a company were organized by like colors. Custer had first done "coloring" of companies in the Michigan Brigade in the Civil War to satisfactory effect. It brought a real identity to a unit and an esprit de corps to the men in it. It had a practical purpose also, allowing a commander such as himself to discern from a distance occurrences and movements on the battlefield. Custer described the process in his book *My Life on the Plains*:

> The troop commanders were assembled at headquarters and allowed, in the order of their rank, to select the color they preferred. This being done, every public horse in the command was led out and placed in line: the grays collected at one point, the bays, of which there was a great preponderance in numbers, at another, the blacks at another, the sorrels by themselves; then the chestnuts, the blacks, the browns; and last of all came what were jocularly designated the "brindles," being the odds and ends so far as colors were concerned—roans and other mixed colors—the junior troop commander, of course, becoming the reluctant recipient of these last, valuable enough except as to color. The exchanges having been completed, the men of each troop led away to their respective picket or stable lines their newly acquired chargers. Arriving upon their company grounds, another assignment in detail was made by the troop commanders. First, the non-commissioned officers were permitted to select their horses in the order of their rank; then the remaining horses were distributed among the troopers generally, giving to the best troopers the best horses. It was surprising to witness what a great improvement in the handsome appearance of the command was effected by this measure.

But it also had a downside. A cavalry horse once assigned to a trooper was his very personal extension in combat. He had to know and trust the horse and, horses being very social animals, a very special bond developed between the horse and the rider. When it appeared the bond was arbitrarily severed to simply "make the regiment look flashier on parade," it could draw anger. Captain Albert Barnitz, a company commander in the 7th, shared in his journal entry on November 12, 1868, just such an emotion: "Have felt very indignant and provoked all evening in consequence of General Custer's foolish, unwarranted, unjustifiable, order with regard to the new horses." To be said another way, Captain Barnitz's company were now mounted on "strangers."

Custer knew the value of good reconnaissance, as he had performed the role often. He knew the command would need it to be effective in the upcoming unfamiliar territory. He also knew the kind of scouting talent they needed did not exist organically in the regiment (at least in a blue uniform). Fortunately, there were many possible civilian scouts available. His first choice as chief of scouts was a man named California Joe Milner, a favorite of General Sheridan but who had a powerful drinking problem he wasted little time displaying. Once on a night march, he got so drunk, he wandered away from the command, got lost and then returned to them coming from the other opposite direction. Custer, in *My Life on the Plains*, described what happened next, "His [Milner's] mule by this time had turned toward the troops, and when California Joe set up his unearthly howls and began his imaginary charge into an Indian village he was carried at full speed straight to the column, where his good fortune alone prevented him from receiving a volley before he was recognized as not an Indian. His blood was up, and all efforts to quiet or suppress him proved unavailing, until finally the officer in command was forced to bind him hand and foot and in this condition secured him on the back of his faithful mule. In this sorry plight the chief scout continued until the return of the troops to camp, when he was transferred to the tender mercies of the guard as a prisoner for misconduct. Thus ended California Joe's career as chief scout." Milner was removed immediately after the incident, and replaced by Ben Clark, another experienced frontier scout. Clark had served in the position previously while Custer was on suspension. He was not as colorful as California Joe, but more reliable.

While the 7th Cavalry continued to prepare for the upcoming winter campaign, a movement was underway to form a volunteer regiment of cavalry from Kansas to augment those regular forces already planned. General Sheridan had been authorized to form a regiment from the state for a length of 180 days service, and turned to the Governor of Kansas, Samuel J. Crawford, for assistance. The request had arrived at Crawford's desk on October 9, 1868, and less than a week later, a brutal Indian attack on a settlement in Ottawa County would serve to help fill the volunteer regiment's ranks. The people of Kansas were tired of Indian depredations, and they were tired of the little effort expended to protect them. Besides several murders, two girls were raped and one woman was carried off as a captive. Within three weeks the regiment was formed. As volunteers were being sworn in, Crawford, who had been a general during the Civil War, resigned his office as governor and accepted command as colonel of what would become the 19th Kansas Volunteer Cavalry.

The Battle of Washita River

Early intelligence to arrive at General Sheridan's headquarters indicated a large concentration of Indian winter villages along the Washita River in the Indian Territory (modern day western Oklahoma). Consequently, on November 1, 1868, Sheridan ordered Custer and Sully to move 90 miles further south, to a point on the North Canadian River. There they waited for necessary supplies, but due to supply shortages the combined command was not ready to move until November 12. Sheridan had hoped the 19th Kansas Cavalry might also be able to join them in movement, but delays in Topeka where they were formed slipped the timeline. On November 17, Sully and Custer arrived at the supply base, fittingly called Camp Supply, to await the Kansans. During the five-day movement to Camp Supply, the command observed considerable Indian signs on the trail, estimated to be as many as 100 warriors. Custer wanted to respond immediately, but Sully disagreed. He preferred to wait for the additional cavalry.

The rift between Custer and Sully would simmer until Sheridan joined them at Camp Supply on November 21. Technically, Colonel Sully, as the district commander, was the senior officer and as such would be in command of the combined force of his infantry and the 7th Cavalry. Custer, chided with the thought of being held back by Sully in the field, appealed to General Sheridan for help. Obscure regulations provided the necessary relief. Colonel Sully clearly had authority over Custer. But, by crossing into the Indian Territory, they were no longer in Sully's command "district." As they were now physically out of district, and because the Kansas Cavalry created a joint force of army regulars and volunteers, the highest brevet rank by regulations prevailed. Therefore, Custer having been a brevet major general of volunteers during the Civil War, technically carried the higher rank. He no doubt helped with the clarification, but Sheridan clearly agreed it would benefit the success of the campaign. Just to ensure there were no future problems with command authority, he sent Colonel Sully back to Fort Harker without delay to "command the district," leaving Custer as on-site commander of the expedition.

General Sheridan spent several days at Camp Supply, visiting with leaders and otherwise ensuring the command was ready to take the field. He impatiently waited for the Kansas volunteers, whose arrival was reported as imminent. The Kansans were lost however, and a link-up which was planned to take a week, dragged into more than three. When the Kansans finally staggered into Camp Supply on November 29, many of their horses were dead or dying, and Custer had already departed five days previous.

Sheridan's orders left little doubt as to the end state he was looking for. Once Custer had located the Indian encampments believed to be on the Washita River, he should proceed to "destroy their villages and ponies, to kill or hang all their warriors, and bring back all women and children." It was the valley of the Shenandoah in 1864 anew. It was total war, the instruction to annihilate all the warriors and warfighting potential—no prisoners. To deny any possible rebuild by destroying the village, its shelter, its food stores and basic survival items, and its ponies. Custer reinforced this point in his own words in *My Life on the Plains*:

> The same spirit who in the Shenandoah Valley campaign of 1864 had so successfully inaugurated the "whirling" movement was now present, and it was determined that upon a slightly modified principle, reinforced by the biting frosts of winter, we should continue to press things until our savage enemies should not only be completely humbled, but be forced by the combined perils of war and winter to beg for peace and settle quietly down within the limits of their reservation.

Finally, by taking captive any remaining women and children, he would send an unmistakable message to others what lay in store for those tribes who refused to be "peaceful." Of course as always, the subtle differences between "peaceful" and "hostile" were often very obscure. On November 22, 1868 Custer penned a letter to Libbie which revealed the launch of the upcoming Washita campaign and his beliefs about the benefit of the winter weather. He wrote:

> Today General Sheridan and staff with two Companies of Kansas Volunteers arrived, I move tomorrow morning with my eleven companies, taking thirty days' rations. I am to go south to the Canadian River, then down the river to Fort Cobb, thence south-east toward the Washita Mountains, then north-west back to this point, my whole march not exceeding 250 miles. The snow is five or six inches deep, and falling rapidly. It snowed all night, and when reveille wakened us at four we found the ground covered to the depth of one foot, and the storm still raging. Little grooming did the shivering horses get from the equally uncomfortable troopers. While they were saddling I galloped across the narrow plain to the tents of General Sheridan who was awake and had been listening attentively to our preparations. His first greeting was to enquire what I thought about the storm. All the better for our purpose, I told him, for we could move in it while the Indians could not.

His opinion about the weather advantage the cavalry had would be challenged the very next day.

Custer and the 7th Cavalry left Camp Supply amidst a blizzard on November 23. The band played "The Girl I left Behind Me" as they departed, or at least attempted to, as valves on brass instruments stuck and lips froze to mouthpieces. Custer loved the band and saw it as a morale booster. During his Civil War exploits, the band was as essential to victory as field guns, regimental battle flags, and war

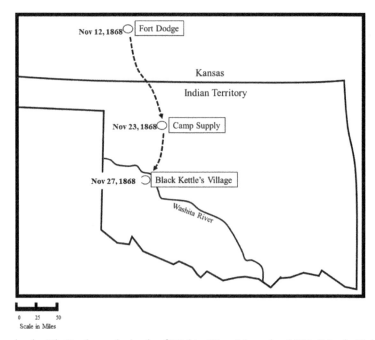

Movement by the 7th Cavalry to the battle of Washita River, November 1868. (Map by Ted Behncke)

correspondents. But, on this cold morning, his critics could see no merit in it, nor with it accompanying the rest of the regiment. After all, there could be little stealth expected from a bunch of rattling musical instruments. There was already a foot of snow on the ground as horse and wagon plowed south. The chief of scouts, Ben Clark, dead reckoned off the Antelope Hills in the distance to support navigation. He was assisted by two other frontiersmen in his efforts and several Osage Indians who were expert trackers. The snow obscured any trail to follow and so the column lumbered on, continuing to head south. Custer later wrote in *My Life on the Plains* that he believed the conditions "favored the Army while disadvantaging the Indians." It was hard to conceive as a mounted trooper, who endured cold temperatures and a driving snow, that his Indian foe, inside a warm lodge and sharing a freshly harvested buffalo, was somehow disadvantaged. Custer at least would admit the conditions were "obstacles." There was a lot riding on his success and he was more tense on the trail than usual.

By November 26, the command was within 20 miles of the Washita River, having traversed over 70 miles, still seeing no appreciable Indian sign. As a result, Custer elected to send out a reconnaissance in force, using three companies under the command of Major Joel Elliott to perform the task. With the assistance of one scout, Elliott was to make his way to the Washita Valley, then follow the river west using the north bank, moving slowly and carefully, without alerting the Indians in the vicinity. Meanwhile, Custer continued south with his main body of troops. Major Elliott soon sent news of a day-old trail leading to the southwest, with evidence of a presence of at least 150 warriors. It was a raiding party returning home. Custer passed instructions to Elliott to follow the trail carefully and Custer would bring the rest of the command to him. Custer immediately had an officer's call to quickly lighten up the regiment and to share a tentative plan for attack.

The command would move from this point in a "light" configuration. The supply wagons were slowing the command down and they only needed ammunition and some other supplies for the upcoming fight. Consequently, each trooper was to carry 100 rounds, either on his person or in saddle bags, and all but seven of the wagons were to be left behind. The seven wagons would receive only the freshest teams to pull them, and inside they were to transport only extra ammunition, rations for the men, and some forage for the animals. The rest of the wagons, supplies and livestock, along with 80 men would remain behind under the command of Captain Louis Hamilton, the officer of the day. According to *My Life on the Plains*, Custer was later approached by Captain Hamilton with a desire to participate with his company on the assault. Hamilton asked if anyone would volunteer to exchange positions. Lieutenant Edward Mathey raised his hand and volunteered. The movement of the past several days had incapacitated him with snow blindness. Mathey, supported by good non-commissioned officers, could aptly protect the trains. Custer agreed, and Hamilton happily mounted his horse and moved out. Interestingly, the move could have saved Mathey's life, as Hamilton would become a casualty of the upcoming battle. Coincidentally, at the Little Bighorn, Mathey would again guard the supply train, saving his life once again.

The sun was setting when Custer, with the remaining eight companies, intercepted Elliott's trail. Custer sent word forward to have Elliott halt his battalion, as Custer would send supplies to feed his men and provide forage to prepare his horses for the coming fight. Fires were lit, and the men prepared dinner. The remaining companies closed on Elliott's camp around four hours later. The men were told to eat and make coffee quickly, for they needed to be prepared to move out within an hour. They were also informed from that point forward the command would have to move with great stealth, no bugle calls, no unnecessary noises, no matches. Where they stood now was behind a tall ridge with the hills running east-west between them and the Indian camp. Once they crossed the ridge, they would be in full view of the Indians.

The village beyond belonged to Cheyenne Chief Black Kettle. Although peaceful himself, it was incredibly difficult for him to contain his younger warriors. In fact, just days before, warriors of his camp were off raiding elsewhere and it was their trail Major Elliott discovered leading back to Black Kettle. Black Kettle had association with non-peaceful elements of his own tribe and they had brought him

The attack of an Indian village as depicted was a rare event, mostly because the Indians were gifted in knowing when they were at risk and chose not to be found. When the Indians were surprised it was often deadly, but more often killed were the innocent, women, children, and the elderly. If villages were attacked in the winter, the inhabitants could also lose the means to survive like those at the battle of the Washita. (National Park Service)

misfortune before. In 1864, his village of Cheyenne and Arapaho near Sand Creek in Colorado, ironically flying a U.S. flag above, was brutally attacked by the 3rd Colorado Volunteer Cavalry under the command of Colonel John Chivington. The infamous and resulting massacre killed hundreds, mostly women and children. Black Kettle and his wife escaped and continued to pursue a peaceful life. Just days before the battle of the Washita, he had visited Fort Cobb along with members of his tribe to draw annuities and protection from Colonel Hazen who refused, warning Black Kettle if he wanted peace he would have to work it out with General Sheridan. Hazen told Black Kettle that Cheyenne and Arapaho raids had made protection at Fort Cobb impossible.

With the Osage scouts leading, the command closed on Black Kettle's village. All were asleep, unsuspecting of any troopers in their vicinity. At any moment, Custer expected to be compromised. Frost covered the noses of the horses, and the sound of horse hooves "punching" through the crust of snow seemed like a cacophony of drumbeats, occasionally punctuated by an individual cough or a low "nicker" from one of the horses. Custer described the advance in *My Life on the Plains*, "The movement of our horses over the crusted snow produced considerable noise and would doubtless have led to our detection but for the fact that the Indians, if they heard it at all, presumed it was occasioned by their herd of ponies." The first indicator of a village was the Indian pony herd, in excess of 900 of them, slowly moving to and fro, a literal "sea of equines" as they pawed the snow for any grass underneath. The Indian ponies were disturbed by the smell of the approaching troopers and their mounts, anxiously giving way like a school of fish in front of a swimmer. Soon a dog could be heard barking, although it was not associated with alarm for the approaching troopers. Finally, an infant could be heard crying—absolute proof Custer had found his target.

The men nervously dropped their haversacks and coats in piles, preparing for the assault. Adrenaline flowed, and the cold was barely noticeable to the men. Although it was quite cold, the protective coats and excessive gear would hinder movement and effectiveness. The more seasoned men led preparations by tightening saddles and checking their weapons, the younger troopers mirroring their actions, hoping it would quell their fear. Custer quietly gave instructions for the attack. Captain

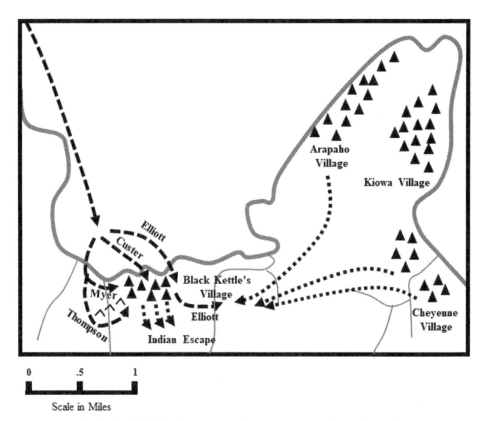

The battle of Washita River, November 27, 1868. (Map by Ted Behncke)

William Thompson and Captain Edward Myer would attack with two companies respectively from the west. Thompson with companies B and F would cross the Washita, coming in on a shallow arc behind the bluffs and provide a flanking attack directly into the west side of the village. Myer, with companies E and I, would initially follow Captain Thompson, but upon Myer's action to the flank, continue further south before arcing to the east into a blocking position on the south side of the village. Major Elliott with three companies, G, H, and M, would move east before crossing the Washita and circling around, ultimately attacking the east side of the village. Custer, with companies A, C, D, and K, along with Cooke's sharpshooters and the scouts would attack from due north, cross the Washita and assault straight through the village. The attack would commence at daybreak or immediately if they were discovered. If possible, the band would play to launch the regiment. Custer asked for any questions, and he recalled in *My Life on the Plains* that Captain Thompson queried, "General, suppose we find more Indians than we can handle?" Custer answered, "All I am afraid of is we won't find half enough. There are not Indians enough in the country to whip the Seventh Cavalry." Great hubris, but the truth was there were enough Indians to whip the 7th Cavalry and they were right nearby. Custer luck and Indian captives would make the only difference that day.

The companies moved into their positions without discovery. As Custer was about to give the order to play, a shot rang out in the village. The order to charge was given, trumpets blared and the band played a few notes of an Irish drinking song "Garry Owen," at least until their instruments froze. Few noticed, the attack was on. It was a complete surprise. With the main attack to their front, most Indians fled their lodges and headed south across the river. Captain Myers and Thompson failed to reach their final positions in time, allowing a seam, an Indian escape route between the cavalry units. Custer led his four companies through the village, destroying everything in front of them. Custer himself rode through and then, selecting a piece of high ground on the south side of the village, rode to it to observe. Captain Hamilton died in the first wave, falling mortally wounded from one shot to the head. Chief Black Kettle died, along with his wife trying to cross the river. Overall, it was a feeble Indian defense, but some warriors found cover in the folds of the earth south of the river and returned fire. One of their bullets found a home in the abdomen of Captain Barnitz. Although in great pain, he would eventually recover, for the bullet had failed to find any of his vital organs. All was going well for Custer and the regiment. There were few losses and within ten minutes, the village was secure. While women and children were being collected, fires were put to the lodges and personal belongings of the inhabitants. Meanwhile, Major Elliott observed a group of Cheyenne escaping through the uncovered seam and then moving east. He collected the regimental sergeant major, along with 18 men and galloped off to the east, giving chase. He was reported to say, as he galloped off, "Here goes for a brevet or a coffin." Neither

Major Joel Elliot was Custer's second in command for the battle of Washita River. It was Elliot who found the village late in the day before the attack the following morning. Elliot and 17 others lost their lives while chasing Indians fleeing the village. Their bodies were not found until two weeks later, and not until Custer was accused of abandonment of these men. The incident would put a dark cloud over the success of the attack and create division among the officers of the regiment. (National Park Service)

Elliott nor his detachment of men would ever be seen alive again. Unknown to them, waiting beyond the ridge were Cheyenne from another larger village, moving to the sounds of the guns. They quickly surrounded Elliott and his men, and killed them all.

The Cheyenne village, which provided Major Elliott his end, was not the only Indian encampment to the east. Further away were two other villages—one Arapaho, the other Kiowa. At the sound of the first shots, a general alarm propelled warriors from all three villages toward Black Kettle's smaller village under attack. Soon the ridges were dotted with warriors trying to discern what was happening and how to get into the fight. When the troopers turned to start killing the Indian ponies, the warriors began to wail at a distance. For a Plains Indian, the fondness for the pony and the culture built on it cannot be overstated. Indian ponies represented wealth, the ability to wage war, the ability to hunt the buffalo, the ability to move and live the nomadic life. Simply, the Indian pony was life itself. Imagine then when the ponies began to be slaughtered, first with bullets, and later with the knife by cutting their throats. The squealing of ponies as they went down had to be heart-wrenching. Custer recounts the episode in *My Life on the Plains*:

> The work of destruction began … and was continued until nearly eight hundred ponies were thus disposed of. All this time the Indians who had been fighting us from the outside covered the hills in the distance, deeply interested spectators of this to them strange proceeding. The loss of so many animals of value was a severe blow to the tribe, as nothing so completely impairs the war-making facilities for the Indians of the Plains as the deprivation or disabling of their ponies.

According to Custer, they slaughtered 875 ponies. Custer chronicled in his official field report the rest of the destruction. They burned or destroyed, "241 saddles, 573 buffalo robes, 290 buffalo skins for lodges, 160 untanned robes, 210 axes, 140 hatchets, 35 revolvers, 47 rifles, 535 pounds of black powder, 1,050 lbs. of lead, 4,000 arrow and arrowheads, 75 spears, 90 bullet molds, 35 bows and quivers, 12 shields, 300 lbs. of bullets, 775 lariats, 940 buckskin saddlebags, 470 blankets, 93 coats, 700 lbs. of tobacco," and every bit of food they could find. Sheridan had asked them to destroy everything and they had completely followed his orders.

While the destruction of the village was being completed, there were concerns the regiment was increasingly in peril. One of the first warnings came from Lieutenant Edward Godfrey. Part of the attack from Major Elliott's in the east, he had pursued some fleeing Indians who disappeared over the crest of a ridge. Suspecting there could be something waiting for them if they pursued, Godfrey dismounted and crawled to the crown of the ridge. Peering over the top, Godfrey was alarmed to see Indians swarming in large numbers, too many to have come from the village they had just attacked. Indian lodges extended as far as could be seen into the wood line. Godfrey found Custer and reported what he had seen. Custer discounted the report but asked Godfrey a series of questions. Godfrey returned a second time to report firing down the valley (the demise of Major Elliott's detachment) but again Custer discounted it by saying it was probably Captain Myers' men as they were operating near the vicinity. It was harder to discount actual events happening in front of them. When the quartermaster came forward to deliver the reserve ammunition, he had to "fight his way in." This clearly meant a forming encirclement, if not yet closed, not long in waiting. The Indians had already captured the temporarily "grounded" overcoats and haversacks the troopers had taken off before the attack. By now it was known that Major Elliott and his men were unaccounted for. Custer dispatched Captain Myer in the last known direction they were seen. Myer advanced a few miles and, not finding anything, returned to the destroyed village.

The regiment needed to move. Conditions were clearly changing and concerns drifted to the safety of the supply trains both near and far. If they were lost, the command would lose their supply base, and they were over 100 miles away from their next closest source of supply and it was winter. The regiment mounted in columns of four, loaded the wounded, and marched the captives in front of them toward the Indian villages to the east. It was a ruse, but as it turned out, an effective one. As the regiment approached the three villages, it threatened to "roll" them as well, trampling them as in the first village, or sending them cascading forward in flight. From the Indian point of view, this group of troopers had just utterly destroyed one village. What would stop them from continuing the carnage? Custer described in *My Life on Plains* what happened next, "they [the Indians] never offered to fire a shot or retard our movements in any manner, but instead assembled their outlying detachments as rapidly as possible and began a precipitate movement down the valley in advance of us, fully impressed with the idea, no doubt, that our purpose was to overtake their flying people and herds and administer the same treatment to them that the occupants of the upper village had received."

Custer and regiment advanced until dark, then did an about-face, moving north. It was cold, especially without winter clothing, but the command continued until 2:00 a.m. on the morning of the November 28, halting to rest. The scouts had advanced forward to the supply train and Lieutenant Mathey. They had not been harassed or molested. The command continued the march, arriving at the supply train at 10:00 a.m. in the morning. The men started fires and cooked breakfast, the only real meal the regiment had had in nearly two days. Custer took the time to scratch a letter to General Sheridan and send off by the courier California Joe Milner. In it were the few words from an ebullient Custer, "We have cleaned Black Kettle and his band out so thoroughly they can neither fight, dress, sleep, eat nor ride without sponging their friends." It was the truth.

General Sheridan wished to send his congratulations back to Custer, knowing the 7th Cavalry would have a difficult march home. Sheridan dispatched Joe Milner back with a letter to Custer on November 29. Sheridan wrote:

> The energy and rapidity shown during one of the heaviest snowstorms known to this section of the country, with the temperature below freezing, the gallantry and bravery displayed, resulting in such signal success, reflects highest credit on the 7th Cavalry ... and the Major-General Commanding expresses his thanks to the officers and men engaged in the Battle of the Washita, and his special congratulations to their distinguished commander Brevet Major-General George A. Custer for the efficient and gallant service opening the campaign against the hostile Indians north of the Arkansas.

The letter from Sheridan reached Custer on the march near the command's arrival at Camp Supply. It completely buoyed his spirits. Custer and the 7th Cavalry rode victorious into Camp Supply on December 2, 1868. Present for the parade were Colonel Sully's infantry companies, the dismounted 19th Kansas Volunteer Cavalry, Sheridan's staff, and General Phil Sheridan himself. It was a well-choreographed event, every bit the definition of who Custer was and would ever be. Preceding the entire command were the Osage scouts, resplendent in their colorful native garb, and communicating a celebration of their culture. Following the Osage, were the frontier scouts, the successful trackers, navigators, the wise counselors to the warfighter. General Sheridan recounted the scouts arrival in *The Personal Memoirs of P. H. Sheridan* in 1885, saying, "As they drew near, the scouts began a wild and picturesque performance in celebration of victory, yelling, firing their guns, throwing themselves on the neck and sides of their horses to exhibit their skill in riding," a performance that would continue past the parade. The lively band arrived next playing "Garry Owen," a lively tune which would forever define the spirit of the regiment, the same song which signaled the charge into the Indian village. Behind the band were Lieutenant Cooke's sharpshooters and following them, a buckskin-clad Custer, leading the triumphant 7th Cavalry. It was a lasting image Libbie had seen many times and captured in *Boots and Saddles* in 1885, "Horse and man seemed one when the general [Custer] vaulted into the saddle. His body was so lightly poised and so full of swinging, undulating motion, it almost seemed that the wind moved him as it blew over the plain." Following Custer was the regiment in columns of four, each company's leader presenting arms with sabre. It was pageant, it was theater, it was martial, and it was victory on parade. And it was typical of Custer. The men, even those that disliked him, loved being a participant.

The parade dazzled those watching, most especially the Kansas cavalrymen, who had never seen or met Custer. By reputation, they expected a towering figure, with great military bearing, basically historical figure. Instead, as James Albert Hadley of the 19th Kansas recalled in the book, *The 19th Kansas Cavalry and the conquest of the Plains Indians*, they were surprised by a "young man of medium height, slender, wearing a buckskin shirt and leggings, much befringed." His unassuming, warrior-like appearance just added to their fascination. Just a little over a year prior, wrapped in scandal, distrusted by his men, fellow officers, and superiors, he left the Army in disgrace, his services undesired. Now, he was again idolized, brave and fearless, an image which restored his balance and ego. He was restored. The Civil War's "boy general" had risen from the ashes.

Following the parade, Custer joined Sheridan to discuss the downside of the campaign. Custer reported one officer (Hamilton) killed, 14 officers and men wounded, and 19 men missing from Major Elliott's detachment. Custer expressed Elliott was lost and would be found, but he knew as did Sheridan, the men were likely dead. For Custer, it was convenient to believe and share the falsehood the men were simply "missing." In such a way, the issue did not detract from the celebration. By Custer's embellished count, the regiment killed just over 100 Indians. There was no accurate count of how many were warriors, but it is very probable the number included many women and children. Fifty-three women and children were captured. Once again, Custer had established he could inspire men to fight for him. In his official report to Sheridan, Custer summed up what the victory meant to him and the Army. "We have taught the Indians that they are safe from us no place and at no season, and also what some of our own people may doubt, that the white man can endure the inclemency of winter better than the Indian." He had accomplished what no other commander had yet achieved fighting on the plains in the two years of pursuing the Indians—he had found an Indian village and attacked the inhabitants without losing the element of surprise. The following rout delivered a psychological blow to the Indians. Every bit of the essentials they needed to survive, their ponies for transportation, their food stores, their clothing, and their hides for lodges, were destroyed and made them destitute in a hostile environment. The attack came in winter when the Indians believed they were always relatively safe. From here forward, the Indian could never be assured of safety.

The Army victory brought immediate praise from supporters of the mission on the plains, particularly in the Kansas press. Custer was once again elevated to hero status in the national press, this time with the title of "Indian fighter" added to his pedigree. The 7th Cavalry would be synonymous with victory against the Indians on the frontier. Predictably though, criticism came soon after the battle, also from peace advocates and Indian sympathizers. Custer and Sheridan had planned and executed another "Sand Creek." The Washita was a massacre in its own right. Chief Black Kettle was a gentle, peaceful, man simply desiring to live in the new Indian Territory.

Custer was also soon embattled with the fate of Major Elliott and his men. The Army did not abandon its own to the enemy. On a visit to the Washita battlefield several weeks after the battle, the butchered and mutilated remains of Major Elliott, the regimental sergeant major, and 18 men were found in a shallow depression in what appeared to have been a last stand defense. Elliott was very well liked by both officers and men in the regiment. He had capably commanded the regiment during Custer's suspension. It was understandable then, when his demise was surrounded by mystery, some division of thought (and blame) would arise.

Captain Frederick Benteen would make sure of it. Elliot had served under Benteen during the Civil War and the two were close. It didn't take much effort for Benteen to get the vitriol against Custer started. He simply took the issue to the anti-Custer faction among the officers. Just to ensure the drumbeat continued, he wrote a letter which was published anonymously in the *St. Louis Democrat*. In it, he openly accused Custer of abandoning Elliott and the other men to their deaths. When Custer learned of the letter, he knew an officer of the regiment was responsible. He summoned the officers, and Benteen admitted to being the author. During a tense standoff observed by other officers, Custer backed away from an earlier promise to horsewhip the author if he found him. The episode ended, but the embers continued to smoke for years after, ultimately playing a role at another battle along a river in Montana.

The takeaways from the battle of the Washita are significant. First, the depression and psychological condition of Custer present a year earlier, was diminished, if not gone entirely. In the field, he made logical decisions on the march in largely unknown territory, and endured extremely challenging weather conditions. He was careful and preserved the element of surprise, which ultimately allowed the attack on the village, but also limited the response of other Indian encampments nearby. The ruse successfully gave the impression of additional offensive army action, preventing what could have been a large-scale Indian counterattack, threatening the survival of the entire regiment. The ample stores of weapons and powder in Black Kettle's village, if equaled in the other villages, certainly could have served to annihilate the command. The timing and nature of the regiment's departure were wise decisions (or luck by some opinion) on Custer's part, securing the victory.

There were some serious concerns among the lessons learned, most significantly among them, poor reconnaissance. Custer found one village among four in the immediate vicinity, and it was the smallest among them. At the time of the attack on Black Kettle's village, there was no knowledge of the others nearby, and they presented a tremendous potential threat. The root cause was reconnaissance conducted singularly to find "a trail" and quickly follow it to "a village" before the Indians camped there could flee. There was no additional reconnaissance conducted by Custer, which would have necessarily developed the entire threat in front of them. It is a fair argument to suggest such reconnaissance could have cost the element of surprise. Certainly, with over 1,000 Indians in the area, it is very probable some aspect of the command would have been discovered if widely deployed, determining the disposition and composition of the Indians in the area. Perhaps not. The conditions of snow and cold, along with an Indian belief they were relatively safe could have lowered their guard. It is important to note Black Kettle's band was not alerted the morning of the battle. The example of poor reconnaissance was repeated years later at the Little Bighorn with disastrous results. Why weren't the lessons learned at the Washita taken into account in further actions against the Indians, most notably at the Little Bighorn? Quite possibly the answer lies in the constant concern that the Indians would flee in both situations and victory could not be assured without the element of surprise. More likely though, it was simply the fact the lack of reconnaissance did not end in disaster at the battle of the Washita. The near miss was simply that, a near miss, and the swift action by Custer to feint an attack against the nearby villages was enough to eliminate the threat.

One final point requires examination, the deployment of the 7th itself in the battle. The regiment essentially conducted an envelopment, attacking the Indian village from all sides. The execution of the plan required a substantial understanding of the terrain around the village, which they did not possess, to be successful, and synchronizing the employment of the companies. In truth the plan was complex, a fact later borne out by the less-than-optimal arrival of Captain Thompson and Captain Myer's companies. They did not reach their intended positions and thus, left a gap in the lines, allowing an unknown number of warriors to escape the encirclement. It was the charge of Custer's four companies across the village from the north which provided the sudden, overwhelming, sweeping collision with sleeping inhabitants of the village. The thunder of hundreds of cavalry

This studio photo of George Custer from a few years before his death aptly captures his frontier persona. Dressed in both buckskin trousers and jacket, with a beaver hat, this look could have been first influenced by scouts accompanying the 1867 Indian Wars Campaign in Kansas. (Little Bighorn National Monument)

horses at the gallop startled everyone in the early morning hours. Major Elliott may not have been lost if his three companies had been in support or blocking positions, rather than chasing small groups of fleeing Indians. Of course the attack succeeded, perhaps the strongest argument for the piecemeal employment of the regiment. It is thought-provoking to consider though, did the success in the piecemeal employment of forces at the Washita, bring doom when repeated in similar fashion at the Little Bighorn? While it is interesting to make those comparisons, many of the variables of the two battles were quite different, too different to support absolutes.

The battle of the Washita changed the operating environment in Kansas and Colorado. The devastation of Black Kettle's village softened the temper of all the tribes in the region and their will to fight. Many tribes were encouraged to move to their reservations, except two—the Cheyenne and the Arapaho. The 7th continued to operate in the field in early 1869, trying to corral the two "hostile" tribes. On January 26, an Arapaho village was found in the western region of the Indian

Territory and Custer was able to convince the tribal leaders to move the group to the newly established Fort Sill, in Oklahoma. The Cheyenne, according to reports, had fled to northern Texas. Custer wanted to pursue but was continually plagued with insufficient supplies. The command endured tremendously difficult conditions in an attempt to find the fugitive Cheyenne bands. Finally, in early February, he was forced to abandon the hunt and return to Fort Sill to rest and refit. He had been away from Libbie for several months and under extremely difficult command conditions. Yet, his ability to cope had changed from 1867. On February 9, 1869, in a 29-page letter to Libbie, he wrote, "To-day is our wedding anniversary. I am sorry we cannot spend it together, but I shall celebrate it in my heart." The words revealed the sensitive, romantic Custer. There was also an acceptance of his situation and mission. The contrast between the fall of 1867 and early 1869 is remarkable. The manic behavior and tremendous need to share company with Libbie could now be satisfied with a lengthy love letter.

The conditions at Fort Sill were quite challenging, bordering on desperate. The men and horses were starving. More importantly, without supplies, the 7th Cavalry and the 19th Kansas (still in service) could not resume operations in the field. It was not until March 2 that the combined force could take the field to continue to pursue the Cheyenne. Of particular importance to the Kansans was revenge against the Cheyenne who had raided settlements on the Solomon and Saline rivers. There were also reports of white captive women from those settlements still with the tribes. On March 15 in the Texas panhandle, a large Cheyenne village was located near Sweetwater Creek. When Custer learned the village contained three white women, the Kansans could barely be contained. For three days Custer negotiated with three chiefs, ultimately keeping them hostage until the women were released. The Cheyenne finally relented. The chiefs did not end their cooperation with the women's release. They promised to report to Camp Supply as soon as the spring grass sprouted, allowing their ponies to strengthen for the trip. Custer agreed, and in good faith promised to release the Indian captives from the Washita when the chiefs arrived at Camp Supply. Custer had been through this before however with Hancock in 1867, when the Indians promised to meet near Fort Larned and promptly rode off during the night with all in their village. Custer kept the three chiefs hostage as insurance. On March 28, they returned to Camp Supply. In a letter to Libbie, Custer reported "I have been successful in my campaign against the Cheyenne. I have outmarched them, outwitted them at their own game." The Indian War in the region had ended. General Sheridan also passed on his congratulations in a letter to his trusted subordinate. Custer recalled Sheridan's words in *My Life on the Plains*, "I am very much rejoiced at the success of your expedition, and feel proud of our winter's operations and of the officers and men who have borne its privations and hardships," a cherished validation of Custer's success in 1868 over the embarrassment and failure of the previous year. He felt redeemed.

Fort Abraham Lincoln

George Custer had hoped, after the success of the battle of the Washita, a promotion might be in order for him. Colonel Andrew Smith, the actual commander of the 7th Cavalry had retired in April 1869 from the Army, leaving a vacancy in the regiment. As the deputy commander, Custer was definitely a consideration for the vacancy. The success at the Washita had propelled him to national attention once again, and he had a strong advocate in General Sheridan, who did "press his [Custer's] case," but it was not to be. General Grant was likely the reason. He never really liked Custer (and would not for the rest of his life) and the episode of 1867, along with Custer's court-martial, cemented it. If the promotion had any active consideration, there was the long line of succession in the officer's ranks—there were many older, longer tenured officers waiting in front of him. Colonel Samuel D. Sturgis, an 1846 graduate of West Point and a veteran of the Mexican War and Civil War, was selected to become the new commander of the 7th Cavalry. He would go on to command the regiment for over 12 years, although often on detached duty.

When passed over for the regimental command, Custer applied for the vacant commandant position at West Point. Considered a dream job by Custer, the former cadet who placed last in his class would have loved returning to lead the "School for Boys on the Hudson." When Emory Upton was selected for the position, Custer settled in at Fort Hays, Kansas, and Libbie joined him. Surprisingly, a pleasant summer passed as Libbie shared with a friend. She and George enjoyed evening horseback rides and he wrote articles for sportsman magazines about various pursuits including buffalo hunting. Custer claimed some notoriety hosting hunts for the famous from back east, including P. T. Barnum and wealthy Englishmen. Libbie played the role of entertainer, even joining in on some of the outings. Mostly though, she stabilized Custer, allowing him to be the charming, social fellow so loved by his friends.

From October 1869 to April 1870, Custer and Libbie lived at Fort Leavenworth, Kansas, the actual headquarters of the regiment. They enjoyed the social life and time with friends, along with the amenities of "civilization." During that time, George and Libbie speculated in land purchases in Kansas, buying two parcels, a 180-acre parcel in Morris County, Kansas (15 miles south of Fort Riley, Kansas) and an 18-acre parcel, the exact location now lost to history, but apparently just off of the Kansas Pacific Railroad. Investing in land was popular and Custer would have had an advantage over other buyers regarding the ground knowledge of the possible value of the property, who were often back East speculators who had never traveled further west than St. Louis. The allure of wealth had always attracted Custer, and in turn Libbie. After the Civil War, Custer had toyed with the idea of working on Wall Street and in business, but could never fully find the right fit. They would continue to experiment with opportunities for the rest of their marriage, but not always successfully.

Custer and Libbie returned to Fort Hays in April 1870, where he resumed field command of the regiment. One of the more interesting stories about Custer purportedly occurred while he was at Fort Hays, a relationship with a young Cheyenne girl named Meotzi, or as whites called her, Monahsetah. A translation of her name was "Young Grass that Shoots in the Spring." She was about 20 years old at the time, the daughter of Chief Little Rock, a warrior killed at the battle of the Washita. By all accounts, she was a beautiful young woman, Custer describing her as "an enchanting, comely squaw." But Custer was attracted to her for a different reason—her ability to act as an interpreter who played an integral role in the release of the three white women the previous year from the Cheyenne camp. Libbie was certainly curious about Monahsetah, especially heightened when George wrote she had given birth to a son in January 1869. Libbie, after meeting Monahsetah, confirmed her beauty, by describing her "as the acknowledged belle among all other Indian maidens." Monahsetah by some accounts gave birth to a second son a year later, called Yellow Swallow, or more commonly Yellow Tail. It was alleged Custer was the father.

There is no question Custer was fond of Monahsetah, but there is scant evidence of any infidelity involving her. Monahsetah's first child could not have been Custer's as he was born just two months after the Washita. There is little evidence of a second child at all, just Cheyenne oral history. These rumors were too irresistible for those in the "hate Custer" crowd though. Captain Benteen picked up the reported relationship and advanced it for sport. It made a great rumor and provided additional support to Benteen's continuing attacks against Custer's character. In reality, there is a very slim chance Custer had a romantic relationship with Monahsetah, and if he did, even less that he fathered a child. First, Custer would have been under constant observation at Fort Hays. Monahsetah spent her time in the stockade with the other Cheyenne

Fort Abraham Lincoln, Dakota Territory (near present day Bismarck, ND), circa 1875. Home of the 7th Cavalry at the time of the battle of the Little Bighorn and the post the regiment departed from to their fate. (National Park Service)

captives, and any visits there would have been accomplished under supervision of the guards. Also, Monahsetah would have normally been in the company of other Cheyenne women. Routine visits by Custer (the ranking officer at the fort) would have been known throughout the command at Fort Hays. Perhaps the most clinical evidence of Custer's inability to have been the father was his contraction of gonorrhea while a cadet at West Point. The resulting infection had made him sterile. The childless marriage between George and Libbie is just further proof, a point of disappointment and anguish for Libbie. She wrote later there were only two regrets in her life, "his [Custer's] death and having no children." Had there been children, the course and direction of their marriage and his career could have been much different.

In 1871, the regiment was parceled out to various locations in the south, providing a stable presence for reconstruction. For Custer and Libbie it meant a move to Elizabethtown, Kentucky. It was a boring time for both, Libbie burdened with making a life in a community and culture foreign to her and Custer often away on detached duty, buying horses for the Army. One detour (at least for Custer) occurred in January 1872 when General Sheridan requested he take part in hosting Russian Grand Duke Alexis for a buffalo hunt. It was a large-scale affair involving over 40 men and a retinue of support wagons and equipment. The Grand Duke had a splendid time, actually killing a buffalo of his own.

Perhaps the most interesting episode of the week-long hunt was the interaction of the Grand Duke, Custer, and the Brule Sioux. Brule Chief Spotted Tail had been invited by General Sheridan from a nearby reservation to give the Grand Duke an experience with the Plains Indians. At a sumptuous evening party on the plains, the Indians performed for the guests with ceremonial dancing. There was an exchange of gifts, the Grand Duke particularly interested in the young Indian girls. Custer, who could communicate in Indian sign language, accompanied the Duke and after a time it was plain to those around them the men were seriously flirting with the young women. At one point it may have gone too far, and after making a gift of earrings to Chief Spotted Tail's daughter, Custer kissed the girl. Custer made light of it, but a reporter for the *Daily State Journal* February 18, 1872, captured the moment and shared it in print:

> Gen. Custer who had been profuse in his attention to her, stepped forward and, taking advantage of his knowledge of the Indian sign language and vernacular, entered into conversation with her [the daughter of Spotted Tail] and requested the privilege of putting rings in her ears, which she graciously accorded. He consumed much time in this pleasant occupation than was necessarily needed, and having adjusted one of them in her ear, without changing his position put his arms around her neck in order to adjust the other. As she made no objection to the proceeding, he claimed the only reward he could request for his pleasing liberty, and the scene ended by him [Custer] kissing her. It was done so graciously old Spotted Tail had no cause to scalp him for his temerity.

Libbie was not present for the affection, and there is no evidence George shared any of the details. However in Libbie's notes about the hunt and Spotted Tail's daughter, she shared, "Young, shy, and pretty, as the Indian girls often are until they become married drudges, she received many gifts." If Libbie felt challenged in any way, her words did not betray her. The hunt ended with the Grand Duke's departure on January 23, 1872. It would be an event he would remember for the rest of his life.

The Custers returned to Kentucky. Probably the most significant aspect of his life occurring in Kentucky were the magazine articles written for two magazines, *Galaxy*, and *Turf, Field, and Farm*. They were well written, about Custer's exploits on the plains, and very popular for the time. So popular, that in 1874, publisher Sheldon & Company, which owned the *Galaxy*, elected to bring the articles together in Custer's first book, *My Life on the Plains*. To capture the public fascination with Custer at the time and his celebrity, this book was a culmination. Among the accomplishments of his young career were: youngest major general in the army at age 23; hero of the Civil War; major contributor of the evolution and use of modern cavalry; Plainsman and Indian fighter; hero of the battle of the Washita; host and friend to the rich and famous; and acclaimed writer and author. He was a media favorite, a legend among circles in the army, and a loyal family man and friend.

In 1873 the 7th Cavalry received orders to leave the south and report to the Dakota Territory. The regiment, which was scattered across the south, mustered in several locations, with the majority forming together at Memphis, Tennessee, before boarding steamers bound for Cairo, Illinois. From there, they would move overland by train to Yankton, Dakota Territory. The move from Yankton to Fort Abraham Lincoln would become an unexpected, epic journey. Early spring snowstorms are commonplace on the plains and one of the worst occurred in April 1873. Upon arrival at Yankton, the regiment moved outside of town into a tent camp called Camp Sturgis. The officers stayed with the men, but their wives moved into the St. Charles Hotel in Yankton. Sunday April 13 started off beautiful and warm, but by evening a heavy rain had begun. During the night, the wind shifted to the north and the temperature plummeted. By early morning on the 14th, a foot of snow was on the ground and the continued high wind turned conditions into a blizzard. Custer came down sick and bedridden, unable to direct things in any way. The storm raged for days and it was not until the 18th that the regiment was dug out. Several men deserted during the storm, probably returning to the south where they were accustomed and the weather more moderate.

The regiment had not been fully together for two years and it was just getting used to operating as a cohesive unit. After the desertions, Custer believed the men needed activity to keep them busy. Consequently, they began drill twice a day, and also began inspections of the companies. No one liked the discipline. Some of the officers complained, but the exercises continued. One officer, Lieutenant Charles Larned, believed Custer's directives were excessive, writing on April 19, he "spends his time in excogitating annoying, vexatious, and useless orders which visit us like the swarm of evil from Pandora's box, small, numberless, and disagreeable." However,

Colonel Sturgis arrived on May 1 to take command of the regiment and apparently found matters agreeable. Nothing changed, and Custer remained in field command. On May 7 the regiment left on the last trip to their destination 400 miles north. They followed the east side of the Missouri River north to Fort Rice, making one layover at Fort Sully en route. They were in the land of the Sioux and, according to Private Charles Windolph, knew they were now operating in "the last of the real Indian country." They were the "mighty 7th" though, and were ready for the challenge.

Quite a number of Indians on reservations were seen on the march. The Sioux were tough and expansionist. Their homeland was in Minnesota, but as civilization advanced west they moved also, trying to stay ahead of the encroachment. The Sioux could not defend their homeland in Minnesota from the endless settlement of the whites, however they were much less intimidated by other plains tribes and took control by force of areas previously controlled by other tribes. One of these was the Crows, who would later ally with the Army, in the hopes they could save their country for themselves. The Sioux were tough to remove and became fearless defenders of their new lands. Hence the reason for the arrival of the 7th Cavalry. The regiment arrived at Fort Rice while the wives made their way north on the Missouri by steamboat. Upon arrival at Fort Rice, the ladies of the regiment found the wives of the fort less than cordial. As the business at hand was a forthcoming railroad survey where the regiment would protect the survey team, the ladies found little purpose in staying. At that point, most headed back east to stay with relatives until the survey returned.

In June 1873, the rest of the survey expedition formed at Fort Rice, including 19 companies of infantry, ten companies of the 7th Cavalry, several cannons, and a long supply train including over 300 civilians. Most of the civilians were engineers and survey personnel necessary for the purpose of the expedition. In overall command was Colonel David S. Stanley, a known drunk, who had risen to command a division of infantry during the Civil War. He was leery of the relationship he might enjoy with Custer. As Stanley wrote in his memoirs, he would try but was not sure he could "avoid trouble with him [Custer]." In charge of the civilian survey team was Thomas Rosser, Custer's old friend from West Point and sometime opponent during the Civil War. The two loved being together, catching up on old times and sharing jokes about Stanley.

Custer and Stanley would clash on several occasions, with Custer placed under arrest at one point. The contentious relationship was fanned by Stanley's intemperance, but also by Custer's contempt for his command and his desire to constantly operate the cavalry on his own bent. They entered the Badlands, beautiful country to Custer who loved the natural world, its creatures, and new experiences. He shared his excitement in a letter to Libbie, "I scarcely know where to begin, where to leave off, what to put down or what to omit." Much of the country would be visited again on another expedition in 1874 and during the Little Bighorn campaign but it was all new ground.

Custer encountered the Sioux on the expedition several times during the survey, enough to develop an appreciation for their tactical ability, and to gauge the regiment's ability to mix with them. On one occasion, while Custer scouted ahead of the column with two companies, the detachment stopped in a thicket to rest their horses. While there, a party of 20 Sioux warriors attempted to scatter the cavalry horses. Custer's detachment mounted and laid chase, before suspecting the command was being led into a trap. Suddenly, the Sioux party stopped and turned to meet the cavalrymen's advance, and then 300 warriors attacked across the valley. The detachment dismounted, forming a skirmish line and began firing, breaking up the Indian charge. The men fell back into the timber, which provided cover for them and their horses. Custer was struck with the Indians' courage. Libbie shared Custer's words in *Boots and Saddles*, they "displayed unusual boldness, frequently charging up to our line and firing with great deliberation and accuracy." The battle waged for three hours with the Sioux lighting fire to the grass at one point to conceal their advance. Finally, running low on ammunition and seeing few options, Custer mounted the detachment and charged the Indians. They broke off their attack. Colonel Stanley, despite the rivalry between himself and Custer, was very accurate about the engagement, capturing the success and even venturing to compliment Custer. In a War Department report on August 4, 1873, Stanley wrote:

> I had sent Lieutenant Colonel Custer ahead to look up the road, a service for which he always volunteered … Three scouts and a Cavalry straggler ran in, and said they had been pursued by Indians … I sent all the Cavalry to support Custer, but an hour before, he had driven all his opponents miles away … He had gained 8 or 10 miles ahead of his train, had unsaddled to graze his animals, when his pickets signaled the approach of Indians. These were only a decoy. When Custer with a few of his officers who had watched their movements declined to follow this decoy to the adjoining thicket of cottonwood, 250 to 300 warriors rode out to the attack. The squadron was about 80 strong, and, the Indians being more numerous, Custer fought defensively on foot, till, finding the Indians had nothing new to develop, he mounted his squadron, and charged, dispersing them in all directions.

Custer had proved the 7th could hold its own against a new enemy. The detachment was outnumbered, but through good leadership and careful deployment, they proved they had the upper hand. On August 11, the command again faced fire from the Sioux, this time from across the Yellowstone River near the mouth of the Bighorn River. The regiment had moved into a position on the south side of the Yellowstone the night before. They had tried unsuccessfully to cross the treacherous river, finally giving up. The next day, they took fire from Sioux warriors from the bluff on the north side of the river. The regiment established a skirmish line and returned fire. What happened next genuinely stunned Custer and the men. The Sioux swam their ponies across the Yellowstone on both sides of the cavalry position and attacked, performing a double envelopment (attacking both sides of Custer and his men). Custer used the only tactic he knew to break their thrust. He mounted the command and attacked in two directions. As bullets flew in each direction, Custer once again demonstrated his courage while having his horse shot out from under him. A reporter accompanying the expedition wrote, "he exposed himself freely and recklessly."

Libbie would not have approved of his recklessness but it served to inspire his men, and the Indians once again broke off their attack. Lessons were learned on both sides, while casualties were light. The Sioux's determination was not lost on anyone. Colonel Stanley commented in his report about the attack, "until the Sioux are quelled, nothing can be done to ever test the capabilities of the country when it is settled." They would have to be removed from their country or be destroyed by force. The Sioux knew their country as well as they did their own capabilities. The double crossing of the Yellowstone River, under fire, and then conducting a double envelopment against the 7th Cavalry, astounded Custer and proved to him without a doubt, the Sioux were a formidable foe.

The regiment pulled into Fort Abraham Lincoln on September 21, 1873. The survey expedition was deemed a success. While the regiment was away on the survey, their barracks and officers' quarters were completed. Six companies of the regiment would remain at Fort Lincoln, while the other six companies would be garrisoned down river at Fort Rice and to the northwest of Fort Lincoln at Fort Totten. Custer had the ability to separate the two factions, both pro and non-pro by geography and took advantage of the opportunity. This would make social life at Fort Lincoln happier, but would also serve to advance the division of the regiment. Captain Benteen and his company would be safely stationed at Fort Rice, away from the day-to-day oversight of Custer. It satisfied both parties. For Custer finally, it provided an opportunity to move into their new home. He made preparations with the assistance of Mary Adams, the couple's servant, and headed west by train to Monroe to get Libbie. On November 16, 1873, George and Libbie moved into their new quarters, serenaded by the regimental band playing "Home Sweet Home," and "Garry Owen." They settled into what would be a happy life on the plains.

The Custers were great hosts at Fort Lincoln and the post enjoyed an unusually vibrant social life. Receptions and parties occurred frequently, and the Custers hosted picnics on the prairies around the fort. Custer and Libbie's mutual interest in the theater gave birth to performances at the fort, several including Custer himself. It was not difficult for him. He had been performing in the theater of life for some time. Reprising an old pursuit, Custer taught school to the children of the fort, thoroughly enjoying it. Libbie painted and sewed her handiwork, but probably more than anything, enjoyed being a mentor to the other wives. Custer pursued his interest in nature, harvesting animals and mounting them. He sent several on to the east to be displayed as the only examples in museums until they contacted him to stop. Libbie commented in *Boots and Saddles* on it all, "The firelight reflected the large, glittering eyes of the animals' heads, and except that we were a jolly family, the surroundings would have suggested arenas and martyrs." He also continued to write, on and off, attempting to complete portions of his memoirs from the Civil War.

On the evening of February 6, 1874, their quarters caught fire and burned to the ground. George, Libbie, and a house guest—Agnes Bates—were unhurt, but the couple lost most of their possessions. The home would be rebuilt, and with appointments specified by Libbie, in the end was a finer, better home. In time, it would again be an expression of their lives.

In 1874, interest in the region around the Black Hills would launch another expedition for the 7th Cavalry. The "Hills that are Black" or "Paha Sapa" as the Sioux referred to the region, were sacred to them. Under the terms of the Fort Laramie Treaty of 1868, the Black Hills formed the western section of the Sioux reservation and were "forever theirs." Indeed, the treaty was quite clear. Whites were to never "pass over, settle on, or reside" in the region. The Sioux fiercely defended their rights, killing an increasing number of invaders, searching for the natural resources (especially gold) they believed to be there. General Sheridan increasingly fielded complaints about the depredations of the Sioux regardless of their clear rights expressed in the treaty. Desiring to establish an Army presence in the region to protect Sioux rights (he actually cared little for Sioux rights, but desired to protect the whites trying to access the area), he sent a request to the commander of the Army, General Sherman,

A posting to a frontier fort usually brought isolation and little access to civilization. Yet, the social life at some of these forts could be quite full, usually a reflection of the commander and ladies of the post. Fort Abraham Lincoln's social life was very lively, and the Custers contributed greatly to it as they enjoyed the arts immensely. Here officers and their wives join the Custers in their home at Fort Abraham Lincoln for a music social. (Little Bighorn National Monument)

to launch an expedition with the purpose of determining locations where forts might be placed. Sherman approved and Sheridan gave instructions to compile a complete and detailed description of the area. Custer and the 7th Cavalry were given responsibility to lead the expedition.

On July 17, 1874, ten companies of the 7th Cavalry, two infantry companies, along with a detachment of Indian scouts, and others including geologists, prospectors, and newspaper correspondents, left Fort Lincoln with great fanfare. Included for the first time on an outing with his older brothers was young Boston Custer, hired as a forage master. In all, the expedition totaled just under 1,000 troopers and civilians. It was estimated the command would be gone for about two months. Custer expected opposition from the Sioux, but the size of the command and the round out of equipment and arms would give them the decisive edge. Custer's confidence would be bolstered by the fact he would be in command.

It was a beautiful country, and, according to most of those along, the trip of a lifetime. Custer shared in a letter to Libbie, "this [is] the best trip ever had." He loved the freedom commanding the expedition offered. While the supply wagons lumbered in the rear, he advanced forward with a detachment equal to a company in size, finding stream crossings, exploring rock formations and caves, even hunting. On August 7 he killed his first grizzly bear. Evenings were looked forward to, as Custer hosted officer calls at his tent. Officers, including old friend and survivor of Beecher's Island fame, Major Sandy Forsyth, and President Grant's brother, Fred, joined in to share tales.

Once the command entered the Black Hills though, Custer was all business, carefully setting up defenses with pickets at night. They saw few Sioux and only encountered one small Sioux village. They had no trouble. The gold prospectors gave their profession a try on July 30, finding some small deposits in a water source called French Creek. They continued their efforts in almost every water course they crossed. According to the two prospectors—Horatio Nelson Ross and William McKay—they prospected 75 dollars' worth of gold in two days.

Excitement ran through the expedition. Custer, quick to get the news out, dispatched scout Charlie Reynolds with the correspondent's stories and his own personal commander's report. In it, Custer shared, "almost every [turn of the] earth produced gold in small but paying quantities." He also caveated his report though, "until further examination is made regarding the richness of gold, no opinion should be formed." Charlie Reynolds delivered the dispatches to Fort Laramie a week later. The news created a sensation. Miners swarmed the Black Hills. Within one year, over 15,000 miners had invaded the region. Conflict with the Sioux would be unavoidable, and for the Indians their future decided. On August 30, 1874, Custer marched into Fort Lincoln in grand procession with the band playing "Garry Owen." It was a proud and happy moment for the men and families of the regiment. At the time, few would have ever predicted it would be the last happy return.

CHAPTER 4

Little Bighorn

I have seen your order, transmitted through the General of the Army, directing that I be not permitted to accompany the expedition about to move against hostile Indians. As my entire regiment forms a part of the proposed expedition, and as I am the senior officer of the regiment on duty in this Department, I respectfully but most earnestly request that while not allowed to go in command of the expedition, I may be permitted to serve with my regiment in the field. I appeal to you as a soldier to spare me the humiliation of seeing my regiment march to meet the enemy and not share its dangers.

TELEGRAM FROM BREVET MAJOR GENERAL GEORGE CUSTER
TO PRESIDENT ULYSSES S. GRANT, MAY 6, 1876

The year 1876 was an election year and the stakes were particularly high for whomever would be selected as the president. There were a lot of leftover, unhealed wounds from the Civil War and the vitriol in politics was very intense. Old southern Democrats went after President Grant and his administration with reckless abandon. There was a lot to attack. Corruption and graft were normal in Washington, each new administration brought their friends and family and placed them in government positions to benefit from winning. President Grant was an honest man but he was surrounded by a level of graft, corruption, and nepotism among his administration that shocked even those who were used to such antics.

One of the more interesting and destiny changing episodes in the life of George Custer occurred in the early spring of 1876, shortly before the launch of the Sioux Campaign. Army posts today are very strikingly similar to their old frontier Army ancestors. In many ways they are a self-contained community with their own culture, nightlife, and retail business activity. In 1876, each post had one store, a general mercantile establishment which provided all sorts of goods for sale to soldiers and their families. These "sutlers' stores" as they were known at the time, carried a little bit of everything a soldier or his family might need. The sutler had a monopoly due to the remoteness of the post and could take advantage if they chose to. Few passed up the opportunity to gouge their clientele. Complaints were numerous, and there was little to be done about it. Post sutlers as well as Indian agents were selected by the Department of War and the Bureau of Indian Affairs in Washington as they were located on military installations or agencies administered through federally funded programs. In these remote locations, sutlers were far removed from close scrutiny.

Interestingly, both the sutler issue and problems with the fair and proper operation of Indian agencies by their agents would touch Custer in profound ways. By 1876, annuity fraud at Indian agencies was at epic levels and had been for years. In fact, as early as 1865 General Alfred Sully, who had been fighting the Sioux on the plains for years, complained in writing because he felt it was a contributing factor to tensions among the Indians. He wrote, "It is my opinion that very little of it [subsidies] reaches the hands of the Indians." The shortage of subsidies and the starving conditions on agencies would eventually lead to the increasing departure of many Indians for historical hunting grounds to feed their families. Custer would of course face these larger numbers of Indians during the Sioux Campaign of 1876 and ultimately, at the Little Bighorn.

Lieutenant Colonel George Custer, 7th Cavalry, photographed in what was the full military dress uniform after 1872. Probably his last formal photo in uniform, this photo was likely shot in 1875 at the famous Mora Studio in New York City. Custer was as much a celebrity as a modern movie or television star today and was popular among the New York Society when visiting the city. (National Park Service)

The sutler issue for Custer had been a frustrating one for some time. He innately hated how the men and their families were taken advantage of. For Custer, the sutler graft violated his principle of fair play. His own family had always struggled with money and worked hard for what they had, and his soldiers had little—he empathized and connected with their pain. Custer had complained openly in the press, in magazines, and in person to his chain of command about it. Nothing changed and in 1870, the Secretary of War required sutlers or post traders to be appointed and operate under license of the War Department. Grant's Secretary of War was William Worth Belknap, a New York-born and raised attorney who had moved to Iowa to practice law before the start of the Civil War. When war broke out he volunteered for service, performing admirably and quickly moving up the ranks.

After the war, Belknap returned to Iowa, where he worked as a federal tax collector. In 1869, President Grant appointed Belknap to be Secretary of War. Grand corruption followed, ultimately involving Belknap's wife Carita who simply cashed in on the profits. Custer argued often with the post trader at Fort Abraham Lincoln where he was the commander. Officers and soldiers there had options however; they could simply cross the Missouri River and visit merchants in Bismarck. The post sutler at Fort Lincoln, R. C. Seip, complained to the Secretary of War about the practice of bypassing his little system. Custer would later testify Seip had been known to "go out and stop an officer's wagon, driven by his servant, and inspect the wagon to see what was in it and threaten to use his influence with the Secretary of War because we traded with a town five miles distant where we got things about half his price." Everyone noticed the exorbitant prices even if they did not understand what had caused them. Sergeant Daniel Kanipe of C Company, 7th Cavalry, recalled of the time, "Liquor was 25 cents a glass, and the glasses were mostly glass—mighty little whiskey." Kanipe's humor aside, soldiers who made just a few dollars a month and endured frontier conditions paid for the graft. Orville Grant, the less than honest brother of the president, owned a portion of three sutler trading posts. Once the press had connected him to scandal, it did not take long for Democrats in Congress to aim at the president himself.

On March 1, 1876, the U.S. House Committee on Expenditures in the War Department investigated the matter. The real target was President Grant and the House wanted Custer to testify. Despite preparations for the upcoming Sioux campaign, Custer was formally requested in late March 1876 to testify in front of Congress about the Belknap matter. Custer, a fervent Democrat, could wear his politics on his sleeve if necessary. Career Army officers inherently knew a neutral position was essential in advancing in rank. In the Civil War, Custer had done this successfully to negotiate confirmation of his position and rank. However, it was not in his nature to leave his strategic belief about who would be best to prevail in the upcoming presidential election. He had never liked President Grant or his policies. If the investigation into the Belknap affair could sway opinion about the outcome of the election and taint Grant's Republican administration, so be it. The sutler issue was a straightforward matter and one which demanded Custer's involvement as a commander. Custer reasoned then, what could be the danger of telling the truth? Still, Custer rightly suspected danger and sought counsel from his superior, General Terry, for advice. Terry, a trained attorney, advised Custer to gather the questions put to him and send them off in written form to Congress. Perhaps that would do it, but in the end Custer went—he could not avoid the political theater. In fact he loved the glare of the spotlight and the media attention his testimony would generate.

Custer arrived in Washington and testified twice to no harm, aside from the final part of his testimony mentioning the president's brother Orville. The testimony angered his commander in chief by so doing, and it would not be forgotten. Custer had failed to foresee the impact of his opinions on others during the Civil War, the Indian wars in Kansas, and he had done so once again. After a short trip to New York to visit friends and attend to business dealings, he intended to return home to Fort Lincoln. Meanwhile, Washington was ablaze with the scandal, and President Grant was furious with Custer. Grant's support for Belknap never wavered, likely a personal position with roots that ran back to Belknap's war service. President Grant had never been an admirer of Custer, and the boy general's court-martial in 1867 cemented it. Allowing Custer to be reinstated in 1868 to participate in the battle of the Washita never changed Grant's opinion of him. To Grant, Custer was a grandstander and a media hog. Grant ordered Custer to be relieved of command of the Dakota Column and for him to return to Washington for further instructions.

Custer had not expected the explosive reaction to his testimony. It was an issue that affected the welfare of soldiers and in that respect a neutral matter, something Grant as a former head of the Army would surely be empathetic to. Custer was not naive about politics but was confused by Grant's personal defense of Orville, rather than the welfare of the Army. Custer needed to leave town and get back to Fort Abraham Lincoln to let things cool off. It was a sticky situation that drove Custer crazy. To relieve the tension he reached out to his chain of command for advice. Neither General Terry nor General Sheridan quite knew what to do. They both liked and supported Custer but were wary of the politics in the case. General Sherman, the commanding general of the Army, ultimately advised a straightforward approach, to let a couple of days go by and visit the president in person. So, Custer waited and then "tail between his legs" visited the White House on the morning of May 1. He would have a long, exasperating wait. Custer waited five hours only to be told the president would not see him. Not knowing exactly what to do, he asked the Inspector General of the Army permission, in a back door move, to leave town, and then left. He traveled to Monroe, Michigan for a short visit with his family before heading on to Chicago to Sheridan's headquarters. Arriving there on May 4, he was summoned back to Washington. Custer knew the reality; as each day went on the likelihood of the 7th Cavalry Regiment leaving on the campaign against the Sioux was more real. He knew he could be left behind, possibly permanently.

As much as Custer was concerned, there was another person more concerned—General Terry. He was no Indian fighter and while he could command the Dakota Column, he was never going to lead the fight in the field. He considered others for the job, but in the end determined Custer was the only one who could lead the 7th Cavalry. Meanwhile, Custer had requested through Sherman that if he was not allowed to accompany the campaign might he be allowed to at least return home to Fort Abraham Lincoln to be with his family. Custer's request was granted, and he departed the next day. Custer arrived at General Terry's headquarters in Minneapolis on May with tears in his eyes, ready to petition his boss for continued help, both needing the same thing—Custer's reinstatement. So together they drafted correspondence to achieve it. In a very well-drafted letter to President Grant, Custer appealed as a soldier to "spare [himself] the humiliation of seeing my regiment march to meet the enemy and not share its dangers." It was endorsed by generals Terry, Sheridan, and Sherman. It was a humble letter and would be difficult to refuse.

Brigadier General Alfred Terry was a Connecticut native who became an attorney and judge before the Civil War. At the outbreak of the war, he raised a regiment of volunteers and led them at the first battle of Bull Run (Manassas). He served successfully for the duration of the conflict and was rare among his peers to be appointed a Regular Army general at the end of hostilities. He was appointed military commander of the Dakota Territory in 1866, and his legal skills were put to use in negotiating the treaty of Fort Laramie in 1866. He led the Dakota Column during the Little Bighorn campaign in 1876 and gave George Custer his final orders. (Library of Congress)

General Sherman responded on May 8 by telegram with news from Washington. It stated, "General Custer's urgent request to go under your command with his regiment has been submitted to the President, who sent me word, that if you want General Custer along he withdraws his objections. Advise Custer to be prudent, not to take along any newspapermen, who always make mischief, and to abstain from personalities in the future." The effort had worked. Terry had his field commander and Custer had command of his regiment. Both were happy. Custer returned to Fort Abraham Lincoln to get ready, concluding an episode, years in the making, which would frame not only the number of Indians against him but if it had gone any other way, prevented his, and the 7th Cavalry's meeting with destiny.

The Great Sioux War of 1876

> I have never dealt with the Americans. Why should I? The land belonged to my people. I never dealt with them—I mean I never treated them in a way to surrender my people's rights. I traded with them, but I always gave full value for what I got. I never asked the United States government to make me presents of blankets or cloth or anything of that kind. The most I did was to ask them to send me an honest trader that I could trade with and I proposed to give him buffalo robes and elk skins and other hides in exchange for what we wanted. I told every trader who came to our camps that I did not want any favors from him, that I wanted to trade with him fairly and equally, giving him full value for what I got but the traders wanted me to trade with them on no such terms. They wanted to give little and get much. They told me that if I did not accept what they would give me in trade they would get the government to fight me. I told them I did not want to fight.
>
> CHIEF SITTING BULL, 1877

The year 1876 was a watershed year for the United States of America. It had weathered 100 years since the revolution, had absorbed endless immigration and westward movements across the continent. It had endured a bloody Civil War which had torn the nation apart. It was now healing and was looking forward to a year of celebration. It was an era of advancement, invention, firsts of many kinds. For the Indians of America, it was 100 years of failed United States government policy toward them. It left them with a pile of broken treaties, all to the benefit of the white man's expansion westward.

For many years leading up to 1876, the Plains Indians were being continually pushed west across the North American continent. Inevitable violence followed as settlers, miners, and railroad men increasingly came into conflict with the Indians, fiercely defending hunting grounds and territory. To prevent the violence between both sides, a series of agencies were set aside for Indians in the American West. The agencies covered a vast territory, most of what is today North and South Dakota (then the Dakota Territory) and northwestern Nebraska. On them, large populations of Sioux, Northern Cheyenne, Arapaho and other smaller tribes were to live on promised subsidies of food, clothing, and other materials. Indians were to become peaceable farmers. They were to give up their nomadic life, violence against their imposing new neighbors and live in peace. Many did, but they constantly dealt with dishonest agents who were the action arm for Indian policy inside the United States government. There were always some tribes who would not surrender, called "roamers." The roamers lived the old life, hunting buffalo, moving often, and avoiding white contact if they could. As the white population stretched further west, more and more altercations between settlers finally demanded government action. In an arbitrary government order issued in late 1875, roamers were to join the agencies by January 1876 or be considered "hostiles." The edict meant nothing, as the roamers had sparse communication with the agencies. Even if they did, the roamers would not understand what was required and when. Sioux bands made up most of the roamers, but some bands of Cheyenne were affiliated along with other smaller groups. They lived there throughout the year, only making limited contact with whites or "Wasichus"—just the way the Indians liked it. This was not to imply there was no contact, there were continual depravities on both sides and violence would inevitably continue.

Every year in the spring, an undetermined number of reservation Indians would travel west to join their "roamer" relatives living the nomadic life. Dishonest Indian agents and the lack of promised subsidies encouraged more to do it. In many cases

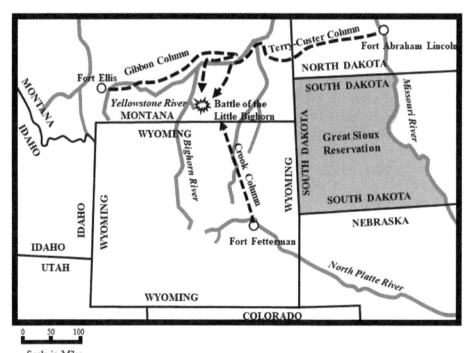

The Sioux Campaign of 1876, leading up to the battle of Little Bighorn, March–June 1876. (Map by Ted Behncke)

starvation became the driving force for reservation Indians to move west. Together, they would hunt and move frequently as resources around them were used up. Of course buffalo were their principal game when they could find them, but they hunted all wildlife, and it was better than starving. Also, they could live the old life and the traditional horse culture they knew so well. The roamers moved often, usually because their ponies had consumed the available grass. When cold weather approached, many would return to the reservation to winter through the frigid plains and to live off subsidies provided by the government. In the spring, they anxiously awaited the spring grass which strengthened their ponies. Without the grass, their normally hearty ponies were simply too weak for any journey. The Indians were not the only ones who knew of this cycle of their lives. Indian agents, the United States Army, and War Department, all knew of this phenomena but just how many Indians left agencies each spring, no one knew precisely.

Roamers felt relatively safe in the far western areas of Montana and Wyoming. Save for a few railroad expeditions, the United States Army remained out of their territory. Dr. Thomas Bailey Marquis in his book *Wooden Leg* said by early 1876, Cheyenne Indians were increasingly warning roamers the "soldiers were coming to fight them." The change in belief was a result of the roamers now being considered hostiles by the Army.

By the spring of 1876, at least 3,000 to 4,000 roamers, including at least 1,000 warriors, were in the vicinity of the Powder and Tongue rivers, and many agency Indians were joining them every day. It was difficult for the War Department to determine just how many Indians had left, and for what reasons. First, there were many separate agencies with hundreds of miles between them. Comings and goings were difficult to measure. Indian agents had little motivation to keep an accurate count. As the subsidies were measured on headcount, the fewer Indians present meant fewer subsidies authorized. To pad the numbers had been a problem for some time, as agents would post a higher number than actually present, distribute subsidies to those on-site, and then sell the rest. The lack of a clear idea of just how many Indians were in the unceded area, both hostile and otherwise, would ultimately be the seminal question for the Army as it anticipated the 1876 campaign.

Pursuit and Discovery

> You felt like you were somebody when you were on a good horse, with a carbine dangling from its small leather ring socket on your McClellan saddle and a Colt army revolver strapped on your hip; and a hundred rounds of ammunition in your web belt and your saddle pockets. You were a cavalryman of the Seventh Regiment. You were a part of a proud outfit that had a fighting reputation, and you were ready for a fight or a frolic.
>
> PRIVATE CHARLES WINDOLPH, COMPANY H, 7TH CAVALRY,
> LITTLE BIGHORN BATTLE SURVIVOR

On May 17, 1876, the 7th Cavalry Regiment under the field command of Lieutenant Colonel George A. Custer paraded from Fort Abraham Lincoln, Dakota Territory

Colonel John Gibbon led the Montana Column against the Sioux in the campaign of 1876. He was twice accused of being timid in the face of the Sioux but ultimately pushed his column toward the Little Bighorn river. Gibbon and his men arrived on June 27, 1876, and relieved the Reno-Benteen defense and discovered the remains of Custer's men. (Library of Congress)

for its campaign with the Plains Indians, and its rendezvous with fate. The organization was impressive in sight and sound for those who witnessed its departure.

Future General Edward Godfrey, then a lieutenant and commander of Company K recalled in his January 1892 *Century Magazine* article, "This expedition consisted of the 7th United States Cavalry, commanded by General George A. Custer, 28 officers and about 700 men; two companies of the 17th United States Infantry, and one company of the 6th United States Infantry, 8 officers and 135 men; one platoon of Gatling guns, 2 officers and 32 men (of the 20th United States Infantry); and 40 Ree [Arikara] Indian scouts." Including a very large supply train which included over 100 wagons, the force numbered 925 officers and men. The parade in its size was an attempt to assuage the fears of families at the fort about the coming campaign. The group also included Mark Kellogg, a newspaper correspondent for the *New York Herald*. Custer had been specifically instructed not to take along any press but Kellogg persisted and came along.

One controversial feature which Custer had done since 1868 was the "coloring" of the regiment's horses. The practice added additional pomp to the parade. That day upon leaving Fort Lincoln: Company A rode dark bays and sorrels; Company C had light sorrels; companies B, F, I, and L all rode bay horses; companies H and M had light bays; Company E had grays; Company D had black mounts; Company G had mixed roans; Company K had standard sorrels. Lieutenants Cooke and Calhoun rode white horses. Interestingly, many of the details about known troop movements the day of the disaster are known because of the color of the horses and their company association. Indian participants paid specific attention to the color of horses, and they have been helpful to fill in some blanks of the mystery of Custer's command. This is particularly true of Company E troopers, who rode grays.

The Dakota Column was under the overall command of General Alfred Terry of the Department of Dakota. Terry was more politician and academic than soldier. With a friendly face and demeanor, he made a most unlikely hardened Indian fighter. The Dakota Column was just a portion of a much larger military force directed by

General Philip Sheridan's military division, which also included columns launched from two other locations. The Montana Column, under the command of General Terry's subordinate Colonel John Gibbon would launch from Fort Ellis, Montana, with over 450 men. Gibbon was an infantry officer who had earned a reputation in the Civil War of being a capable commander. He had limited to no experience fighting the Plains Indians though. In reality he tended to be timid. Twice during the Sioux Campaign of 1876 he had the opportunities to fight the Sioux before the arrival of the Dakota Column, but passed. From Fort Fetterman, Wyoming Territory, Brigadier General George Crook, operating as part of the Department of the Platte, would move northward with a combined force of over 1,000 men of infantry and cavalry.

Despite the reputation of Custer and the 7th Cavalry as being the premier Indian fighters since the battle of the Washita in 1868, it was Crook who had proven himself the more successful in the southwest fighting the Apache. Crook was not much to look at, often wearing a preferred combination of unmarked canvas clothing and a non-regulation hat. He was known for having an unruly beard with long dundreary tails. At a glance, Crook gave off no outward signs of being a soldier, much less a general. He rode a mule because they were surer footed and he was the first commander to use mules for pack animals instead of wagons. The use of mules allowed his forces to be very agile and quick, and speed was especially useful against his first Indian opponent—the Apache. Crook's speed, coupled with his use of Apache scouts to "hunt their own" was innovative and, in the end, very successful. He would bring his success into a new fight with the Plains Indians. So, strategically and in concert, the three columns would focus on the area where the "hostile Indians" were known to reside and hunt during the summer months.

The Montana Column was already in the field near the Yellowstone River and the Wyoming Column was leaving Fort Fetterman when the Dakota Column slowly made their way west. On June 1 the Dakota Column encountered a freak snowstorm, giving some idea of the peril of operations on the plains. The conditions made it miserable for soldiers and their horses alike. Gibbon's force had already had contact with the Sioux. The Indians stayed at a distance though, picking off occasional stragglers. Lieutenant James Bradley, Gibbon's chief of scouts, would be the first observer of all three columns to garner some idea of the Indian strength in the region. On May 16, he and his Crow Indian scouts discovered a large encampment on the Tongue River. The camp was then 35 miles from the rest of Gibbon's force and also separated by the Yellowstone River, a formidable obstacle. Nonetheless, a plan of attack was formed which first required the north-to-south crossing of the river by the troops. Gibbon intended for his horses to swim connected in series, one halter rein to another, with the first held by a soldier in a boat. Lieutenant Edward McClernand, Gibbon's chief engineer, aptly described the ineptness of the crossing in *With the Indian and Buffalo in Montana 1870–1878*, writing "To get the horses to cross, a number were tied head to tail … but as soon as the horse on the lariat entered the main current he pulled loose from the soldier in the boat and turned downstream, followed, of course, by those in the rear." Those men affected were caught in the maelstrom and drowned. The loss of troops put a halt to the mission and the attack was canceled. To the Sioux, who observed the debacle from the other side of the river, and had crossed the river many times on their ponies, the whole episode must have left the impression of incompetence on the part of their foe.

While Gibbon's force remained in place, Lieutenant Bradley continued his scouting operations. Between May 24–26 he discovered an even larger camp of Indians, the result of even more agency Indians joining the roamers. This time the Indian camp was only 18 miles from Gibbon on the Rosebud River. The strength of the encampment was estimated to be 800–1,000 warriors, and Bradley's Crow scouts sensed real danger in the Sioux numbers, and they desired to leave the area immediately. Bradley once again reported the encampment to Gibbon. Because of the proximity, Bradley expected an immediate movement to attack, but once again he would be disappointed. While Bradley was away on the scout, Gibbon had heard from Terry and interpreted his orders to stay put. Gibbon's perceived delay to action left many with the impression he was incompetent. Some applied a less flattering assessment—cowardice. The result was the same, the camp was let go and allowed to grow with more agency arrivals. Twice, Gibbon had the opportunity to attack. Twice he had failed. Had Gibbon even disrupted these camps, it could have prevented their eventual growth, which came to be the immense village which Custer would find. Perhaps even worse, the intelligence gained by Bradley's scouts was not relayed to General Terry. Whether Gibbon believed the intelligence was of little value, or whether he thought if it had been forwarded to Terry it might raise questions about his inaction will never be known. For the historical record, the information was essential to a shared picture of the Indians' activity in the region. Further, if timely engagement had occurred, it would probably have changed the direction of the overall campaign. Similar events with the Wyoming Column would follow.

On May 29, Crook headed north from Fort Fetterman with his large column. They traveled to Goose Creek near modern-day Sheridan, Wyoming, and established a base camp to operate from. On June 16 they continued north with an approximately 1,300-man fighting force including Crow and Shoshone scouts. The column followed the Rosebud River, another tributary of the Yellowstone. The column immediately found buffalo, a sign they knew would soon mean finding the roaming Indian bands. Later, they started finding evidence of abandoned Indian camps. These were previous stays of both Crazy Horse and Sitting Bull's bands as they hunted and moved north. The Crook Column and the growing Indian encampment near the Little Bighorn were relatively close. In fact, both Sitting Bull and Crazy Horse knew of the Crook forces but Sitting Bull did not desire to engage them.

Brigadier General George Crook shown during the Indian War years in dress uniform. George Crook compiled an excellent record fighting the Apache Indians in the American southwest before fighting the Plains Indians. Crook used unconventional techniques like using pack mules instead of supply wagons and Indian scouts as trackers. While on campaign he dressed comfortably in canvas clothes with no rank or any other outward indication of being a soldier at all. He was surprised on Rosebud Creek and defeated by the same warriors who attacked Custer. Unfortunately, that intelligence never reached Terry or Custer. (Library of Congress)

The Crook Column continued north and went into camp. Crook dispatched Captain Anderson Mills and a scouting party to move forward for a few miles. Within an hour, gunshots were heard from the north. It was the Indian scouts who rose to meet the attacking Sioux first and who were credited with saving the slow-responding command. For the next six hours, the battle of the Rosebud raged, and a furious fight spread across the hills and ravines of the area. There was no specific strategy on the part of the Indian forces, just charges of warriors and soldiers of both sides. The tremendous persistence of the Indian fighters should have been observed by Crook. As Lieutenant John Bourke, a member of the Crook Column remembered, the Indians "were extremely bold and fierce" and "advanced in excellent style." After several hours of fighting, Crook left the field with moderate losses, but he had been significantly engaged—and he knew it. He felt no choice but to return to his base camp at Goose Creek and await reinforcements.

Two important elements of the battle of the Rosebud would have been critical intelligence to the Dakota Column and Custer if they had been shared. First, the fierce "stand and fight" nature of the engagement by the Indians was unexpected. The Indians had not done this before, and Crook had been solidly whipped. He retreated and abandoned the campaign. Of more importance to the overall campaign would have been sharing the sizeable increase in the strength of the roamers and their agency additions. As Lieutenant Bourke later said, "It was patent to everyone … that not hundreds as had been reported, but thousands of Sioux and Cheyenne were in hostility and absent from the agencies." The unknown presence of "thousands" of Indians changed everything, but the news came too late to help Custer and the valiant 7th Cavalry.

Prelude, the Reno Scout

While the Montana Column was plagued with its self-imposed inactivity and the Wyoming Column bloodied, the Dakota Column had moved steadily west, through the Dakota badlands and on into Montana. The column advanced on supplies and successive depots (first the Glendive Depot and then the Power River Depot), supplied by the steamer *Far West*. General Terry traveled with the column itself and was increasingly frustrated by the lack of intelligence of forces further west and south. He had written to his sister of his increasing worry that the Indians might scatter, and he "might not be able to find them at all." Gibbon was supposed to define the far western extremes of the campaign's theater, to find the Indians and contain them. Gibbon, despite being in the field since April, had done little but hug the Yellowstone and provide conflicting reports of Indian strength and possible locations. Upon arriving at the Powder River and going into camp, Terry was not even sure where Gibbon was located on the Yellowstone. As for the whereabouts of the Wyoming Column, he knew nothing of their advance.

Terry took matters into his own hands once he reached the Powder River on June 8. He knew, thanks to his Arikara scouts, the steamer *Far West* was 20 miles downriver at the confluence of the Yellowstone at the Powder River Depot. While the rest of the 7th Cavalry refitted and rested, he took two companies and headed downriver to the steamer, and used it to find Gibbon on the Yellowstone. While he was gone, Terry ordered the supply trains of the 7th to de-wagon and fit mules with supplies to be more mobile. They had never used mules before, so it would prove quite interesting. Custer would stay behind, writing letters and preparing the command for operations.

The next day, June 9, Terry linked up with Gibbon just five miles downstream, and Gibbon came aboard. For the first time, Gibbon was able to relay the intelligence about the large Indian encampment seen by Lieutenant Bradley on May 24. Terry in turn instructed Gibbon to return to his basecamp at the mouth of the Rosebud, and as soon as he was ready, dispatch his cavalry south on the Rosebud. With his new knowledge, Terry believed the Indian roamers and their agency arrivals to be further west than first thought. They would have to be along the Rosebud or more likely, further west along either the Bighorn or Little Bighorn rivers, or even the Tongue River. As no one had seen the encampment in two weeks though, it was

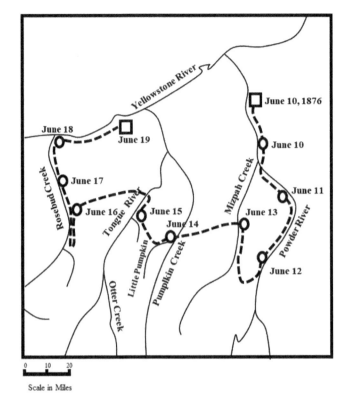

Reno's Scout, June 10–11, 1876. (Map by Ted Behncke)

only one possible direction. The Indians would only remain as long as the game was plentiful. Terry would also have to rule out a move to the east as well.

Upon returning to the Dakota Column, Terry prepared to launch a reconnaissance with a portion of the 7th Cavalry. Custer, of course, assumed he would lead the effort, as he had done throughout the past five weeks on the march out from Fort Lincoln. He was stunned to learn Reno would be given the command.

While Terry never explained his decision, it may have had to do directly with his beliefs about his subordinate commander. Custer had a propensity to wander while leading the command, following his instincts rather than orders. It could also have been related to Custer's belief the scout was unnecessary. He had been vocal in opposition to Reno leading the scout, offering instead a reconnaissance in force with the entire 7th Cavalry, with him leading. Custer reasoned they could then rapidly pitch into what they found, preventing movement of the Indians and any possible escape. It was most probable that Terry feared Custer would move to fight too soon. The area of operation was extraordinarily large and his forces relatively small. Terry had to be sure of where the Indians were before committing the Montana and Dakota columns. He had still heard nothing from Crook and the Wyoming columns—Terry was taking the safe, prudent course.

Major Reno launched his reconnaissance on June 10 with five companies of the 7th Cavalry, a Gatling gun, 12 days' rations on a pack train of mules, and a complement of Indian scouts, including the very capable Mitch Boyer, who was of French and Sioux descent but also spoke Crow. He was a contemporary of mountain man Jim Bridger and knew the area better than anyone in the command. Reno's orders from Terry were to proceed down the Powder River to the mouth of the Little Powder. From there, head west to Mizpah Creek, then move north to where it meets the Powder River (a complete loop), then west again to Pumpkin Creek, crossing it and continuing west to the Tongue River. From there, head north to the Yellowstone River and then east to return to camp. Actual knowledge of the area being limited, this long, looping movement would eliminate the possibility of the Indians moving their camp east. Terry could then adjust the entire Dakota Column further west. With Gibbon's forces further west on the other side of the Indians, they would be inside Terry's tightening noose. With Crook moving north with his column, there would be no escape.

Major Reno's scout would include five capable cavalry companies, with some of Custer's favorite officers. Company B commanded by Captain Thomas McDougal,

Major Marcus A. Reno was the senior surviving officer of the 7th Cavalry when George Custer was killed at the battle of the Little Bighorn. Accused of being drunk the day of the battle and after, Reno never escaped suspicions of cowardice and incompetence. He was removed from the Army in 1880 and died penniless in 1889. (National Park Service)

Company E commanded by Lieutenant Algernon Smith, Company F commanded by Captain George Yates, Company I commanded by Captain Myles Keogh and Company L commanded by Custer's brother-in-law, Lieutenant Jimmie Calhoun. Rounding out the five was Company C, Captain Tom Custer's normal command, however, he was on detached duty with regimental headquarters. In his stead, young Lieutenant Henry Harrington would command Company C temporarily. The command left optimistically under clear skies, but quickly it started to rain. It would rain intermittently for the rest of the scout.

Before leaving the Powder River Camp, the 7th Cavalry Regiment left one particular defining weapon of the cavalry behind—the sabre. The weapon was used extensively in the Civil War but over time had seen little use in the Indian Wars. Besides being heavy, it was noisy (an issue when stealth was necessary for the element of surprise) and was often in the way. One was reported to have been retained by Lieutenant Charles DeRudio, who liked to use it "for killing snakes" but his mount was lost in Reno's charge and thus, there is no evidence to support his claim. None were found on the battlefield after the fight and no Indians observed one used in the fight against them. Despite popular depictions of his last stand, Custer did not use his sabre when his ammunition ran out, because he didn't carry it into the battle.

After two days of marching, the command reached the mouth of the Little Powder River. And then onto Mizpah Creek. Upon reaching the Mizpah, Reno's orders were to descend the creek to where it reached the Rosebud. However, the relatively high ground between the two north–south waterways and good visibility allowed Reno to observe no Indian activity. As a result, he disregarded his orders to move to Pumpkin Creek and went onto the Tongue River. In the meantime, Boyer and the scouts had found the site of the formerly occupied Indian village near Rosebud Creek which Lieutenant Bradley had located several weeks earlier. This was the first concrete intelligence of Indian presence observed. Where exactly the village had moved was unknown, but to know which direction the Indians had moved would be important to General Terry. Reno decided to disregard orders to scout the Tongue further north and instead followed the Indian trail.

On June 17, the command halted a few miles short of Rosebud Creek. The scouts fanned out, looking for Indian signs. Boyer and the scouts found evidence of two other camps and a new trail—all headed south. Boyer believed the Indian camp was likely several days' ride further west. By the increasing signs of other smaller trails converging with larger trails, there were many Sioux present. Worried about increasing Indian signs, the command went into camp (with higher security) to determine the next move.

Just seven days out from the planned 12-day scout, the soldiers and their horses were tired. Interestingly, the Indians they worried about were not in the immediate vicinity, but already further west on the Little Bighorn River and fighting Crook. Of course Reno did not know this, but he had seen enough. For the next two days they headed north to the mouth of the Rosebud on the Yellowstone River. Colonel Gibbon's Montana Column was just across the river on the north side. Custer and a refitted remainder of the 7th Cavalry and General Terry were now just a few miles downriver and upon news of Reno's position, would move west toward him.

Reno had sent a message to General Terry shortly after his arrival on the Yellowstone and Terry was not happy with the news. Reno had disregarded his orders and perhaps doomed the entire campaign. The major purpose of Reno's scout was to determine where the Indians were not. That is, Terry presumed the Indians had moved further west, but he could not risk the possibility of them potentially slipping by the Dakota Column by moving south and east. Terry still did not know where the Indians were.

Custer too was angry. In an anonymous letter to the *New York Herald* in June 1876, he wrote, "Had Reno, after first violating his orders, pursued and overtaken the Indians, his original disobedience would have been overlooked, but his determination forsook him at that point, and instead of continuing the pursuit, and at least bringing the Indians to bay, he gave the order to countermarch and faced his command to the rear." Custer's words confirm the instincts he had followed throughout his career, always bold, always on the offensive. Pursue the enemy and pitch into them. He had followed the same tactics throughout the Civil War and during the Indian Wars. The battle of the Washita was a textbook example. His words also confirm why General Terry did not want him commanding the scout. If Custer had been given the mission and followed his instincts, the battle of the Little Bighorn would have simply happened earlier, albeit with a slightly smaller force. Reno's information though would require a change of plans and General Terry set about doing so.

Arrival at the Little Bighorn

Onboard the steamer *Far West*, General Terry's temporary headquarters, members of the separate columns and Terry's staff met on the afternoon of June 21 to finalize elements of the modified plan. Terry's scouts believed the Sioux were likely encamped somewhere along the Little Bighorn River or even as far as the larger Bighorn River. This meant the entire campaign should shift west. The smaller Montana Column, slower mostly because of its infantry, would best serve as a blocking force. As a result and without delay, General Terry had ordered Colonel Gibbon and the Montana Column (minus its cavalry) to travel west along the Yellowstone River. It would travel to the mouth of the Bighorn River and await Terry and the *Far West* to assist them in crossing the Yellowstone before moving south along the Bighorn River. They would then continue further south if necessary to the confluence of the Little Bighorn River with an expected June 26 arrival. The 7th Cavalry would serve as the larger and more mobile attacking force.

Departing the present camp near the Yellowstone River and Rosebud Creek on June 22, the 7th would travel down Rosebud Creek to its headwaters before moving west toward the Little Bighorn, ensuring the Indians were not escaping east or south. It was estimated this trip would take four days of march allowing the convergence of the two columns in the region on or about June 26. Before leaving, Custer was offered the four companies of the 4th Cavalry from the Montana Column to augment the 7th Cavalry along with two Gatling guns. He passed on both. He believed the towed Gatling guns would slow him down. Also, he would be traveling over a lot of the same ground as the Reno scout and the reports of the challenges they faced only confirmed his beliefs. The pass on additional cavalry is seemingly nonsensical. The additional four companies would give the attacking force potentially 18 companies of cavalry—the more the better. But, the refusal represented Custer's thoughts about the upcoming engagement.

First, Custer believed there were far fewer Indians present among the roamers than the rather large actual group. Custer shared before leaving their last camp on the Yellowstone River that he believed the Indian strength was at 1,500, with even less warriors. The well-equipped 7th Cavalry, he reasoned, could handle those numbers easily. Additionally, he did not want the mixing of regiments. As bizarre as it seems, the addition of troops and leaders from another regiment which he did not know well could serve to reduce the 7th Cavalry Regiment's combat effectiveness. Custer also knew he did not want any more unknowns than he was already dealing with. Custer also did not want to share the glory of a successful Indian campaign with anyone but the 7th Cavalry. The 4th Cavalry returned to the Montana Column and would be among the first to find the horrific scene of the Custer disaster a few days later.

There has been extensive analysis of General Terry's written orders just before Custer leading up to the battle of the Little Bighorn. True to his nature, Terry's orders reflected more attorney than military commander—noncommittal instructions right down the middle. The greater risk facing Terry was a failure, not success, and he knew it. He commanded the campaign but was no Indian fighter. He was reliant on Custer for his experience.

Terry wrote, in camp at the mouth of Rosebud River, on June 22, 1876:

> The Brigadier General commanding directs that as soon as your regiment can be made ready for the march, you proceed up the Rosebud in pursuit of the Indians whose trail was discovered by Major Reno a few days ago. It is, of course, impossible to give you any definite instructions regarding this movement, and were it not impossible to do so, the Department commander places too much confidence in your zeal, energy, and ability to wish to impose upon you precise orders which might hamper your action when nearly in contact with the enemy. He will, however, indicate to you his views of what your action should be, and he desires that you should conform to them unless you shall see sufficient reason for departing from them. He thinks that you should proceed up the Rosebud until you ascertain definitely the direction in which the trail above spoken of leads. Should it be found, as it appears to be almost certain that it will be found, to turn toward the Little Big Horn he thinks that you should still proceed southward, perhaps as far as the headwaters of the Tongue, and then turn toward the Little Big Horn, feeling constantly, however, to your left so as to preclude the possibility of the escape of the Indians to the south or southeast by passing around your left flank.

Terry's concern was the escape of the Indians, as indicated by the last few lines of his orders. Less certain, were his instructions for the offensive part of finding and attacking the Indians. He was relying on Custer's expertise for that. In the end, his orders were neither directive nor confining. If the campaign were successful he could claim credit, if it failed they could not blame his orders as the cause. While final preparations were underway to leave Powder River Camp, Custer took a few minutes to write what would be his final words to Libbie. In a letter dated June 22, 1876, from the camp at the junction of the Yellowstone and Rosebud rivers, Montana Territory, Custer characteristically tried to abate her fears:

> My darling—I have but a few moments to write as we start at twelve, and I have my hands full of preparations for the scout. Do not be anxious about me. You would be surprised how closely I obey your instructions about keeping with the column. I hope to have a good report to send you by the next mail. A success will start us all toward Lincoln.

The letter was telling about how well Custer knew Libbie and how sensitive he was to her fears. His optimism about his return to her concealed what he knew would be the tough and dangerous culmination of the campaign. His sentiments revealed something further, the desire to return home. Custer could get homesick for Libbie as is well documented, but once he was on the campaign his focus was on completing the mission. Returning to Fort Lincoln seemed to be the mission in this letter and "success" the necessary task to perform to get there.

As Custer was writing to Libbie from the Montana Territory, Libbie was penning a June 22 letter from Fort Lincoln to Custer too. She wrote:

> My own darling—I dreamed of you as I knew I should. Colonel P. has sent word by scouts that the Post is to be attacked. I don't feel alarmed, because we have so cool and cautious a commanding officer. He is vigilance itself. I am getting this off by to-morrow's mail to [Fort] Buford. Oh, Autie how I feel about your going away so long without our hearing … Your safety is ever in my mind. My thoughts, my dreams my prayers, are all for you. God bless and keep safe my darling. Ever your own, Libbie.

She had always feared for Custer, and these letters exchanged 12 years after their marriage confirm the love they still shared. Libbie's mention of the possible threat to Fort Lincoln needed not to be mentioned as she had already professed the confidence she had in the commander of the fort. It was a light "touch" to remind Custer that she needed him home to feel truly safe.

In the words of the 7th Cavalry's surviving senior officer, Major Marcus Reno, stated in his *Official Report of Major Marcus A. Reno,* dated July 5, 1876, at the Powder River Camp:

> The Regiment left the camp at the mouth of the Rosebud River … on the afternoon of the 22nd day of June, and marched up the Rosebud 12 miles and encamped; 23rd, marched up the Rosebud, passing many old Indian camps, and following a very large pole-trail, but not fresh, making 33 miles; 24th, the march was continued up the Rosebud, the trail and signs freshening

with every mile, until we had made 28 miles, and we then encamped and waited for information from the scouts. At 9:25 p.m. Custer called the officers together and informed us that beyond a doubt the village was in the valley of the Little Bighorn, and to reach it was necessary to cross the divide between the Rosebud and the Little Bighorn, and it would be impossible to do so in the day-time without discovering our march to the Indians; that we would prepare to march at 11 p.m. This was done, the line of march turning from the Rosebud to the right up to one of its branches which headed near the summit of the divide. About 2 a.m. on the 25th the scouts told him that he could not cross the divide before daylight.

The scouts were cautious, they had seen enough signs to know the Indian village before them was arguably the largest they had ever observed. They also did not share Custer's confidence in certain victory. Custer brought his officers together for an officer's call. Lieutenant Godfrey was among those present and remembered the curious event in an article for *Century Magazine* in 1892:

> All officers were requested to make to him [Custer] any suggestions they thought fit. This "talk" of his, as we called it, was considered at the time as something extraordinary for General Custer, for it was not his habit to unbosom himself to his officers. In it he showed concessions and a reliance on others; there was an indefinable something that was not Custer. His manner and tone, usually brusque and aggressive, or somewhat curt, was on this occasion conciliating and subdued. There was something akin to an appeal, as if depressed, that made a deep impression on all present. We compared watches to get the official time, and separated to attend to our various duties. Lieutenants McIntosh, Wallace [killed at the Battle of Wounded Knee, December 29, 1890], and myself walked to our bivouac, for some distance in silence, when Wallace remarked: "Godfrey, I believe General Custer is going to be killed." "Why? Wallace," I replied, "what makes you think so?" "Because," said he, "I have never heard Custer talk in that way before."

There was something different about Custer. Outwardly, on the surface, not too much. He was 37 years old though, and a seasoned soldier. He had fought in numerous campaign battles during the Civil War and with the Indians on the plains of Kansas. He was tired, and only in a way 15 years in the saddle could make someone. He maintained the same vigor in front of the men, but there were many unknowns for Custer about this campaign. Moreover, Custer knew it. In part, this explains his solicitation from his officers—a novel event for him. But lieutenants Godfrey and Wallace identified something further. Custer, in the entire time they had known him, was never indecisive. Custer appeared so now, and it made his officers nervous.

From the Crow's Nest, a well-known viewing point on a high ridge, Custer's scouts desired precise knowledge of what lay in front of them. By the early hours of the 25th, the scouts could see for the first time an enormous pony herd grazing and the smoke of campfires. The chief of scouts, Lieutenant Charles Varnum and Custer came forward to see for themselves. Through using borrowed field glasses they could see nothing. The scouts were insistent the village was there and it was large. A heated conversation then began between the half-Sioux scout Mitch Boyer, borrowed from General Terry, and Custer, who was heard to say "I've got as good eyes as anybody and I can't see any village Indians." Lieutenant Varnum added he could not see either.

At which point Mitch Boyer said, "Well General, if you don't find more Indians in that valley than you ever saw together, you can hang me." Upon Custer's return from the Crow's Nest, he learned the command had surely been discovered. A detail sent looking for lost supplies found Indians on a back trail and they had to come from a nearby village. Any hope of surprise was fleeting.

Both horses and troopers were exhausted as they crossed into the valley of the Little Bighorn. Lieutenant Godfrey recalled in *Century Magazine* in January 1892 about the Little Bighorn area at the time of the battle:

> The Little Bighorn River, or the "Greasy Grass" as it is known to the Indians, is a rapid, tortuous mountain stream from twenty to forty yards wide, with pebbled bottom, but abrupt, soft banks. The water at the ordinary stage is from two or five feet in depth, depending upon the width of the channel. The general direction of its course is northeasterly down to the Little Bighorn battle-fields, where it trends northwesterly to its confluence with the Bighorn River. The other topographical features of the country which concern us in this narrative may be briefly described as follows: Between the Little Bighorn and Bighorn rivers is a plateau of undulating prairie; between the Little Bighorn and the Rosebud are the Little Chetish or the Wolf Mountains. By this it must not be misunderstood as a rocky upheaval chain or spur of mountains, but it is a rough, broken country of considerable elevation, of high precipitous hills and deep, narrow gulches.

Edward Settle Godfrey (shown here as a general later in his career) was a 1st Lieutenant and Company K's commander at the Little Bighorn. He performed admirably in the Reno-Benteen defense, calmly covering a retreat from Weir Point that could have cost the regiment the loss of two more companies to the attacking Indians. After the Little Bighorn, Godfrey authored several accounts of the battle that provided scholars with valuable details of the fight. (Little Bighorn National Monument)

It was terrible ground for cavalry operations and no one in the command had spent any great amount of time there—they knew nothing about the ground they would fight on.

Near noon the regiment was called to a halt and reorganized. Custer, accompanied by Regimental Adjutant, Lieutenant William W. Cooke, rode off alone to determine just how the regiment would be tactically formed to maximize its strengths for the coming fight. Custer's thoughts on organization were influenced by several factors. First, his greatest concern was the likely escape of the Indian encampment. The Plains Indians were gifted at dissolving and disappearing before a fight could be brought. Arguably the finest light cavalry in the world, the Indians wanted a fight on their terms but also were concerned primarily with the protection of the women, children and the elderly. Time and time again on previous campaigns, Custer and other commanders were left attacking empty camps, detecting trails which led away, and finally trails which disappeared altogether. The 7th Cavalry had been successful at the Washita because of cold winter weather and the element of surprise. Of course, the summer weather would not provide an advantage in limiting the Indian movement, but Custer believed he might still achieve surprise. This was a much bigger camp, with more warriors than at the Washita, but it also had more non-combatants who would be vulnerable. If they could be captured, it may persuade the permanent roamers and their summer additions to yield and return to their respective agencies. The plan would require several elements creating a fixing force and several other elements designed to envelop and exploit the opportunities which developed (an evolving offensive battle). Custer knew who these elements would be.

Custer would always be predisposed to select his "favorites" or sometimes referred to as the "Custer Clan" in his division of troops. These were the commanders he considered the most reliable and he wanted them under his direct command. Of course this would include his brother Tom, recently promoted to captain, the commander of Company C. First Lieutenant James "Jimmie" Calhoun, his sister Margaret Custer's husband, considered to be the most handsome officer in the 7th and commander of Company L. Also included was the Irishman Captain Myles Keogh, the commander of Company I, a veteran of the Papal wars and a brevet lieutenant colonel of the American Civil War. Keogh was the senior captain of the Custer wing and only 36 years old, one year younger than Custer. Finally, two other officers, First Lieutenant Algernon Smith of Company E, a badly wounded veteran of the Civil War, but well respected by his troops, and First Lieutenant George Yates, a Michigander whom Custer knew during the Civil War and had helped earn a commission in the 7th. These five companies and their commanders would form the Custer Battalion.

Captain Frederick Benteen would command a second battalion consisting of his own Company H along with companies K and D, numbering over 100 men. Benteen's subordinate commanders were an odd lot. Captain Edward Godfrey, who commanded Company K, would later be promoted to a general officer before the end of his career, and would also earn the Medal of Honor during the Indian Wars. Captain Weir of Company D by reputation was a solid officer, but had a tremendous thirst for the bottle.

Major Marcus Reno would command the final battalion, companies A, G, and M. The three respective company commanders enjoyed good reputations in the regiment.

Captain Thomas French, commanding Company M, was a competent officer and arguably one of the best shots in the regiment. 1st Lieutenant Donald McIntosh commanded Company G. Well-liked by his men and officers alike, "Tosh" as all called him, also had the distinction of being part North American Indian. Lieutenant Myles Moylan, commanding Company A, was a former enlisted man serving with Custer during the Civil War. Custer had recommended him for a commission and he did not disappoint. He had a reputation as a very capable officer.

Reno, in contrast to his commanders, had a mixed reputation. He had established a good record during the Civil War rising to the rank of brevet colonel in the regular Army and brevet brigadier general of volunteers. But, he was dark, moody, and difficult to like. It was probably well earned. He had a reputation as someone who liked to drink and was an angry drunk. Second, in seniority next to Custer in the regiment, he neither inspired others nor left them with confidence in his leadership.

Rounding out the division of the command was the supply wagon train under Lieutenant Edward Mathey, but protected by Company B, commanded by Captain

Many of the Custer Clan are included in this rare 7th Cavalry Officers group photograph taken in 1873 at Fort Abraham Lincoln in front of the Custer residence prior to the Little Bighorn campaign. Pictured in uniform second from left is Lieutenant George Wallace, with Lieutenant Colonel George Custer and Lieutenant Benjamin Hodgson appearing jauntily to Wallace's right. Captain George Yates appears seated in the center of the picture, with Margaret Custer Calhoun seated to his left and rear. Captain Tom Custer stands at the top of the stairs in the final row at the far right. Captain Thomas Weir is standing just right of the stairs, partially obscured, and Lieutenant Donald McIntosh at the far right. (State Historical Society of North Dakota)

Thomas McDougall. Each company in the regiment would detail seven troopers to the pack train to provide extra support. The pack train, in addition to extra rations, contained the invaluable reserve ammunition. The troopers only carried with them 100 rounds of the Model 1873 Springfield single-shot carbine ammunition and another 25 rounds of Model 1873 Colt pistol ammunition, and the reserve ammunition would be required for an extended engagement. The supply wagons and Company B would follow the entire regiment. The supply wagons trailed the main column on average 2–3 miles behind.

The village lay some 15 miles ahead, west and slightly north, but Custer had not determined the location precisely. The trail was the freshest in the direction of the Little Bighorn River valley but there was also a noticeable lesser trail leading south. He strongly suspected the village was west and he was instinctively inclined to move in that direction immediately with the entire command. He had chastised Major Reno (both inside of the command and anonymously in the press) for not pursuing immediately when there was evidence the Indians lay within his grasp. General Terry's orders to scout the southern region of his area of operations to ensure the Indians would not elude them were quite clear however and he could not risk the possibility entirely. As a result, as soon as the command cleared the divide around noon, he sent Captain Benteen with his three companies to the south. Benteen's orders were to take his companies several miles to the south to a line of bluffs about two miles distant. From there, move west through a series of hills, reporting anything he came across. As he moved further west, he should begin to observe the valley of the Little Bighorn more definitively and any of the information would be of value to the command. Additionally, he was to "pitch into" anything he might come across. Benteen responded predictably, he protested. He hated Custer and saw this move (a detour) as an opportunity to keep him and the companies in his command out of the coming fight.

Benteen had other complaints. He was being sent out into uncharted country no one in his command knew anything about and it could be full of Indians. With the enormous amount of Indian signs the scouts had shared, the potential number of Indians could easily be more than his men could handle. Likewise, he reasoned if Custer encountered the large Indian village, wouldn't it be more prudent to keep the regiment together? The two commands would be putting more ground between their mutual support and him, which was never a good idea. But Custer had done exactly that at the battle of the Washita and it worked. He believed it would work here as well. He was not worried. As Benteen marched away with his three companies, he was covering Custer's orders from General Terry and any concern about any Indian escape to the south. If Custer came across an emerging need he could quickly recall Benteen in time. His decision indicates he had to pay attention to possibilities in the south and he also couched a calculated risk in the space between the commands. It made tactical sense to Custer and was perfectly in step with his experience.

As Benteen disappeared to the south, the rest of the regiment headed west. Custer gave instructions to Major Reno as well. He was to take his battalion, companies A, G, and M, cross Sun Dance Creek to the south side and parallel the rest of the regiment (the five companies Custer retained in his immediate command) which would remain on the north side of the creek and advance west. The scouts, under the command of a now-exhausted Lieutenant Varnum, were out front of the regiment, reconnoitering everything in the immediate vicinity. Staying ahead of the increasingly impatient Custer was a problem. Frustratingly, the additional few miles of movement west had revealed nothing about a village. The ground on which they traveled was a series of north–south running gullies and ravines, each one requiring a climb and descent only to encounter another. Custer realized the phenomena were also plaguing Benteen and sent several couriers to him with messages to be less thorough and deliberate on his movement.

Reno and Custer kept sight of one another for over half an hour until they came across the remains of a small village containing one standing tepee, which contained a Sioux warrior on a funeral stand in beautiful attire, a recent casualty of the battle of

With friendly smile and prematurely gray hair Captain Frederick Benteen appears more like a grandfather than the officer more often referred to as the "Savior of the Seventh." Indeed, Benteen demonstrated exceptional leadership and courage at the Little Bighorn, assuming pseudo command for the Reno-Benteen defense. Taciturn and vengeful, he hated Custer from their first meeting, and challenged him at every opportunity. Some in the Army and the public knew of Benteen's feelings about Custer and sought to hang the Little Bighorn disaster on him for failing to come to Custer's aid. (Little Bighorn National Monument)

the Rosebud with Crook's Wyoming Column. While the Indian scouts made quick work of desecrating the tepee and warrior, the rest of the command tried to discern the meaning of what they observed in the recently abandoned village. Campfires still smoked, and the site gave every indication the Indians who had just left had departed quickly. Were the Indians already starting to scatter? Were they moving west and north up the valley? Custer had to know and act quickly. He already suspected it may be too late to capture them. Nowhere in his thought process was the belief these small bands observed by the scouts exiting the area, were moving west to join an immense village—the largest Indian village ever observed on the North American plains.

Reno's Charge

> I, however, soon saw that I was being drawn into some trap, as they would certainly fight harder and especially as we were nearing their village which was still standing; besides, I could not see Custer or any other support, and at the same time the very earth seemed to grow Indians. They were running toward me in swarms and from all directions. I saw I must defend myself and give up the attack mounted. This I did.
>
> MAJOR MARCUS RENO, 7TH CAVALRY REGIMENT, ABOUT HIS CHARGE IN HIS OFFICIAL REPORT, DATED JULY 5, 1876, AFTER THE BATTLE OF THE LITTLE BIGHORN

While Custer and the rest of the command were getting ready to move, the Indians encamped along the Little Bighorn were going about their normal daily life. It was already proving to be a hot day and many were taking advantage of the cool water of the river to bathe. The "hostile" Indians, principally Sitting Bull's Hunkpapa band of Sioux and a band of Northern Cheyenne associated with Crazy Horse had never succumbed to agency life. Instead, these two bands and a few others roamed the unceded region hunting buffalo and pursuing the old life. Normally, these two bands would add up to perhaps a few hundred warriors together with their families. In his book *Wild Life on the Plains*, 1885, Captain Frederick Benteen relates the bands came together "by a mere alliance of convenience" rather than any particular "patriarchal ties." The winters of 1874 and 1875 being harsh, and agency Indians receiving less than promised rations, the numbers swelled significantly during the summer. Benteen estimated "The village of Crazy Horse, at the close of 1875 was found to contain one hundred and five lodges, which at the ordinary rate of five or six warriors to a lodge … furnished a force of about five hundred warriors." He continued, "Sitting Bull's band probably then numbered at least one hundred and fifty lodges, he being a more famous chief than Crazy Horse." By the following summer of 1876 both Sitting Bull's and Crazy Horse's groups had grown significantly with the nearly constant arrival of more agency Indians.

On the morning of June 25, 1876 as Custer's scouts peered through trees on a ridge above the site of the lone tepee, they could see just the beginning of the

Indian encampment. Lieutenant Edward Godfrey recalled in 1892 about the camp, "For two or three days their camp had been pitched on the site where they were attacked. The place was not selected with the view to making that the battle-field of the campaign, but, whoever was in the van [the lead] on their march thought it a good place to camp, put up his tepee, and the others, as they arrived, followed his example. It is customary among the Indians to camp by bands. The bands usually camp some distance apart, and Indians of the number then together would occupy a territory of several miles along the river valley, and not necessarily within supporting distance of each other."

The nearest to them was Sitting Bull's Hunkpapa band, one of six "circles" of lodges nestled among the timber, each next to the south side of the bends of the Little Bighorn River. Other Hunkpapas were represented by chiefs Gall, Crow King, and Black Moon; Oglala under Crazy Horse, Low Dog, and Big Road; the Miniconjou followers of Hump; Sans Arc, Blackfoot, and Brule Sioux. There were also Northern Cheyennes under Two Moon, Lame White Man, and Dirty Moccasins, and a handful of warriors from tribes of Eastern Sioux. Robert S. Utley, Chief Historian at the Custer Battlefield Monument from 1947–52, wrote in his three-volume set, *Custer Battlefield Monument—Montana* from 1942, "all together they numbered perhaps 10,000 to 12,000 people mustering a fighting force of between 2,500 and 4,000 men. Many had firearms—some the Winchester repeating rifle obtained, quite legally, from traders and Indian agents for hunting." The sprawl of the village extended some three miles in length throughout the river bottom, with lodges interspersed among trees and vegetation. In between the village and extending over a bench of land to the south was an enormous pony herd of over 10,000 animals grazing on the summer grass.

George Herendeen, the interpreter for Custer's scouts, peered over the ridge above the village and he had seen enough. He communicated to Custer he believed the Indians who had just left the lone teepee site along with those further west were fragmenting. He could see dust clouds ahead of him drifting to the north and west. Major Reno and his three companies had crossed the creek at the teepee site and were at a halt, several troopers watering their mounts. Soon, Adjutant William Cooke galloped up to Reno, stopping his horse in a cloud of dust—he had orders. Reno was directed to cross over the creek, progress down the left bank, then cross the Little Bighorn River. After, he was instructed to charge the village with his three companies. Custer offered further that "he [Reno] would be supported by the whole outfit."

Reno turned in his saddle and off the battalion went at a trot. Cooke and Captain Myles Keogh accompanied Reno until they approached the river, and then Cooke and Keogh returned to Custer. This is important, as these two seasoned officers would share all they had seen up to their return to Custer. Meanwhile, Lieutenant Varnum, who had been scouting the left side of the creek, had returned with news about what lay in front of Reno. Excited, but exhausted from nearly a full day of being in the saddle, he reported to Custer, "The valley in front is full of Indians."

With Reno's battalion attacking, Custer's observation was that this was a rearguard action to protect the village, a predictable reaction. This meant the non-combatant women and children were fleeing upriver. The capture of the women and children being decisive to success, persuading the warriors to lay down their arms, Custer's plan had to change to seize upon this opportunity. With the bluffs to his immediate right front and the other end of the village beyond the bluffs, Custer's only feasible course was to deploy around the bluffs to the right and move upriver, looking for the first fording opportunity further to the west. From there he could envelop or penetrate the other end of the village, cutting off the line of escape.

Reno's charge or "fixing" action could keep the warriors home, fighting the troopers who were the immediate threat to them. Satisfied with Varnum's report and feeling he had a good grasp for what lay in front of him, he released Varnum and the scouts to Major Reno. Shots could be heard coming from the direction of the valley. No word from Captain Benteen. Turning to Lieutenant Cooke, Custer

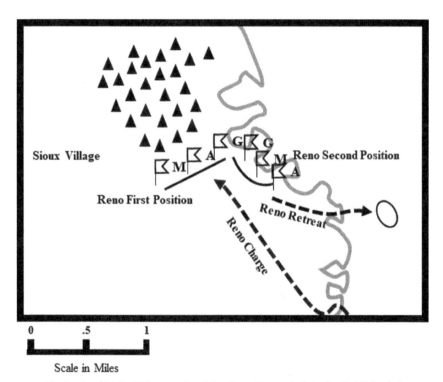

The battle of Little Bighorn, valley fight, June 25, 1876. (Map by Ted Behncke)

gave the order for the column of five companies to start a movement to the right, up the bluffs, and beyond.

After a two-and-a-half mile movement at a fast gait, Major Reno could see the tops of the Indian lodges coming into view ahead. There were many lodges and they were intermixed with the cottonwood trees and continued far into the distance. There was smoke coming from the Indian campfires and Reno could see women and children moving about. The village had a sleepy feel to it and inhabitants were unaware of the storm coming their way. Reno had a clear line of vision and the ability to maneuver, so he deployed his companies from a column of four troopers abreast into a skirmish line with Company M on the left of the line, Company A in the middle and Company G on the right, just touching a stand of timber near the river. The Indian scouts were released and went to collecting ponies out of the Sioux Indian herd on the far left of the battalion skirmish line. Each trooper had dismounted, giving the reins to the fourth man or horse holder, who remained behind with the responsibility for his buddies' horses and their equipment, the other three troopers moving forward to the skirmish line. The tactic was Army drill, but it reduced the troopers available to engage the Indians by 25 percent. With approximately 140 troopers in Reno's battalion, this meant only a little over 100 troopers were on the skirmish line firing. The horses were moved to the rear for protection as the first few trooper bullets whizzed into the village. The initial damage was to splintered lodge poles and holes in the lodge skins. As the troopers' fire increased, women and children were increasingly hit, innocent and unintended casualties. Warriors started running toward the sounds of the firing and began firing back. Soon there was so much smoke lingering in the air from the shooting, it was difficult to see more than a few feet. Warriors were yelling war whoops to encourage others, escalating the overall level of fright and terror. Two cavalry horses were too terrified to stop and carried their riders into the village, never to return. First Sergeant John Ryan of Company M recalled one of these terrifying accounts for the June 22, 1923 edition of the Hardin, *Montana Tribune*, "Private James Turley of my troop when we arrived at the timber and had orders to halt, could not control his horse which carried him towards the Indian camp. That was the last I saw of him." Turley may have been the very first casualty, disappearing into the smoke of the village, likely being dragged from his horse and killed in the village.

The arrival of the troopers genuinely surprised the village. Sitting Bull, in an interview in 1877 said, "I was lying in my lodge. Some young men ran into me and said: 'The Long Hair is in the camp. Get up. They are firing into the camp.' I said, all right. I jumped up and stepped out of my lodge." The old men, the women and the children had already begun fleeing away from the firing. Low Dog, an Oglala chief, also commented in 1881 on the village's surprise, "I heard the alarm, but I did not believe it. I thought it was a false alarm. I did not think it possible that any white men would attack us, as strong as we were."

Major Reno had interpreted his orders to mean Custer would be following him into the fight, most likely with the other five companies of the regiment. He was ordered to charge the village, but unexpectedly the Indians were now moving toward his battalion and in disturbingly large numbers. Sitting Bull described their early movements. "Oh, we fell back, but it was not what warriors call a retreat; it was to gain time. My people fought him here in the brush."

Lieutenant Luther Hare, second in command of the scouts, later testified during the Reno Inquiry that shortly after the skirmish line was established "four to five hundred Indians came out of a coulee four hundred yards in front of us." Soon outnumbered, Reno believed conditions to remain on the offense were beginning to change. The firing from the troopers was "hot" and for the moment the situation was stable, but Reno wondered how long they could hold. Sitting Bull for his part thought they (the Indians) were "whipped" in the opening moments but his read on the situation changed after a few minutes. In fact, he later stated about the fearful opening moments, "There was so much doubt about it that I started down there [west end of the village] to tell the squaws to pack up the lodges and get ready to move away." The warriors in the village were marshaling ponies and equipment during the chaos, and with the women and children behind them, they could move forward to concentrate on the troopers. Cheyenne Chief Low Dog's *Leavenworth Times* account from August 18, 1881, recalled the moment clearly, "When I got my gun and came out of my lodge the attack had begun at the end of the camp where Sitting Bull and the Uncpapas were. The Indians held their ground to give the women and children time to get out of the way. By this time the herders were driving in the horses and as I was nearly at the further end of the camp, I ordered my men to catch their horses and get out of the way, and my men were hurrying to go and help those that were fighting." The increasing Indian numbers and rifle fire were making a difference and the pitch of the battle would soon change.

Custer had not shared his movement to the right of the bluff with Reno. The battle was evolving, and it was not uncommon for Custer to keep his subordinates in the dark as long as he felt in control. Several members of Reno's battalion knew where Custer's command had gone though, they could see the gray horses of Company E, part of the Custer Column, on the ridge beyond the bluffs. Lieutenant Charles DeRudio with Company A and fighting in the center of the skirmish line on the valley floor, said he saw Custer and Lieutenant Cook on the bluff waving their hats and cheering to the troops below. Lieutenant DeRudio's observations are significant. Custer, from his position, could see Reno on the skirmish line and the Indians moving with growing in numbers to his front. Custer could also discern the fighting was heavy and, as Reno had stopped his "charge" short of the village, there would likely be no more advance. Finally, Custer's enthusiasm observed by Lieutenant DeRudio, strongly suggested he thought the action in the valley was serving the developing battle plan. While Reno's charge had sputtered, it was still serving very well as a "fixing" movement and drawing warriors to him. Custer could see the large numbers of Indians below him and it reinforced this belief. Custer intended to find a river crossing further upriver and envelop the village at the other end. There, he reasoned, would be the vulnerable fleeing women and children so essential to a victory. He was still on the offense and events as they were evolving fit his overall battle plan. He ordered his five companies further north and west along the bluffs.

Down in the valley, Lieutenant Benjamin "Benny" Hodgson, Reno's adjutant, was "trooping the line," moving up and down the skirmish line, sharing guidance from Reno and collecting a status of ammunition and situation reports from the company commanders. The skirmish line had advanced only about 100 yards since the dismount even though the firing was steady. The increasing Indian fire threatened the horses, so the horse holders moved to the shelter of the timber on the right side of the line near the river. Company M on the left and Company A in the center were holding their own, but Lieutenant Donald McIntosh of Company G reported Indians were infiltrating the timber on his right. The Indians were using the ground vegetation and the turns of the riverbanks to their advantage, covering their movements.

Captain French commanding Company M on the left of the line reported the Indians might soon be able to "turn his corner," flanking him. The Indian firing on the left was coming dangerously close to his men and was increasing. The horses which had been safe only minutes before when taken into the timber were now increasingly in danger again. To counter the Indian infiltration, Reno gave orders for Company G to fall back off the skirmish line and establish a defensive position in the timber, focused west. The new "right flank" created by the move was done to deny the Indians an infiltration route and protect the troopers from the Indians' increasing fire.

Canadian-born 1st Lieutenant William W. Cooke was a Civil War veteran and a member of the Custer Clan. During the Indian wars in Kansas he served in a number of roles including commanding a detachment of sharpshooters at the battle of the Washita. At the Little Bighorn, Cooke served as adjutant, scribbling the last communication to come from the Custer battalion. His body was found just feet from Custer's on Last Stand Hill. (Little Bighorn National Monument)

The troopers of Company A were shocked to see the sudden movement of Company G into the timber, but even more concerned about the identifiable gap in their already thin skirmish line. After almost 30 minutes of continuous firing, troopers across the line were also running out of the 50 rounds of carbine ammunition with them. By ones and twos, the troopers were randomly and independently returning to their horses for their reserve ammunition in their saddlebags. To the Indians facing the skirmish line, the sudden departure of troopers to the rear for ammunition looked like a retreat. The holes left by troopers in the skirmish line encouraged the warriors to step up their fight. Trooper casualties were also starting to mount up, particularly in the vulnerable center of the line where Company A was taking fire from both ends of the Indian lines. No one had yet been killed, but suddenly Sergeant Myles O'Hara dropped to the ground with a mortal wound to the abdomen. O'Hara had recently been promoted to sergeant while on the march and was well-liked. The sergeant's death shook the resolve of many on the skirmish line. The troopers were starting to "bunch up," an innate self-preservation phenomenon, each trooper seeking the support of one another. The integrity of the skirmish line was disintegrating.

By now Major Reno was aware Custer was not going to support him from the rear. Reno also knew his "charge" had faltered, and the skirmish line was becoming more untenable by the minute. If Reno did not do something and do it immediately, he might lose his battalion. The only cover available was in the timber with Company G. He gave the order for Company A and Company M to abandon the skirmish line and fall back into the timber. The troopers of Company A were the first to sprint to the tree line, anchoring a position now on the left of the line on the bank of an old dry bend of the river. Company M fell back into the center of the position tying in with the same dry riverbank and finding some well-received cover behind it. The new defense looked like a "half-moon" with the companies arranged A-M-G, with Company G being the most northerly positioned. All companies had the Little Bighorn River to their backs. They had left wounded behind on the valley floor to their doom to the advancing Indians, but for the moment the surviving troopers had improved their position. It would not last.

Five miles away to the southeast of Reno, Captain Benteen and his men were emerging from some hilly, difficult terrain. Benteen's horses were tired and thirsty, and he had no idea that Reno was engaged in an attack on the village. Benteen's orders were to "pitch into anything he found" and then report to Custer, but he had done neither. His actions had no malice nor neglect, Benteen had found nothing and he had nothing to report. He had heard nothing from Custer either, and so far Benteen rightly believed he had been sent on a wasted mission. The lack of activity left him curious as to what was happening. The Benteen battalion caught the noticeable trail of the rest of the regiment ahead of the supply train which they could see about a mile distant and off to the east. A lone rider could be seen coming in their direction, probably an orderly dispatched from Captain McDougall. Surprisingly, the rider turned out to be Custer's younger brother Boston, hurriedly moving to

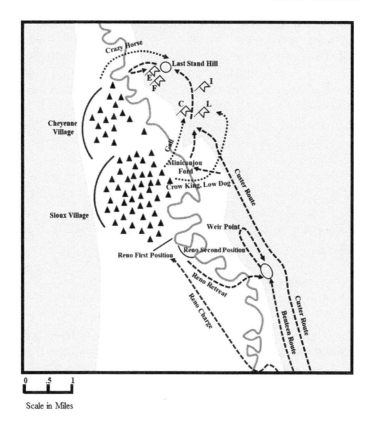

The battle of Little Bighorn, June 25–27, 1876. (Map by Ted Behncke)

the north and west. Boston had been with the pack train but was now moving to join his older brothers, no doubt believing he would miss the show. With a hearty wave but exchanging no words with Benteen, young Boston moved on his way to his eventual death on Last Stand Hill. Shortly after, Benteen stopped at a morass where the groundwater was good to water the horses. He was still several miles away from Reno and further away from Custer.

Meanwhile, Custer had begun his move above and beyond the bluffs with his five companies. Now nominally split into two wings, Company E and F formed one wing traveling together, Captain George Yates in command, while the other wing consisted of companies C, L and I with Captain Myles Keogh in command also traveling together. Custer, with the command group and immediate staff, moved to the edge of the bluffs on the east side of the river, while the two wings came to a halt. For the first time, Custer could see portions of the village through the trees and occasionally glimpse women and children running toward the west and north. Sergeant Daniel Kanipe, a 23-year-old Company C trooper assigned to Custer's headquarters detachment, recalled, "Reno and his troops were again seen to our left, moving at full speed down the valley. At the sight of the Indian camps, the boys of our five troops began to cheer. Some of the horses became so excited their riders were unable to hold them in ranks, and the last words I heard Custer say were, 'Hold your horses in, boys, there are plenty of them down there for us all.'" Few warriors could be seen, but Custer had seen enough to know the village was far larger than they had expected. Lieutenant Colonel Custer quickly grabbed his brother Tom to send a message back to the pack train. They were now about half a mile away from the river on the east side. Tom Custer called Sergeant Kanipe to carry the message. It was a verbal message to "Go back to [Captain] McDougall and bring the pack train straight across the country." He continued, "Tell him to hurry the pack train to Custer and if any of the packs get loose cut them and let them go; do not stop to tighten them." Without any hesitation, Sergeant Kanipe turned his horse and galloped off to the southeast. Kanipe would find no Indian resistance yet in the country ahead of him on the return trip to the pack train—the command remained on the offense.

Sergeant Kanipe's last image of the living Custer was far different than the familiar version in the press and to the American public. Gone was the boy general with the flowing locks of golden hair. His hair, while still gold, was already thinning at 37 years old and cropped short, which was more practical, and much cooler on the campaign, especially in the hot weather in June. Despite wearing a large, white brimmed, non-regulation hat, Custer still suffered from sunburn to his face. His fair complexion was now marked by a bright red nose and cheekbones. Like his hat, Custer wore a non-regulation uniform, one he found comfortable. On campaign, he wore doeskin fringed trousers substituted for blue wool trousers, and a blue navy shirt with a dropped collar instead of a heavy wool shirt. He had a matching doeskin jacket, but on this hot day it would have been tied on the saddle of his favorite horse, Vic. Around his neck, he wore a red ribbon, a throwback to his days in the Michigan Cavalry Regiment in the Civil War. Many of Custer's leaders liked the look of their commander and emulated him with their dress, especially those in his clan. Custer rounded out his equipment with two British Webley "Bulldog" pistols and a Remington .50 caliber hunting rifle.

In the valley below, conditions were rapidly changing. The ordered "charge" by Major Reno had fizzled, transitioning from an advancing skirmish line to a clear defensive action by falling back into the timber. The Indians had started to turn Reno's left flank before moving his battalion into the momentarily safer tree line. Reno's troopers had exhausted a considerable amount of their ammunition, and there were growing trooper casualties—including Sergeant O'Hara—who were lying dead or dying near the skirmish line. Indians on horseback were beginning to dash in front of the command, carefully concealing themselves behind their ponies as they were moving and screaming in a fashion Plains Indians were well known for.

Sioux Chief Low Dog led warriors across Miniconjou Ford as Custer's battalion climbed the ridge in an attempt to attack the village further upriver. His warriors made repeated attacks on companies C and L, frightening cavalry horses and stranding their troopers to a die in place during their defense. (National Park Service)

In the timber, it was getting increasingly difficult to command and control the defensive action they found themselves in. Several officers, including Company A's commander Captain Moylan and the scout's commander Lieutenant Varnum, thought the position was becoming impossible to hold. On a trip into the wood line, Lieutenant Varnum met the battalion adjutant Lieutenant Benny Hodgson who he thought was acting peculiar. Hodgson continually asked Varnum if Hodgson's horse had been wounded. There were no wounds present, and Hodgson seemed to be off-balance. He and Major Reno were observed earlier passing a bottle among them—fear, panic or inebriation, it could have been all were starting to show.

If Major Reno was still in command of anything, it was impossible to know. The men in the timber were in singles and bunches, many not knowing the distance between others. Between the dust, the sound of firing, and the growing terror of the horses, there were no clear signs of order. Reno would say later in his official inquiry in 1879, "[He] could not stay there unless I stayed there forever." The command was in confusion. Word had passed there was going to be an attempt to leave the timber and the troopers should find their horses. Amid the panic, few troopers were returning fire, some troopers never got the word to find their horses, and several were concerned their officers were already mounted, Captain Moylan and Major Reno among them. While Reno was conferring with a scout named Bloody Knife who was mounted next to him, an Indian bullet smashed into Bloody Knife's brain, splattering blood and brains across Reno's face. Wiping the blood off with his pistol, Reno gave the commands to "dismount," and then, "mount," in rapid succession. He was entirely flustered and erratic. Finally, he said, "Men who wish to make their escape, follow me." With that, he headed to the rear and for the river. There was no plan and no covered retreat. It would become a mass of panicked men, horses, and death. If Reno appeared to have lost control and lacked resolve in pressing his fight, it was not just his men who noticed. Chief Low Dog, an Oglala Sioux who opposed Reno in the valley fight offered his thoughts to the *Leavenworth Times* in August of 1881. Low Dog shared, "I do not say that Reno was a coward. He fought well, but our men were fighting to save their women and children, and drive them back. If Reno and his warriors had fought as Custer and his warriors fought, the battle might have been against us."

While the valley situation was in chaos, Custer was unaware of the extent of it, so he continued his movement further west. With Sergeant Kanipe on his way for more ammunition, Custer moved his five companies along the bluff, looking for a way down to the river and to find a ford, allowing a flanking attack into the village. At the end of the ridge, a clearing among the trees allowed a full view of the village for the first time. It was shocking. Hundreds of lodges were in view, organized into circles. Few warriors were noticed, mostly women and children excitedly moving about. Some Indians appeared to be moving north and west away from Reno's fixing action, but some appeared to be simply staying put. Custer had found what he was after—the women and children, who, if captured, could end the warrior resistance no matter how strong. The number of lodges was disturbing however. He knew the math; with this many lodges there were many thousands in this camp and more warriors than they had estimated.

When he sent Kanipe for the pack train and the reserve ammunition, he knew they would need it for the fight, but he did not send any news or requests to Benteen. Custer knew now he needed more men and he needed them quickly. He briefly discussed it with Lieutenant Cooke, who in turn called for a messenger. Trumpeter John Martin (born Giovanni Martini), an Italian immigrant, reported to Cooke, who shouted a verbal message to Martin—find Captain Benteen, have him bring the pack mules, and to come quickly. With Martin's poor command of English, Cooke reached for his notebook and scribbled a note for him to carry. He wrote "Benteen, Come on. Be quick. Bring Packs. p.s. Bring Packs. WW Cooke." Martin stashed the note and reining his horse around, headed off to the south and east to find Benteen, with full awareness this was a critical moment in the engagement.

While the full strength of warriors present or the precise numbers of Indians in the village were not known, much intelligence was known and much of it shared already in some form, whether inductively or deductively. Major Reno's "charge" was neither a charge nor even an offensive maneuver for any great length of time. The arrival of Major Reno's three companies did surprise the village, but the Indian reaction was unexpectedly strong and fairly rapid. Substantial groups of warriors reacted with immediate return of fire and maneuver, probing both of Reno's flanks. Significantly, the Indians clearly counter-attacked and pushed Reno's skirmish line back and then again pushed the three companies into a hasty defense. Sitting Bull reported the same in the village, "[I] started down to tell the squaws to strike the lodges. I was then on my way up to the right end of the camp, where the first attack was made on us. But before I reached that end of the camp where the Miniconjou and Hunkpapa squaws and children were and where some of the other squaws—Cheyennes and Oglala—had gone, I was overtaken by one of the young warriors, who had just come down from the fight. He called out to me. He said: 'No use to leave camp; every white man is killed.'"

Custer did not fully know Reno had fallen back into the timber, but he did know Reno was significantly engaged with Indians coming toward him, not running in the other direction. Custer also knew the numbers of warriors were far above what was believed, significantly higher. Lieutenant Varnum had reported to Lieutenant Cooke both the greater numbers and their movements. Two couriers were also dispatched from Reno to Custer with similar messages and it is known both reached him, their bodies found with him on Last Stand Hill.

Custer wanted a decisive action on the southern edge of the village, to panic and push vulnerable non-combatives in a northwestern direction upriver. He believed the warrior reaction suited his purposes perfectly and also fitted well with his understanding of other Indian engagements. Reno had not successfully charged into the village as envisioned, but for Custer it had "fixed" them and served his purposes to be successful. He took the five other companies and headed up the bluff with this knowledge and proceeded further downriver. By his actions, he believed he was on the offense and could be successful—classic Custer. He did not fear what might be behind him. The first message carried by Sergeant Kanipe asked for ammunition only, not men. It was not until perhaps 15 minutes later, with the full knowledge of the size of the village, that he needed additional forces and hence the message to Benteen.

Captain George Yates commanded Company F and was a loyal member of the Custer Clan. Company F rode gray horses, the only company to do so in the 7th Cavalry. They were often referred to as the "Band Box" company, a period expression for being showy and sharp in appearance. Much is known of Company F's movements during the Little Bighorn because of the gray horse distinction and Indian observations of where they were seen. Yates died with Custer, but a large number of his men were killed in a ravine near the river, perhaps in a desperate attempt to escape. (Little Bighorn National Monument)

Reno had the Indians concentrated on his attack on the village, and he could hold. The village could be taken and to do so, he needed to attack it by envelopment further down the river. He needed ammunition and additional troopers. Both the pack train and Benteen's battalion were close enough to help and could reach him in time for the assault. Finally, his line of communication with Benteen and the pack train was secure. If they could come in time, Custer's luck would hold.

Offense Becomes Defense

As Custer surveyed the landscape in front of the command, his first thoughts were that it was not ground suited very well to cavalry operations. The rolling hills and ravines were treeless, and there were no concealments for his movements. His horses and men were tired and the endless climbing and descent from one hill to another was wearing out the mounts. Several had already fallen out, leaving at least one desperate trooper behind to try and coax his horse to continue.

Custer needed a good path to the river and as yet there appeared few options. Boston Custer, the lieutenant colonel's brother, had succeeded in joining the command. He reported no difficulty in the travel from the pack train and reported his contact with both Captain Benteen's battalion, and trumpeter Martin, whom he had also passed. The news was well received. Both Benteen and the pack train were close and they could easily reach the command in time. Custer's combined force would then number eight companies. Finally, a ravine appeared to the left, suitable for movement to the river. The east–west running depression in the ground, today called Medicine Tail Coulee, showed signs of use and appeared to lead to a ford in the river. It could be the opportunity the command needed to envelop the village. Custer called Captain Yates forward for a discussion. Yates, a blond, balding former enlisted man and Civil War veteran, was a reliable Custer favorite. A reconnaissance of the potential attack route down the coulee was needed, so Yates was given command of Company E along with his own Company F. Together, the two companies were to form a wing and travel the length of the coulee to its confluence with the Little Bighorn River, find a ford, if there was one in the vicinity, and determine the level of Indian resistance present.

While Yates moved his command toward the river, gunfire, first a few shots and then increasing, spoke to the presence of warriors across the river. All five companies of the command were under constant surveillance during its movement. Major Reno had drawn the majority of the first response from the village, but with his departure from the timber, more and more warriors were responding now to the new threat to the village—Custer's force. By the time Yates reached the river, it was very clear any ford there would be impossible, because of the increasing intensity of the Indian response. This was the Hunkpapa Chief Gall who was marshaling warriors at the ford, providing strong rifle fire against any attempt to cross the river. Yates had dismounted his company and established a skirmish line to mount a necessary response. He had taken a few casualties, including possibly Company E Lieutenant James "Jack" Sturgis, who was a recent graduate of West Point and the son of the formal commander of the 7th Cavalry Regiment, Colonel Samuel Sturgis. His body was never found after the battle, but there were reports his severed head was found in the village afterward. If he fell at the ford, the proximity of his body to the village could easily explain these reports.

Custer waited for word from Yates on the possible ford, but the significant fire experienced in the area probably ended active consideration. The fire also communicated growing Indian opposition there, which was not expected. Indian women and children do not normally have firearms, so the shooting came from warriors. Not known to Custer, Crazy Horse and his warriors had already started movement downstream, also anticipating the troopers may attempt to cross the river further down. Custer must have theorized the vulnerable Indian women and children had probably moved further west and north. Throughout the Yates's reconnaissance to the river, Custer had remained at a halt, probably for as long as 45 minutes. During the wait, his force was basically unmolested. He had released his Crow scouts at the beginning of this long delay, leaving only his half-Sioux scout Mitch Boyer for consultation.

Sitting Bull, from his vantage point on the west side of the river, said the Indian reaction to Custer only happened after Reno retreated. Sitting Bull erroneously believed both Custer's group and Reno's group was the same force. So, with his wings relatively safe and Major Reno pressing the valley fight, Custer gave instructions to Captain Keogh, to move the command further west. He was to take his three companies and move up a ridge, today called Sharpshooters Ridge, and then travel west along Nye-Cartwright Ridge, keeping the village in continuous view. Yates and his two companies would travel up a depression in the ground leading away from the river called Deep Coulee, and join the rest of the command where it intersected Nye-Cartwright Ridge. Together, all five companies would continue further west, looking for another ford. The lines of communication were still open for Captain Benteen and the pack train. They had only lost a few troopers and they were still on the offense. Their

The last surviving member of the 7th Cavalry to see George Custer alive, Sergeant John Martin (Giovanni Martini), pictured years after the Little Bighorn battle. Martin carried the famous written message from Adjutant Cooke to Benteen. Martin reported Custer was attacking the village and the Indians were "skedaddling." Martin's horse suffered a bullet wound during his journey suggesting a more dire situation. (Little Bighorn National Monument) lines were stretched however, and new gunfire behind them indicated warriors were now infiltrating across the river and up the hills. It was distant fire and inaccurate, but it was increasingly probable they would have to forcibly hold the lines open for the imminent arrival of Benteen's battalion.

Captain Benteen had reached the area of the now-burning lone tepee when Sergeant Kanipe from his company approached. He said he had a message for Captain McDougall from Custer. Benteen pointed in the direction of the pack train, indicating it was just a mile further east on the trail. Kanipe left and a few minutes later trumpeter John Martin rode up with the message for Benteen from Custer. Benteen read the message and then asked Martin what else he knew about Custer. Martin, in his limited English, said the Indians were "skedaddling." When Benteen pressed Martin for more information about what Custer was doing, he said, "I guess he is attacking the village." Benteen noticed Martin's horse had a bullet wound on its hip and said, "Your horse has been shot."

What Benteen had seen and read were conflicting. If Custer needed him, and the message indicated he needed him quickly along with the ammunition, the fight was on and Custer was in the middle of it. Yet, trumpeter Martin did not indicate for certain Custer was engaged at all and the Indians were fleeing. If they were fleeing, why would he need Benteen's three companies and the reserve ammunition? Also, if there was limited contact, how did Martin's horse get wounded and why did Martin not know it? The orders were clear and he had no others. He directed the command forward, Martin fell in and followed.

A few minutes later, Benteen reached the Little Bighorn River where Reno had crossed to attack the village. He could hear gunfire to the west, down the river bottom, where the men of Reno's battalion were in disarray. There were two distinct groups—one fighting near the river and another on the east side trying to scale the bluff. Lieutenant Winfield S. Edgerly from Company D said he saw

Chief Gall as he appeared years after the Little Bighorn in a photo taken by renowned photographer D. F. Barry. Gall was a sturdy and fierce warrior. On the morning of the attack by Reno in the valley, he had two wives and three children killed in the opening moments. Enraged, he led a devastating attack against Myles Keogh's battalion. (National Park Service) "fighting going on in the valley and very shortly saw a body of men … make a break for the bluffs." Captain Benteen later testified in the Reno Inquiry that he observed the broken elements of Reno's command near the river, "There were 12 or 13 men in skirmish line that appeared to have been beaten back. The line was then parallel with the river and the Indians were charging and recharging those men." The men on the valley floor were doomed and Benteen knew it. Chief White Bull, a Sans Arc Sioux, recalled, "Then the Indians charged them. They used war clubs and gun barrels, shooting arrows into them, riding them down. It was like a buffalo hunt. The soldiers offered no resistance." Benteen had to focus on the larger group of men now on top of the bluff. He turned his battalion toward them and climbed the bluff.

Nearly everyone involved in Reno's scramble to the top of the hill described it as the interpreter George Herendeen did, a "stampede." The Cheyenne Wooden Leg, who laid chase to the fleeing troopers, called it a "Buffalo Hunt." There were two groups as Captain Benteen had identified—those left on the valley floor still in the timber, some with or without mounts, and those who headed for the river in an uncovered retreat. Four troopers had either died or were wounded on the skirmish line or after reaching the timber. The dash to the river or the crossing cost three officers killed, including lieutenants Donald McIntosh and Adjutant Benny Hodgson, along with Assistant Acting Surgeon James DeWolf. Twenty-nine enlisted men total had been killed as a result of the "charge" and another seven wounded. Also, two Arikara scouts, Bob Tailed Bull, and Little Bull had been killed, along with two interpreters, Isaiah Dorman and Bloody Knife, and guide "Lonesome" Charley Reynolds. There were also soldiers left behind and missing from the command. They included Herendeen, Lieutenant Charles DeRudio and another ten soldiers. The missing, whether they had mounts or not "went to ground," figuring their odds were better to wait than to try for the river. A few Indians crossed the river in pursuit of Reno's command but soon ended it as the troopers topped the bluff. Word was passing of another threat from another group of soldiers on the other side of the river—Custer.

Crazy Horse, the chief of the Northern Cheyenne, had been patient in preparing to fight the soldiers, but by Reno's departure from the valley, was ready. He crossed the river near the ford at Deep Ravine and led a band of warriors to Custer's ridge, to attack the coming soldiers. They rode and positioned themselves in the folds of the earth on the sides of the ridges. Gall, a fierce Sioux chief, led another group across Miniconjou Ford to pressure the rear of Custer's five companies now heading up the ridge to the west. The Indians were massing on the east side of the river in large numbers and they had the advantage, whether mounted or not. The ground lent itself to infiltration among the many ravines and gulches. They were well armed, many with repeating rifles, some with older muzzleloaders and many with bows and arrows. Custer's battalions were "sky lining" on the ridges as they moved and were, in contrast to the Indians, at a considerably inferior position.

Captain Tom Custer circa 1871–72 shown as a 1st Lieutenant and wearing both of his Congressional Medals of Honor. Fearless, he commanded Company C on the Little Bighorn campaign, although he was detached to the Regimental Staff. A prankster like his older brother George, he would sometimes violate the lines of official military decorum to be just "Brother Tom." (Little Bighorn National Monument)

Benteen crested the bluffs to arrive in the middle of a chaotic scene. There were men collected in bunches, appearing to have collapsed as the point man and his mount reached the top of the bluffs. The ground was a poor spot for defense but there they were and commanders were attempting to form a defensive circle. The spot offered little cover and no concealment. The bluffs protected their southwest side and a depression in the center provided some cover for the wounded men, but high ground existed on the other three sides which aided the Indians. Only aggressive fire and the denial of the higher ground could prevent deadly fire from raining down on the defenders. Yet, here they were and there seemed to be some respite. The Indian attack had ceased, there was no gunfire, and no immediate pressure. Several of the officers were in a hysterical state. The Company A commander Myles Moylan and the scout commander Lieutenant Charles Varnum were both sobbing quietly, the latter between rifle shots exchanged with some distant Indians. As Benteen rode to the center, Major Reno, with a handkerchief around his head and without either his carbine or Colt revolver, came forward in an extremely excited state. Reno reportedly stated, "For God's sake Benteen, halt your command and help me." Reno went on, "We have been whipped." From what he had seen, Benteen was inclined to agree, but there were his orders from Custer.

Captain Benteen calmly pulled Custer's message from his pocket and handed it to Reno, who read it quickly, re-read it and looked up as if it meant nothing. Benteen pressed him, "Have you seen Custer?" Reno had not seen him in the last hour and when he did it was on the very same ground they occupied. There were no other messages or communications. Benteen, with orders in hand from a superior, should have acted immediately to move on. His companies had not faced the enemy yet, were relatively fresh compared with the rest of the command, and still had their entire combat load of ammunition. The pack train was close behind and Custer must be ahead, somewhere off the line of vision. Also, there was distant firing going on further down the river—that must be Custer. Lieutenant's Varnum, Hare,

Edgerly, and Godfrey among others heard the firing distinctly. Reno pleaded with Benteen for him to stay, explaining he had lost Lieutenant Hodgson but believed he might still be alive. He wanted to go and find him before he was discovered by the Indians and killed. Benteen relented. Later, both Reno and Benteen explained at the Reno Inquiry they believed Custer, with approximately 225 men, could take care of himself and the message from him implied he wanted the ammunition pack close to him. While Reno went in search of Hodgson, Benteen organized the hasty defense of the hill and his companies cross-leveled their ammunition with Reno's men. Lieutenant Luther Hare, Reno's hastily appointed "new" adjutant, borrowed a horse and went in search of the pack train, now a mile and a half away.

The search for Hodgson lasted only 30 minutes. The young lieutenant was found but had been dead for a time. After collecting a few personal effects for Hodgson's family, Major Reno returned to the top of the hill. Lieutenant Hare had not yet returned and the pack train had not closed on the hasty defensive position. During this time, the Crow scouts—Goes Ahead, Hairy Moccasin, and White Man Runs Him, who had been with Custer until he had dismissed them—came into the defense. They knew little about the whereabouts of Custer as they had left him before any real engagement and wanted nothing to do with fighting the Sioux. They left 30 minutes later for their camp on the Yellowstone.

In the meantime, the six companies had loosely formed a lazy non-concentric circle, trying to make the best use of the terrain. There seemed to be no sense of urgency to do anything. There was, however, an abundance of discussion among the officers and men about why they were not moving toward Custer and the sound of the distant firing. Captain Myles Moylan and Captain Thomas Weir particularly debated about what had become of Custer and what the "battle plan" might be. Moylan had served as Custer's adjutant at the battle of the Washita in 1868 and knew him about as well as anyone on the campaign. Moylan spoke with Weir, remembering Custer never revealed what he was going to do in battle. Rather, he reacted and adjusted as events developed. This no doubt had roots in Custer's Civil War experience, where plans were made "on the hoof." The use of cavalry by the war's end compared little to pre-war tactics and Custer had played a significant role in the evolution of cavalry tactics. His actions as the war went on, but also in the Indian Wars, reflected this change and growth of knowledge. War was dynamic, particularly in fighting the Plains Indians. Custer would never be locked down with doctrinal tactics—then or now. Captain Weir was growing impatient about not moving to the fighting. They could still hear the shots in the distance and wanted to be part of it. Weir's Company D was hopping, ready to go. Captain Weir, his second in charge Lieutenant Winfield Edgerly, and his First Sergeant Michael Martin had all seen the distant dust clouds and firing, believing it was Custer. They all believed the company should move and join him and the fight.

Major Reno had returned from reaching Lieutenant Hodgson's body and stood in a circle with Captain Benteen and Captain Moylan. Captain Weir approached them with a suggestion they move out to reach Custer. Major Reno responded, it was impossible, they were surrounded and the pack train had still not arrived. They needed to remain. Captain Benteen concurred, they needed to wait. Weir was then reported to say, "If no one else goes to Custer, I will go." With that he walked over to his horse, mounted, and started in a northerly direction toward the firing in the distance. He intended to find out what was going on by himself, however, Lieutenant Edgerly, seeing his commander's actions, assumed Captain Weir had the authority to leave. Consequently, he mounted all of Company D and moved out quickly behind their captain. Interestingly, no one, including Captain Benteen, made an effort to stop the departing company. There were wounded from the valley fight to think of and tend to.

A few minutes later, the pack train with Captain McDougall arrived, the mules with the reserve ammunition arriving first. While the ammunition was being distributed, McDougall asked why they were not preparing to move to Custer? He later testified that the firing from Custer's direction could be distinctly heard, yet Major Reno seemed disinterested in their situation. He perceived Reno had been drinking, perhaps heavily and was incapable of making a command decision. To press the issue, Captain McDougall looked to the north and pointed, saying, "We ought to be down there." Whether it was the arrival of the pack train or McDougall's persuasion, Benteen finally gave orders to Lieutenant Godfrey and Company K, and to his own Company H to mount their troopers and prepare to move. In defiance of Reno's demands to stay, Benteen's battalion was finally moving together toward the sounds of the firing.

On the other end of the battlefield, Custer and his staff, including brothers Tom and Boston, nephew Autie Reed, correspondent Mark Kellogg, the regimental sergeant major, Dr. Lord, the regimental surgeon, Sergeant Robert Hughes, his color bearer, and others moved quickly in front of Captain Keogh's

One of the Custer clan, 1st Lieutenant James "Jimmie" Calhoun was one of George Custer's most loyal officers and was also his brother-in-law. Married to Margaret Custer, he had first met Custer during the Civil War. Jimmie would command Company L as part of the Custer battalion, and his company was the first to be annihilated while attempting to hold the line of communication open for reinforcements and ammunition. (Little Bighorn National Monument)

wing of three companies. Keogh's Company I led the wings movement in columns of four, followed by Company C with Lieutenant Henry Harrington in temporary command and with Lieutenant Calhoun's Company L, following up the rear. They had faced no opposition to this point, but troopers in the rear of Company L were reporting fire from the ravines leading away from the river. There was increasing Indian presence to their rear and it was strong enough to be concerning. By the time they reached the crest of the ridge it was growing apparent their line of communication with Captain Benteen could be interrupted. The command could continue, but with every bit of movement further north and west, they were putting greater distance between them, Benteen's three companies and the ammunition. They needed both now. Custer halted the command and called officers forward.

Besieged

> The column took the gallop with pistols drawn, expecting to meet the enemy which we thought Custer was driving before him in his effort to communicate with the pack train, never suspecting that our forces had been defeated.
>
> LIEUTENANT EDWARD GODFREY, COMMANDER COMPANY K

Custer must have wondered where Captain Benteen and the pack train were. Brother Boston had left Benteen nearly an hour and a half ago and rode straight to Custer. Boston most certainly reported the pack train was about a mile behind Captain Benteen's battalion. They were both near. Something had happened, but what? The situation around the Custer command was starting to deteriorate. Captain Yates had not been able to cross the river at Miniconjou ford and Indian opposition there was not what they had expected. Not only was opposition fierce at the crossing, but once Yates's wing left the river, Indians crossed over and started to infiltrate the ravines leading away. Even though their fire was inaccurate, it could soon mean the line of communication to Benteen might be closed by this new Indian presence. Cavalry is an offensive arm of the Army and not well inclined to the defense. Therefore, it is a rare occurrence, used only if it is essential to allow a return to the offense. Custer historically rarely assumed the defense and if he did, it was usually in the direst of circumstances. Several times it was necessary in the Civil War and in both cases he fought his way out. It was Custer luck and he was going to need it again on this day if the 7th Cavalry was to survive.

Given the situation, Custer must have felt offensive operations were still possible. He also knew, with recent developments, it might mean Benteen may not be able to fight his way through to the command. He still had companies E and F advancing forward of the command further north and west, experiencing little contact. They could remain on the offense, searching for another ford. Meanwhile, if he placed Keogh's wing on the ridge in a nested, hasty defense, he could hold the line of communication open for Benteen, then they could still join and continue the attack of the village further on. Cavalry tactics of the time called for a layered defense (nested) with the successive depth of units, in this case companies. Further, the defense should always call for the most senior commander to be in the position furthest to the rear, to better command and control those units in front of him. In this case, the senior commander was Captain Keogh (the wing commander) and Company I, which then would assume the rear position. Company C, and the recently promoted Captain Tom Custer, would be the next most senior officer, and would assume the next position forward. Tom Custer was on detached duty with the regimental staff, so the leadership position fell to his subordinate Lieutenant Henry Harrington. Finally, the most forward and closest to the Indians called for the most junior of the commanders, in this case, Lieutenant Calhoun and his Company L. The arrangements of companies made sense tactically. Tactics always placed the most seasoned commander in depth of one another in succession. If one fell in battle, the next one with more seasoning would take command of the combined forces. Captain Keogh and his wing's mission would be to "keep the door open" for Benteen to allow the link-up of forces. After the link-up, all eight companies could capture the village, and the fight could still be won.

Indian accounts of what happened next speak to both the bravery of the troopers, but also the story of the disintegration of the command. While the hasty defense in Keogh's sector was being set up, companies E and F, along with Custer's command group, were arriving further to the northwest along the ridge. According to Cheyenne Indian accounts, the two companies followed an old buffalo trail leading down to the river. It was an organized reconnaissance of a ford located there, one to be used no doubt for follow on forces. Indian fire did not prevent the movement, but once they arrived at the river, Indians fired on them. Cheyenne warrior Hanging Wolf later recounted they hit one horse but no troopers. The trooper whose horse was hit was saved by his fellow soldiers, but both companies moved back up the

A youthful Captain Myles Keogh, 7th Cavalry probably circa late 1860s. An Irish immigrant, he served with some distinction during the Civil War earning a brevet to Colonel. A 7th Regimental favorite and also one of Custer's, he would fall commanding Company I, dying with his men. There is some evidence he was wounded early with leg wounds that would have prevented even standing to lead his company effectively. (Smithsonian)

hill toward the ridge. There, both companies and Custer stayed approximately 20 minutes, according to a Cheyenne warrior present. The command was not under any immediate pressure and was likely waiting on Keogh with Benteen's battalion. They would never come.

Pressure on Keogh's battalion, particularly Calhoun's position, was becoming intense. Keogh had placed Calhoun's Company L in a depression immediately behind the crest of a small hill, which today bears Calhoun's name. It was a solid military move, positioning on the "military crest" of the hill (the rear side) as it provided some cover from direct fire. There, Calhoun placed his men on several successive skirmish lines to provide volley fire if necessary to break any Indian resolve to threaten the position. Behind the position, in a small depression, every fourth man held the company's mounts. Company C was here also as a reserve. Company I stretched further up the hill within the observation of the other wing. The entire position was increasingly taking fire from a ridge to the southwest, today known as Greasy Grass Ridge. Direct Indian fire from this ridge threatened the whole of the position. While the majority of the Indians there were led by a Sioux chief named Gall, there were Cheyenne warriors there as well. The number of Indians swelled by the minute, as warriors who had fought Reno's battalion broke away after his retreat. The pressure became so intense on the hasty defense that Company C mounted and charged the Indians there. The action worked, as the Indians moved out of range of the troopers, falling further down the hill. The troopers remained mounted, but they were separated now by about 500 yards from Company L. Cheyenne warrior Yellow Nose, who was one of the hundreds of warriors present, moved with the others, but waited patiently for the opportunity to begin moving back up the hill.

Company C dismounted to deal with the regrouping warriors. They established skirmish lines as directed by Lieutenant Harrington, their only officer. The troopers, along with their mounts, were now horribly exposed. Chief Gall realized the precarious position of the troopers and knew their mounts were the key to their defense. In an interview in 1886, Gall said, "They fought on foot. One man held the horses while the others shot the guns. We tried to kill the holders, and then by waving blankets and shouting we scared the horses … where the Cheyenne women caught them." Dismounted, the troopers were extraordinarily disadvantaged. They were outnumbered and outside of the ability of Company L to help them. Although not known by Gall at the time, the trooper's reserve ammunition was in the saddlebags of the mounts. Without it, the troopers' few rounds would run out in a matter of minutes, leaving them on foot and without arms to defend themselves. Following Gall's action, the Indians, in singles and in groups, advanced, some waving blankets to scare the already terrified mounts. Each horse holder, dealing with the frantic movements of four horses, all weighing over a half a ton apiece, many of them wounded, fighting to break free of their tethers, found it impossible to control them. Horses broke free and ran in every direction. It would be only a matter of a few minutes before the position was overrun. Finding the position now untenable, troopers abandoned their positions, running to the rear to join the safety of the Company L defensive line. Some made it, including sergeants George Finckle and Jeremiah Finley, whose bodies were found among the Company L dead.

Company L may have been the unit which made the most effective stand for the day. A grass fire in the area in the 1980s prompted an archaeological study of the area. The results were very revealing, showing artifacts including a 7th Cavalry Springfield carbine, and Colt Army revolver casings, but also Indian bullets which impacted the area. First, there was clear evidence of several linear skirmish lines in depth, demonstrating discipline and firing among the defense. Many of the individual positions showed more casings than the basic load of an individual soldier, implying these soldiers continued to fire long enough to transition to

Comanche, the personal cavalry horse of Captain Myles Keogh, was found badly wounded near the site of the abandoned Indian village several days after the battle. Placed on the steamer *Far West*, Comanche was transported back to Fort Abraham Lincoln where he was restored back to health. Often recognized as the sole survivor of the Custer battalion, he was celebrated by the 7th Cavalry Regiment and the public. Eventually, Comanche moved to Fort Riley and was given the freedom to move about the post becoming a bit of a pest, begging for fruit, biscuits, and even beer from soldiers who loved to imbibe him. He died in 1891 after a long life. (Little Bighorn National Monument)

their reserve ammunition. Further, the dead were found where they fell, generally along these lines. Their officers, lieutenants Calhoun and James J. Crittenden, were found to the immediate rear of their lines, positioned perfectly to direct their company's fire. They had to have fallen at or near to the same time as their men. If panic had consumed them, this integrity would have been lost. The impacted bullets found during the archeological dig, which were fired from Indian positions within firing range, helped to further define Company L's tactical lines by outlining or shadowing them. The number of Indian arms was also significant. There were many types of weapons, including revolvers, single-shot weapons, and repeaters, and even outdated muzzleloaders, suggesting the Indians were well-armed. Some of the single-shot bullets were from the cavalry Springfield carbine, meaning troopers were facing fire from weapons lost by their men who either fell in battle or had lost them elsewhere.

The final evidence of a disciplined defense came from the Indians they were facing. Red Hawk, a Sioux warrior who was in the fight, said the soldiers "made a very good fight." There is little doubt the loud volley firing lieutenants Varnum and Godfrey had heard happened during the lull after the Benteen battalion arrival on the bluffs and Reno's search for his missing adjutant, Lieutenant Hodgson. The loss of companies C and L followed shortly, exposing Captains Keogh's Company I and their thin, extended defense of the ridge leading to Custer.

Captain Keogh did not have the luxury of good ground to defend on. His role in the defense was to provide command and control of the wing's defenses and reinforce it as required. In doing so, he, at least in the beginning, was mounted on his horse Comanche. There was no pressure initially where he and his company were located. Visibility of the sector from the ground there was not good, so being mounted gave him a better view in both directions—toward Calhoun and Custer. With the disintegration of companies C and L his view east became increasingly poor, a combination of the smoke of gunfire and the dust of movements. He must have seen the move north from the river, of Indians attacking his wing, the charge of Company C, and the eventual loss of the mounts of both companies. The wild movements of over 100 cavalry horses in the scene must have added to the confusion. Cavalrymen on foot are infantry at once, and inefficient infantry at that. It was quite natural for the troopers in those two companies to want to run to the rear, as it was the only place they could expect any relative safety. Now, dozens of men were headed in his direction, chased by Indians mounted and on foot themselves. They were running through Keogh's men, challenging their ability to engage the Indians interspersed among the fleeing melee in the dust and smoke. The Indians soon surrounded his position, shooting from concealed positions in the grass, on both sides of the ridge. Chief White Bull, who was mounted, remembered, "Here and there through the fog, you could see a wounded man left behind afoot. I saw one bleeding from a wound in his left

Early depictions of the battle of the Little Bighorn rarely got the details right but aptly captured the utter chaos of the last few minutes. The public had an insatiable appetite for the answers about the disaster, and lithographs like the one above tried to provide answers. With no survivors to tell the tale, imaginations ran wild, often providing in print false detail that only served to further obscure what had happened. (Public Domain)

thigh. He had a revolver in one hand and a carbine in the other. He stood all alone shooting at the Indians. They could not get at him. I rode at his back. He did not see me coming."

Keogh located his men near the top of the ridge in an exposed position taking fire both ways. At some point Keogh took a gunshot wound along with Comanche. After the battle, Keogh's body had shown a debilitating bullet wound to the leg that matched a bullet wound on Comanche. The collapse of the Keogh sector happened very quickly, but it could have been this wound which caused him to lead from the ground in a seated position. Visibility would not have been very good and being reliant on others for what was happening made matters worse. The end came quickly though, and Keogh died surrounded by his soldiers.

Custer would have observed the disintegration of Keogh's wing, but he had similar events going on to his front. Indian pressure was strong facing the river, so strong Custer deployed companies E and F in a layered defense, to check it. This was Crazy Horse's Northern Cheyenne and other affiliates, some on horseback, others advancing up the ravines on foot leading to Last Stand Hill. Much like

Keogh's defense, it was deployed with the more junior commander in front, meaning Lieutenant Algernon Smith's Company E, and Captain Yates's Company F behind them. Company E was in skirmish lines, volley firing and at first it was very effective at keeping the Indians at a distance. Again, archaeological work done after the 1983 fire revealed collections of shell casings in linear skirmish lines. It was evidence of orderly fire, first with the single-shot Springfield carbine and later by the Colt pistol. As the Indians advanced, the placement of casings showed when the Indians had crept closer and closer to them. The trooper transition from a slower rate of fire carbine to the more rapid rate of fire pistol was clearly necessary. Crazy Horse, riding back and forth, directing his warriors and inspiring them by his close encounters with the troopers, was slowly turning the right flank. Warriors on foot were slowly turning the left flank. The position was becoming untenable and the call to fall back was given. The Custer command was out of options.

The final scenes would have been extremely chaotic. Troopers from Keogh's sector were running on foot through the smoke and dust toward Custer's battle flag fluttering in the hot wind in the sweltering afternoon sun. Custer had to know Keogh's defense had failed, and with it, any possibility for Benteen's battalion to reach them. His three companies would have to fight their way to Custer now and if Keogh's three companies could not hold the Indians at bay, Benteen could not fight his way in. The other wing of companies E and F were now falling back to Last Stand Hill. There were few tactical options left, only defense. The command to shoot the remaining mounts for breastworks meant the end of any hope of victory, leaving just a desperate possible survival. Led into a circle around the hill, 50 horses were killed in place to provide some cover for the troopers to fire from. Behind them, surrounded by his two brothers, nephew, the scout Mitch Boyer and the survivors of five companies, Custer's final stand was made. It is often conjectured exactly when Custer himself fell. Indian accounts suggest rushes on troopers on Last Stand Hill did not end the fighting. In the final closing minutes, an effort was made by some 20 troopers from Company F to run down Deep Ravine in an attempt to reach the Little Bighorn and a possible escape. They were followed and quickly killed by the numerous Indians in the area in the ravine itself.

Chief Gall was one of the warriors who led the attack on last stand hill and answered questions for the readers of St. Paul Pioneer Press in 1886: "How long before all the soldiers were killed?" The chief made the sign of the white man's dinner time which means noon, and then with his finger cut a half, which would signify half an hour consumed in slaughtering everybody. "Did the red men shoot guns or arrows?" "Both. We soon shot all our cartridges, and then shot arrows and used our war clubs." "Did the soldiers have plenty of ammunition?" "No. They shot away all they had. The horses ran away, carrying in the saddle pockets a heap more. The soldiers threw their guns aside and fought with little guns [Pistols]."

It was the final mopping up of the killing on Custer Hill which Captain Weir witnessed, as he rode up to the little pointed hill which today bears his name—Weir Point. Although he could not identify the human figures in the distance some three miles away, he observed gunshots in multiple locations on the ridge and the discharge of firearms by mounted figures into the ground. Lieutenant Edgerly was not far behind with the rest of Company D. The company was alone, and when they arrived near him, he dismounted the company. Lieutenant Edgerly placed them into a skirmish line focused north. Weir watched the distant battlefield for a few minutes. He could see company guidons stuck in the ground and fluttering in the hot wind. The guidons normally followed company commanders, so their presence usually meant company positions. Weir was troubled though, as what he observed did not seem to be normal cavalry operations at all. Were they observing soldiers moving about, and doing what? Sergeant James Flanagan who had been observing the movements in the distance through field glasses, called for Captain Weir, saying, "I think those are Indians." If this was Custer, he had lost several companies and a disaster had occurred. Oglala Chief Crazy Horse shared in 1877, "Outnumbering him [Custer] as we did, we had him at our mercy. The smoke and dust were so great that foe could not be distinguished from friends. The horses were wild with fright and uncontrollable. Indians were knocking each other from their steeds, and several dead Indians were

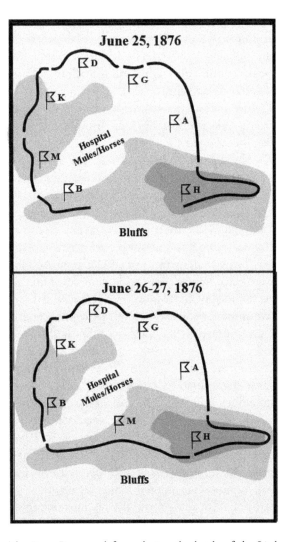

The Reno-Benteen defense during the battle of the Little Bighorn, June 25–27, 1876. (Map by Ted Behncke)

found killed by arrows. Just like this [intertwining his fingers], the Indians and white men. The chiefs suffered a loss of fifty-eight killed, and over sixty wounded. Many of our wounded died."

The remainder of Captain Benteen's battalion (companies H and K) was closely on the heels of Captain Weir, having left the hasty Reno defense after topping off ammunition from the first mules to arrive from the pack train. He did not discuss his departure with Major Reno nor asked for permission to leave. Captain French and Company G followed, along with a few troopers with mounts from Company M, leaving only Major Reno with Company A and its commander, Captain Moylan, to help tend the wounded. Reno tried to halt the movement west with bugle calls, but no one stopped. After the pack train arrived at last, Reno mounted the remaining troopers, fashioned litters for the wounded, and started a reluctant movement toward Benteen and the others. Major Reno gave instructions, ordering Lieutenant Hare to find Captain Weir and instruct him to open a line of communication with Custer. What remained of the 7th Cavalry Regiment, now seven companies somewhat battered and tired, were strung out but united.

Captain Weir and his company were in a superior position to view the entire landscape up and down the valley of the Little Bighorn. They could see the extraordinarily large Indian village, the Indians in the distance fighting Custer or a portion of his wings, and the bare landscape of their area of operations. Unfortunately, his company was also visible to the Indians who were wrapping up their fight with Custer and were ready to take on any new threat. Soon, approximately 1,000 to 1,500 warriors were headed in their direction. Captain Benteen's arrival at Weir's position steadied the nerves of the company. He quickly established additional skirmish lines on both flanks of Weir's already deployed company. Soon, realizing a big fight was coming, and the ground they were on would not support success, Benteen told Captain Weir he was riding back to Major Reno and suggest they return to their start point on the bluffs and establish a defense there. While not perfect defensive ground, it was better than the present, and they may have stood a chance there. When Benteen departed, Weir went with him, leaving his troop behind. The troopers of Company D, now under the temporary command of Lieutenant Edgerly, started firing along with Captain French's Company M at the advancing Indians.

Major Reno needed little persuasion from Benteen to retreat. He immediately gave the order, but few were responding to him. The afternoon's events left others with little confidence in him. Benteen took over nominal command and the companies were soon headed south. Companies A and B were the first to arrive as they were the closest, having just departed from the spot. Companies M and H followed, leaving Company K with Lieutenant Godfrey on a ridge behind the forward-deployed Company D with Lieutenant Edgerly and Company G with Captain French. None of the three companies were operating in concert with each other and they all were without clear orders about how and when to retreat. The Indians were now within rifle range of the companies out front and unnerving the troopers with their fire. It was not a surprise then when Lieutenant Edgerly and Captain French mounted their companies and in succession passed Lieutenant Godfrey and his troopers to the rear at a speedy gallop. The Indians behind them were in hot pursuit. Godfrey remembered years later, "The Indians almost immediately followed to the top of the bluff, and commenced firing into the retreating troops, killing one man, wounding others and several horses. They then started down the hillside in pursuit. I at once made up my mind that such a retreat and close pursuit would throw the whole command into confusion, and, perhaps, prove disastrous. I dismounted my men to fight on foot, deploying as rapidly as possible without waiting for the formation laid down in tactics."

Had it not been for Lieutenant Godfrey's quick thinking, the situation may have ended badly for the entire command. Godfrey knew the Indians excelled at the mounted chase as it mirrored the hunt for buffalo. As they closed on the companies, they would cut down the troopers on the run. In the end, it would also leave Godfrey and his troopers surrounded. So, Godfrey quickly organized his troopers into two squads capable of providing volley fire in succession. When the forward squad fired, they would retreat, passing the squad behind them, who then were ready to fire next. The first strong volley worked, scattering the Indian advance. Godfrey repeated the sequence, again and again, providing a disciplined example of a textbook rearguard action. When finished, Godfrey's troopers dashed the last few hundred yards back to the defensive lines. Not a single trooper was lost.

The 7th Survives

It was about 6:00 p.m. when Lieutenant Godfrey's troopers closed on the defense site on what today is referred to as Reno Hill. The position consisted of two parallel running ridges which lay east–west, with a slight depression in the middle. The defense would have to be loosely circular. The area deemed the most vulnerable to attack was facing north, so the strongest company, Captain Weir's Company D, was given that area to cover. Lieutenant Godfrey's Company K would tie in on the left of Company D facing west. Captain French's Company M would also defend west, tied into Company K on the right and Captain McDougall's Company B on the left. On the south side of the area was the bluffs, which were difficult to climb and there could be some risk accepted there, so the area was initially left undefended. Lieutenant Wallace's Company G, badly mauled in the valley fight with a strength of only three troopers, would tie into Company D on the northeast side of the circle and cover a very small frontage. Captain Moylan's Company A would tie into Company G on the left and cover nearly all of the east side of the circle. Finally, Captain Benteen's Company H secured a narrow finger tying into Company A and extending to the east a few hundred yards. It was badly exposed on all sides with high ground all around, but it was a ready avenue of approach to the defense and had to be denied to the attackers. In the depression in the defense's center, Dr. Porter established a field hospital inside of the mules and cavalry mounts. The entire area was barren, with little vegetation, dry as a bone, hot, and with no available water. Dr. Porter, the sole surviving surgeon of the regiment (Dr. James DeWolf had been killed on the retreat from the valley with Reno and Dr. George Lord would perish with Custer) would ultimately serve 30 wounded before the two days of siege would end. Porter had laudanum and morphine sulfate to ease the pain of the wounded. After removing as much debris from wounds as possible, he would use a carbolic acid solution to sterilize wounds. He also performed one leg amputation and the amputation of badly damaged fingers before it was over. It is indeed astonishing that he performed most of the medical care without water and while dodging bullets and arrows from all sides.

The Indian attack began even before all the companies were in their positions. The warriors, flush with the cavalry weapons they had taken from the valley fight and the Custer dead, were now being used against the Reno defense. The gunfire was heavy and with no cover, casualties started immediately. There was simply no cover for the troopers. Digging fox holes for protection was difficult in the hard dirt. Further, being lightly provisioned for the campaign, there were only three shovels in the entire command. As a result, troopers were desperately digging with anything they could find, knives, tin cups, and eating utensils. Ammunition and ration crates, saddles, anything which could deflect a bullet were put to use. It did little good. As casualties mounted, so did the demand for water but they had none. Several had tried to reach the river below but they were under constant fire in trying to do so. The horses tied off in the center of the defense were also targeted and suffered greatly. It had been a hot and long day for all.

Major Reno and Captain Benteen trooped the line with striking differences. Reno was drunk and he had been drinking even before the campaign began, and continued throughout the day. It was apparent to all, officers and the enlisted men, he was coping with the challenges of leadership by staying inebriated. Captain Benteen, in contrast, was inspiring. He walked along with the defenses, consistently exposed to Indian fire. He coached the men and leaders on the defenses, assigned priorities, but perhaps most importantly, giving them confidence in their leadership and that they could survive.

The Indian attacks were frequent and intense. The pattern was similar to what had worked with the demise of Custer's companies: lay down an intense fire, creating smoke and disorder, then charge forward. The attacks came on different sides as the Indians tested positions. Soldiers began to go down. The fire on the horses and

Assistant Acting Surgeon Henry R. Porter was the only doctor to survive at the Little Bighorn from the three assigned to the 7th Cavalry Regiment. A Georgetown Medical School graduate, he performed yeoman work with scant help in a makeshift hospital inside the Reno-Benteen defense including two field amputations. (Little Bighorn National Monument)

mules was particularly fierce. As the animals died they were dragged for breastworks around the hospital. By 6:00 p.m. the sun was setting and provided some respite. In the three hours spanning their arrival in defense and sundown, Reno stated in his official report, 18 troopers had died from wounds, and another 43 had been wounded, in addition to the seven already being treated by Dr. Porter in the makeshift hospital. The numbers were exaggerated on both counts, but there was a lot of uncertainty, given the number lost in the valley fight and retreat.

The Indian firing nearly stopped completely when night came. Work continued digging in or preparing fighting positions. For the first time in over nearly a day, there was time to relax and try to eat. Rations were hard to find and most resorted to finding food where they could, even if it was not theirs. It was hot and water was limited in supply, just what was left in canteens if any. The priority for any water they could find needed to go to the wounded.

The favorite topic of discussion—what had become of Custer? Most believed he had been pushed back but had linked up with Terry, then he would return to defeat the Indians and rescue those holding out. Captain Benteen could think of nothing other than Custer's abandonment of Major Elliot at the battle of the Washita. Elliot's detachment had been separated from the main body of the attack and killed. They were not found for another week. Benteen always believed Custer could have done more to save him and his dozen men. Was the same fate in store for the embattled command? Why didn't he fight his way back in? How could the rest of the 7th Cavalry Regiment allow them to be exterminated? No one in their wildest thoughts believed the rest of the regiment was already dead.

At one point after dark, Lieutenant Varnum asked for permission from Major Reno to try and find Custer. Reno denied the request. Later, Captain Weir informed Varnum that Major Reno would support an attempt to find Custer if it were performed by the remaining two Arikara scouts. A short time later, Varnum presented the idea to the two scouts, both of whom were wounded, but they agreed. The scouts departed but were only gone a short time before returning. The mission was impossible. Sioux were swarming the entire area.

For his part, Reno spent most of the day lying prone behind a pack-saddle next to Captain Weir. The coupling seemed odd at first appearance. They did not like one another normally, but then there was the love of the bottle. Apparently, the drink (or the sharing of it) overcame any opposition to each other's company. Major Reno found time to visit the supply area, reportedly to chase off those trying to make off with supplies. The truth more likely was a resupply of his flask from a container he had in the pack train. He was observed many times with a flask, even getting into an altercation with two civilian packers and spilling the alcohol contents on one of them. Down in the darkness of the valley, the wounded and weary troopers could hear the noise of celebration from the Indian village—beating drums, what sounded like singing, and wailing. Lieutenant Godfrey remembered, "They [The Indians] were a good deal happier than we were; nor did they strive to conceal their joy. Their camp was a veritable pandemonium. All night long they continued their frantic revels: beating tom-toms, dancing, whooping, yelling with demoniacal screams, and discharging firearms. We knew they were having a scalp dance. In this connection the question has often been asked, 'If they did not have prisoners at the torture?' The Indians deny that they took any prisoners. We did not discover any evidence of torture in their camps. It is true that we did find human heads severed from their bodies, but these had probably been paraded in their orgies during that terrible night."

There were odd visions as well. Some troopers reported seeing columns of mounted men, perhaps it was Custer—ghosts of the deceased 7th Cavalry. There was even one report of a bugle call. All, of course, were emanating from the village and beyond, but it was entirely the actions of the Indian village, celebrating victory on one hand and the mourning of their dead in the fight on the other. Day two, June 26, began with the heavy firing on all sides of the defense. The firing was particularly heavy in the southern area of Benteen's Company H. The high ground, all the way around his position, allowed for a withering and deadly fire on his men. So many troopers had been hit, some uninjured members of the company were hiding out at the hospital. Benteen found them and moved them back to the skirmish line, warning them he would kill anyone who left the line. He then went to Major Reno to request more men to fill his sector. Reno reported he had none to spare. Benteen pointed out if he lost the southern end of the defense, the Indians would "roll" the entire position. Reluctantly, Reno gave him a portion of Captain French's company as replacements. Over the day Benteen conducted two charges to put off Indian pressure on both ends of the defense.

In *The Field Diary of Lt. Edward Settle Godfrey*, Godfrey remembered one of the charges:

> Benteen came back to where Reno was, and said if something was not done pretty soon the Indians would run into our lines. Waiting a short time, and no action being taken on his suggestion, he said rather impatiently: "You've got to do something here on the north side pretty quick; this won't do, you must drive them back." Reno then directed us to get ready for a charge and told Benteen to give the word. Benteen called out, "All ready now, men. Now's the time. Give them hell. Hip, hip, here we go!" And away we went with a hurrah, every man of the troops B, D, G, and K ... Our men left the pits with their carbines loaded, and they began firing without orders soon after we started. A large body of Indians had assembled at the foot of one of the hills on the north intending probably to make a charge, as Benteen had divined, but they broke as soon as our line started.

Captain Benteen stood in the middle of bullets whizzing in every direction, targeted toward him for the entire day. He was hit only once on a boot heel, while he was lying down. Major Reno barely left his spot on the ground; everyone knew who was in command. About noon some courageous water carriers were successful in getting badly needed water from the river for the wounded and other men. By 3:00 p.m. all but a few of the Indians had stopped shooting. The Hunkpapa Chief Crow King shared in 1877, "We fired at them until the sun went down. We surrounded them and watched them all night, and at daylight we fought them again. We killed many of them. Then a chief from the Hunkpapa's called our men off. He told them those men had been punished enough, that they were fighting under orders, that we had killed the great leader and his men in the fight the day before, and we should let the rest go home." That evening none of the celebrating heard the night before occurred. There was also a clear indication of tremendous activity in the village below them.

The command desperately needed water for the wounded. Major Reno testified in the *Reno Court of Inquiry* on January 13, 1879, "The question of obtaining water was then becoming vital for the wounded, and the water being on the front of Company H, about 600 yards distant, a skirmish line was formed under command of Colonel Benteen to protect the volunteers who went for water. Of these one was killed and six wounded. Water was obtained, and though the Indians remained annoyingly about us during the rest of the day." This was the first resupply of water the command received since the morning of the 25th, a full day and a half in the hot sun.

At 6:00 p.m. a procession of horses, travois and Indians began departing the village, in a southerly direction. The Indians had set fire to the grass between the Reno-Benteen defense and the village, to help obscure their intended movement. Reno recalled in the *Reno Court of Inquiry* in January 1879, "I saw them making a big fire in the valley, raising great clouds of dust and smoke. The fire was evidently encouraged by the Indians, and about six o'clock we saw their column come out from behind these clouds of smoke and dust on to the bluffs, moving in regular military order in the direction of the Bighorn Mountains, which were about thirty miles distant." The village was breaking up. The formation of Indians, their ponies, and possessions on the move stretched for several miles. The pony herd alone was estimated at 20,000 animals.

Captain Benteen, who had seen large units on the move during the Civil War, said the scene rivaled a Union cavalry division (normally numbering 4,000 soldiers) on the march. With estimates of the Indian inhabitants of the village being approximately 7,000, the comparisons are understandable. Leaders and troopers alike could not imagine they had stood off an Indian force that large. All were relieved at the village departure but still endured a restless night.

At about 3:00 a.m., several separated men of the valley fight made their way back to their command. Lieutenant DeRudio, Mr. Girard, Private O'Neal, and the scout Jackson slipped through the lines, to share tales of their harrowing time hidden in the brush near the river. After dodging Indians near the river, they crossed through their own nervous sentries. DeRudio shared in the *New York Herald* on July 30th, 1876:

> We proceeded a little further and heard the bray of a mule, and soon after, the distinct voice of a sentry challenging with the familiar words "Halt. Who goes there?" The challenge was not directed to us, as we were too far off to be seen by the picket, and it was too dark; but this gave us the courage to continue our course and approach, though carefully, lest we should run into some Indians again. We were about 200 yards from the fire and I cried out: "Picket, don't fire, it is DeRudio and Private O'Neill," and started to run. We received an answer in a loud cheer from all the members of the picket and Lieutenant Varnum.
>
> This officer, one of our bravest and most efficient, came at once to me and was very happy to see me again, after having counted me among the dead.

On the hill, the stench from the dead troopers and horses was growing unbearable. The dead troopers were buried together in the prepared rifle pits, and the defense shifted a bit further south to avoid the smell of the horses and to locate closer to the water sources. There was no more enemy activity during the night. June 27 dawned still, hot, and dry. Major Reno was informed of dust being raised in the distance to the west and north. Believing it had to be Custer or General Terry, he drafted a note and sent it with two Arikara scouts to deliver it. It essentially read there had been a terrible defeat, the command had many dead and wounded, and was unable to continue their mission. They did not know the whereabouts of Lieutenant Colonel Custer and needed relief. The scouts were instructed to find General Terry, but instead they ran into one of Terry's scouts, Muggins Taylor. He had been sent by an anxious Terry to learn of developments. He continued to link up with the Reno Command with a note from General Terry, seeking news from Custer. Neither command knew where he was located. Meanwhile, three of Custer's Crow scouts—Hairy Moccasin, White Man Runs Him, and Goes Ahead—had made it west, running into Terry's commander of scouts, Lieutenant James Bradley. Custer's scouts were despondent, reporting a seemingly wild tale about the 7th Cavalry being routed with great loss, with only a small portion surviving, who were surrounded by the Sioux and still fighting for their lives. Reporting the same to General Terry, Bradley and the entire Montana Column found it impossible to believe a great disaster had befallen the entire 7th Cavalry Regiment. Terry pushed on.

About 1:00 p.m. on the 26th they had reached the Little Bighorn River. Crossing over and traveling on the east side, the command with Bradley's scouts out front started to see parties of Sioux, first small but as they advanced further east, large Sioux parties establishing skirmish lines across the Little Bighorn valley. These rearguard warriors, protecting the departure of the village, knew Terry's troops were in the vicinity. Confusing however, were reports of columns of mounted cavalry, complete with uniforms and guidons in the same area. Something had clearly happened, but with darkness coming on, the command went into a bivouac for the evening. The next morning, Lieutenant Bradley and his scouts were exploring the east side of the Little Bighorn River and stumbled into the abandoned site of the Indian village. Still smoking from the fire set the previous day, it contained the normally discarded items consistent with the hurried departure of the large encampment. Among the normal items, the scouts started finding bits and pieces of cavalry equipment and personal items of troopers themselves. Most disturbing were three severed heads of white men and clothing having belonged to lieutenants Sturgis and Porter and Captain Yates. Porter's recovered jacket indicated he suffered a gunshot wound to the chest, a fatal one. Exploring up the hills, his scouts started finding naked bodies of troopers, counting 197 of them. Many were mutilated and dismembered beyond recognition, but Bradley believed he had even seen Custer himself. Bradley shared the news with General Terry. The Crow scout reports were true, Custer's troops had befallen a terrible tragedy.

General Terry's arrival on the Reno-Benteen defense came with a mix of emotion. On the one hand, elation about a rescue for the battered command, and on the other hand, astonishment about the fate of Custer. General Terry cried when delivering the news. George Custer was a larger than life figure to his leaders and troopers—like him or not.

A gifted leader, Custer had fought his way out of many tough situations in the Civil War and after, during the Indian wars in Kansas. He was a man of incredible personal endurance, passion and intellect. His men couldn't believe he could be gone. Lieutenant Varnum turned away and openly sobbed with the news. Custer's striker John Burkman walked away to be alone. Always a loner and somewhat odd soldier, he was devoted to Custer, taking care of his animals and camp. In an instant his life changed and his importance was removed. Captain Benteen's astonishment was real, but his reaction to the news was predictable. Benteen not

Charles C. DeRudio was a 2nd Lieutenant assigned to Company A and was left behind in the hurried retreat by Reno from the valley fight. Hiding in the woods with several other troopers he was able to elude Indians about the area and successfully reunited with the Reno-Benteen defense a day later. DeRudio was labeled "Count No Account" by Captain Benteen because DeRudio immigrated from Europe prior to his service in the 7th Cavalry and had a habit of telling large tales about his past. (Little Bighorn National Monument)

only believed Custer was alive, but he also suggested he had to be somewhere away from the command. Benteen for years had held Custer responsible for the loss of Major Elliot and his command at the battle of the Washita. If he would do it once, why not again? Benteen could not let it rest, always believing Custer was up to something contemptible. General Terry again said General Custer is dead. Turning to Lieutenant Bradley, Terry instructed him to take Captain Benteen and any others who wanted to accompany him, down the ridge to investigate the scene for themselves, and verify what many refused to believe—that Custer's luck had finally run out. A few minutes later, with Bradley leading Benteen, Captain Weir and Lieutenants Nowlan and DeRudio, they followed the evident trail of the Custer command, first down Medicine Tail Coulee to the attempted ford and then up to Calhoun Hill. From there through the Keogh sector and finally to Last Stand Hill. There they found Custer, lying dead and naked but not mutilated among his leaders, family members, and the troopers of his five companies. The end for a national hero and the greatest victory for the Plains Indians.

Conclusion

The wounded survivors of the 7th Cavalry were placed on board the steamer *Far West*. Thanks to the competent and heroic piloting of Grant Marsh, the riverboat reached Fort Abraham Lincoln in record time. While the spouses of those killed were being given the terrible news, the newspapers in the east were already spreading the story and assigning responsibility for the disaster. Of course, if Custer had delivered a victory, there would have been no great surprise. He and the 7th Cavalry were expected to win. But, this horrible and complete loss left all (except the Indians) reeling for an explanation.

The nation was in the middle of a celebration 100 years in the making—the centennial of American independence. Grand parties and activities were being held across the country and the commander of the Army, Lieutenant General William T. Sherman was in Philadelphia attending an exposition. The tragedy was incongruent with the celebration and most of the official news arrived on July 4. Sherman received two reports from General Terry, one more apologetic report meant for the public, the other condemning Custer and the "sacrifice" of the 7th Cavalry. In a twist of fate, the condemning report was sent to the press accidentally, setting off a firestorm. The reaction was divisive and swift, those who blamed Custer and his braggadocio and vainglorious reputation, while on the other side his friends, the public, and much of the press who saw him and his men as victims of a failed Indian policy. Facts were in poor supply. Even the participants of the battle, who were on the periphery of Custer's Last Stand, knew few comprehensive details of what had really occurred. The 7th Cavalry was quickly reconstituted in the field and, along with additional forces, made busy hunting down the Indians responsible. The horses, equipment, and artifacts of the slain, serving as a DNA of sorts, led the Army to Indian participants in the battle. Within a year, the victors would become the vanquished. The battle of the Little Bighorn, the greatest victory of the Plains Indians, would also be their last, and with it, a great culture and way of life ended.

Libbie Custer went about her duties as a commanding officer's wife by personally notifying the wives of those slain in the regiment. Despite the personal pain of by losing a husband, she also lost a way of life and her security. She was "out of the Army" as it were and there were few benefits available to the survivors of those lost in the line of duty, except a modest pension to support her. Custer had also left debt that she became responsible for. She moved back east to stay with friends and put a devastated life back together. She never remarried, supporting herself with her literary talent, writing several books that sold well. Her life's work became her defense of Custer. Through public appearances, her writings, and prompt action to negative stories that emerged, she was largely successful. She above all knew her husband, and was devoted to his memory and reputation. While many who knew and served with Custer may have been critical of his actions at the Little Bighorn, they avoided public condemnation, out of respect for the beloved Libbie.

If there is a key to understanding the real personal side of George Custer, it is trying to rationalize many profound and diverse dichotomies in his life. Custer certainly had many realities. I think it is tempting to say he had many "personalities," but the term suggests schizophrenia, which is not correct. Perhaps the confusion has persuaded some historians to suggest schizophrenia or even madness. Custer was completely rational, but the polar ends of his behavior could always be confusing.

Take one of the first and very apparent dichotomies—his rebut of even the mildest discipline imposed on him, while at the same time expecting the full embrace of his orders and discipline from others. Custer was a precocious and incorrigible youth. He was constantly breaking the rules, performing pranks on others, and testing the limits of intransigence. In his early courtships with young women, he skirted the watchful eye of their parents. If they imposed prescripts, he found his way around them. The trait followed him to West Point, where he was constantly at work pushing the limits of what might be accepted, dangerously riding the edge of a razor. Time and again he faced expulsion only to narrowly slip by. In an environment where discipline was considered obligatory, indeed necessary to be successful, he would not conform. His last memorable experience at West Point was not of celebratory graduation but rather a court-martial and narrow escape.

Nearly every episode of his life included non-conformance of one form or another. He was unconventional on the battlefield as well. In the Civil War, where other leaders led from the rear, Custer tested fate with great courage by leading from the very front. Over a dozen horses paid with their lives carrying him into battle from the front, a testament to the real and ever-present danger he courted by his style of leadership. His unconventional and unanticipated cavalry tactics snatched victory from defeat time and again. The press and nation adored him for it. His cavalry tactics redefined the use of cavalry in the Civil War and beyond. In the subsequent Indian Wars in Kansas, Custer again and again made decisions which defied the intent of the orders given him by superiors. Custer crisscrossed Kansas, seemingly pursuing elusive bands of Indians, while at the same time inappropriately exhausting his troops just to be with his young wife, Libbie. He was court-martialed a second time and was suspended from duty for a year, hardly the behavior of a national hero and brevet major general. Custer fought authority throughout his time assigned to the plains, even up to the last few days of his life. Custer's early attack on the Indian village at the Little Bighorn (June 25), was a violation of the intent of General Terry's orders to bring the Montana Column and the Dakota Column together. The five companies under his direct command that day lost their lives as a result. Convexly, Custer demanded absolute loyalty and discipline from others. If he did not get it, he became angry and vindictive. He had a bad habit of mistreating his soldiers far and above the limits acceptable for a commanding officer. In the case of deserters he had heads shaved, hard labor performed, and in some cases, men shot. Even if the men had good reasons, like the case of starvation at Army forts in western Kansas in 1867, there was no exception given by Custer. The contrast between the discipline Custer ignored and the discipline he demanded was remarkable.

Custer had a comparable contrast in his view of southern culture and, on the other hand, his support for the end of slavery. Custer not only had affection for southern culture, he preferred it to his own experience growing up in the north. Take his close associates at West Point. He not only preferred the company of his fellow cadets from the south, but he also preferred to be billeted with them. Even as he advanced from a first-year plebe, where he had no choice about his barracks buddies, to an upperclassman where he did, he chose to stay with his southern friends. The root of his affection probably had to do with his innate love of chivalry, which he viewed was more evident in southern culture. A visit to a southern plantation of a friend during a break from West Point, would not change his feelings, even in the presence of slavery. When secession occurred and his southern friends left West Point for commissions in the Confederate Army, he understood. During the war, he treated captured and wounded Confederate officers he knew with great care, even to the point of writing letters to their families if they were wounded, died in battle or were taken prisoner, and loaning money to them. Custer's elaborate and elegant bow on horseback to his former West Point roommate and Confederate friend Thomas Rosser, before the battle of Tom's Brook, may best epitomize how he felt about his southern friends. It seems illogical then to know how opposed Custer was to slavery, and how hard he fought to end it. To Custer, it was improper to hold any man in bondage simply because of his race. He had great empathy for the slaves who moved north fleeing plantations and then would surround his camps for protection. But, his feelings only went so far, as he unconsciously shared many of the bigoted views of those from the North who fought for the Union. For many Union officers, preservation of the Union was foremost, the freedom of slaves secondary and he did not see freed slaves as equals. Yet, Custer fought fiercely in battle to defeat slavery, violently ending the lives of southern men who came from the culture he admired, only to free the lives of enslaved men he did not completely understand. If there is an explanation, it is complex and confusing.

In many ways Custer's feelings about the Plains Indians contain befuddling views as well. He admired the Indians in many ways. Not surprisingly, he related to their free lifestyle, immersed in the vast stretches of the west. He loved many of the things they loved, hunting, horsemanship, their love of family, even the thrill of warfare. When Custer first saw Cheyenne warriors in their tribal regalia as part of the Hancock command in 1867, he was astonished beyond words. Custer's appreciation for pageantry and parade were central to his reaction. For Custer, the beauty of the spectacle was visceral, innate, and inescapable. He loved and admired the Indians' simple existence, unencumbered with material pursuits. Custer related to the Indians and their fierce opposition to living on a reservation, and how, if faced with similar circumstances, he would fight it with every measure of his being. It was a great paradox then when Custer took up arms and led forces to destroy the very characteristics of Indian culture he so appreciated. It went further than that though. It would be accurate to say he tracked, pursued, oppressed, maimed, killed, and annihilated the Indians to carry out the orders given to him, all designed to compel the Indians to an existence he found so abominate. It is illogical, and Custer made a career of it.

George Custer loved attention and made a life's work of seeking and obtaining it. At first, as a youngster, it was simply performing pranks, but over time it grew to increasingly dangerous exploits. Today they would refer to Custer as an adrenaline junkie, insatiably desiring more and never getting enough. When he entered the Civil War, dangerous exploits could mean death, but he soon learned they could also bring a new form of attention to him, the admiration of the press. The focus of the press was a new paradigm for him. The exposure was shared with thousands across the whole country, hungry for news via the mass media of the day, limited to newspapers and magazines, photographs and wood-cut illustrations. And Custer's exploits were great copy. They were authentic, they captured success, and his youth and distinctive uniforms were accelerants. He was soon the media darling, and the public adored his success. Custer loved the media too, but for a different reason—the well-written word.

With the mentorship of his division commander, General Pleasonton, Custer learned good exploits could be enhanced by well-written reports, and in turn become spellbinding. A vainglorious twist on "the pen is mightier than the sword," even if the facts got skewed along the way. With practice, and exaggeration, Custer became an excellent writer. His continued success in writing magazine articles and his first book introduced him to an even larger, enamored audience. It was intoxicating and the press was always indulgent. It seemed the press only worked one way—his way.

It is interesting to see the other Custer when the press turned on him. After his court-martial in 1867, the press hammered on his reputation incessantly. Not only did he abhor it, but he also could not understand the reaction, and it cut through his ego like a Bowie knife. Moreover, criticism like Captain Frederick Benteen delivered after the battle of the Washita over the Major Elliot abandonment and then published in the press, worked Custer into a fury, nearly resulting in a duel until calmer heads prevailed. It was a striking contrast, that a man so finely tuned into the salient points of influencing the press for personal gain, could be reduced so quickly to blind emotion and furor when the same was delivered against him.

Custer could be equally blind to politics. He grew up the son of a Jacksonian Democrat and the conveyance of Jacksonian principles, like self-reliance and responsibility, clearly took with Custer. It elevated him in some circles, especially while assigned to the staff of General McClellan, a fellow Democrat, constantly at odds with Republican President Lincoln. After Custer's fame propelled him to the national stage after the war, he tried unsuccessfully to use his capital to support President Andrew Johnson's plan for the speedy restoration of the south. Custer and Johnson failed. But he could not give up on his deeply set political opinions, especially if the target was irresistibly rich.

When Orville Grant, President Grant's brother, became hopelessly entangled in the Belknap affair in early 1876, Custer could not help but get involved. Custer reasoned the issue at the center of Orville Grant's conundrum was essentially a straightforward neutral matter of corruption (the post sutler selection scandal). Custer being an Army officer with an interest in it for his men would naturally be seen as germane, there wouldn't be a problem. He foolishly played the political pawn to Democrat senators wishing to tarnish the president. It was a field fraught with danger, but he testified anyway and lost. President Grant was so angry, Custer would have to gather the help of General Sherman, General Sheridan, and General Terry, employing their ample lobbying efforts just to allow his accompaniment of the Dakota Column. Given these big stumbles, it is interesting to see his deft, successful navigation of politics when he badly needed an essential outcome.

His successful entry into West Point was clearly his first attempt at currying political favor. Despite the well-known Custer family's Democrat leanings, Custer, undaunted, convinced Republican Congressman John Bingham to appoint him to the academy. Later, during the Civil War, Custer was in a tough spot to garner Senate confirmation of his appointment as a brevet major general in the Regular Army. Custer coveted the position, but once again his politics preceded him, and his war record was of limited help. In the end, Custer had to provide a carefully written letter which did not surrender his political beliefs but still satisfied influential members of the Senate. The letter was a stunning piece of literary achievement, and more importantly it worked. He portrayed a functional Republican in prose, only to be drawn by political gravity back to his Democrat foundation. This perplexing back and forth would continue nonsensically his whole life.

The capstone dichotomy of George Custer's life is the battle of the Little Bighorn itself, the combatant sides providing striking contrasts. In 1876, the 7th Cavalry represented the premier unit of its kind in the Army. Recently outfitted with the new Model 1873 Springfield carbine, and the equally new Model 1873 Colt revolver, the regiment bristled with armament. It was a well-supported unit on the campaign, with a long supply tail which utilized steamboats to push supplies to them as they probed deeper into the frontier, on the hunt for Indians. The 7th had impressive leadership, starting at the top. George Custer was as seasoned as a commanding officer could be. He had a West Point education, had four years' experience and success in the Civil War (all with cavalry), and he was one of the few leaders in the Army who had real success fighting Indians. The other officers of the 7th Cavalry were above average as well. Many had served in the Civil War, and many others had seen service in Kansas and supported the victory at the battle of the Washita.

Sioux Chief Sitting Bull pictured in the 1880s after his surrender. Though not leading warriors in the Little Bighorn fight, he led a band of roamers into Canada to live in peace. Eventually starvation of his people led him to return to the United States and surrender at Fort Buford in 1881, the last band of roamers to do so. (National Park Service)

The 7th also enjoyed good non-commissioned officers (sergeants), with a great many having been at the Washita, and served on the two expeditions of the 1870s. They knew victory and had tasted it before. The enlisted men were somewhat green but eager. The Army had poor intelligence of what was in front of them, but the circumstance was not all that unusual. For Custer, he more often than not made up battle plans as he went along. Unpredictability can be a combat multiplier.

The grouping of Indians encamped on the Little Bighorn in June 1876 were different in almost all ways to other Plains Indians. They were at their core "roamers," moving every couple of weeks as their logistical support (the land beneath them and natural resources within their reach, such as the buffalo herds) was exhausted quickly. The agency arrivals loosely fitted in but there was not optimal inclusion, just a bunch of independent bands of Indians sharing the same ground. The large village was full of vulnerable women and children, always of great concern to the warriors. If an attack were to come, their only option was flight, requiring warriors to cover them to buy time. The Indians were armed mostly with their traditional weapons, bows and arrows, clubs, and lances. Some had repeating arms but not excessively so. Archaeological evidence suggests the Indians had a lot of weapons ranging from repeating arms to muzzleloaders, pistols, and everything in between. The bulk were older weapons, and they had limited ammunition for them. Some of the bands, but not all, had courageous leaders. Sitting Bull was certainly among them but only in an advisory role. Other leaders like Crazy Horse, Gall, Crow King, and Low Dog were combat leaders and very good. Crazy Horse stood above the others as he had played an important role in the Fetterman massacre and other engagements. The Indians knew the ground they were on very well and had generally good intelligence about potential foes in their region.

With the sharply contrasting capabilities of both sides and a definite advantage for the 7th Cavalry, the outcome at the Little Bighorn shocked the nation. As historian Robert Utley said so well, "The Army lost because the Indians won." True, but the Indians never won again. From the Little Bighorn on, the Indian bands present there were hunted down doggedly until all had capitulated. When Sitting Bull's band, the last of the last roamers, walked into Fort Buford in 1881 to surrender, they were thoroughly defeated. So, what was the window of opportunity for Indian victory at the Little Bighorn then, one day or a day and a half? The Indians did not want to fight and did not seek it that day. Custer, in his pursuit of the village, set the day of the fight, and in turn, the conditions for it. If he were not himself, enduring in the saddle, persistent, working the odds, pushing, constantly adjusting—all of those things which made him successful in the past, and defined him—there would have been no fight on June 25, 1876, and perhaps not the next day or the next week. The Little Bighorn would not have occurred. If he had waited for the rest of the command to catch up, his presence would have been discovered, and the Indians would have fled that night, scattering in all directions. The best combat leader in the

Army, commanding the best fighting regiment in the Army, with the best possible support available to them, contrasted with the most vulnerable of people, caught by surprise, equipped with outdated arms, with their backs against the wall, and nowhere to go but stand, fight and win. The result? The most disastrous defeat in the history of the Army, and at the same time, the greatest dichotomy in the life of George Armstrong Custer.

Bibliography

Ambrose, Stephen E. *Crazy Horse and Custer: The Parallel Lives of Two American Warriors*. New York, NY: Doubleday & Co, 1975.

Ballard, Ted. *The Battle of Antietam*. Fort Lesley McNair, Washington, DC: Center of Military History Publications, 2008.

Barnett, Louise. *Touched by Fire: The Life, Death, and Mystic Afterlife of George Armstrong Custer*. New York, NY: Henry Holt and Company, 1996.

Beecham, Captain R. K. *Gettysburg. The Pivotal Battle of the Civil War*. Chicago, IL: A. C. McClurg and Company, 1911.

Bluhm, Raymond Jr. *The Shenandoah Valley Campaign, March to November 1864*. Fort Lesley McNair, Washington, DC: Center of Military History Publications, 2014.

Bolton, H. W. *Personal Reminiscences of the Late War*. Chicago, IL: H. W. Bolton, 1892.

Bourke, John G. *On the Border with Crook: General George Crook, the American Indian Wars, and Life on the American Frontier*. New York, NY: Charles Scribner's and Sons, 1891.

Boyd, James P. *The Gallant Trooper: General Philip H. Sheridan*. Philadelphia, PA: P. W. Ziegler and Company, 1888.

Bradley, James H. and Edgar Stewart, ed. *The March of the Montana Column: A Prelude to the Custer Disaster*. Norman, OK: University of Oklahoma Press, 1961.

Brady, Cyrus T. *The Sioux Indian Wars: From the Powder River to the Little Bighorn*. New York, NY: Indian Head Books, 1992.

Brininstool, E. A. *Troopers with Custer: Historic Incidents of the Battle of the Little Bighorn*. New York, NY: Bonanza Books, 1952.

Brooke-Rawle, Colonel William. *The Annals of the Civil War, written by Leading Participants, North and South*. Philadelphia, PA: The Times Publishing Group, 1879.

Butler, M. C. *Battles and Leaders of the Civil War*. New York, NY: The Century Company, 1888.

Camp, Walter and Kenneth Hammer, ed. *Custer in 76: Walter Camp's Notes on the Custer Fight*. Provo, UT: Brigham Young University Press, 1976.

Carpenter, Louis H. "Sheridan's Expedition Around Richmond, May 9–25, 1864." *Journal of the U.S. Cavalry Association*, vol. 1, no. 3 (November 1888): 300–324.

Carroll, John M. *Custer's Chief of Scouts: The Reminiscences of Charles A. Varnum*. Lincoln, NE: University of Nebraska Press, 1987.

Carroll, John M., ed. *The Benteen-Goldin Letters on Custer and his Last Battle*. Lincoln, NE: University of Nebraska Press, 1991.

Carrington, Francis G. *My Army Life and the Fort Phil Kearney Massacre*. Philadelphia, PA: J. B. Lippincott, 1910.

Cheney, Newel. *History of the Ninth Regiment, New York Volunteer Cavalry, War of 1861 to 1865*. New York, NY: Poland Center, 1901.

Chief Low Dog. "Low Dog's Account of the Battle of the Little Bighorn." *Leavenworth (KS) Weekly Times*, August 18, 1881.

Coppee, Henry, ed. *History of the Civil War in America, Comte de Paris*. Philadelphia, PA: Joseph H. Coates and Company, 1876.

Cross, Walt. *From Little Bighorn to the Potomac: The Story of Army Surgeon Dr. Robert Wilson Shufeldt*. Stillwater, OK: Cross Publications, 2010.

Custer, Elizabeth B. *Boots and Saddles*. New York, NY: Harper and Brothers, 1885.

Custer, Elizabeth B. *Tenting on the Plains*. New York, NY: Charles L. Webster, 1887.

Custer, Elizabeth B. *Following the Guidon*. New York, NY: Harper and Brothers, 1890.

Custer, George A. *My Life on the Plains*. New York, NY: Sheldon and Company, 1874.

Custer, George A. "Battling with the Sioux on the Yellowstone." In *The Custer Reader*, ed. Paul Andrew Hutton. Lincoln, NE: University of Nebraska Press, 1992.

Devens, R. M. *The Pictorial Book of Anecdotes and Incidents of the War of the Rebellion*. Des Moines, IA: W. E. Bliss and Company, 1884.

Dixon, Dennis. *The Hero of Beecher's Island: The Life and Military Career of George A. Forsyth*. Lincoln, NE, and London: University of Nebraska Press, 1994.

Donovan, James. *A Terrible Glory: Custer and the Little Bighorn—The Last Great Battle of the American West*. New York, NY: Little, Brown, and Company, 2008.

Du Mont, John S. *Custer Battle Guns*. Canaan, NH: Phoenix Publishing, 1988.

Duke, Basil W. and R. W. Knott. *The Southern Bivouac*. Richmond, VA: B. F. Avery and Sons, 1886.

Farley, Joseph Pearson. *West Point in the Early Sixties*. New York, NY: Pafracts Book Company, 1902.

Fox, Jr. Richard A. *Archeology, History, and Custer's Last Battle: The Little Bighorn Reexamined*. Norman, OK: University of Oklahoma Press, 1993.

Garst, Shannon. *Crazy Horse*. Cambridge, MA: Houghton Mifflin, 1950.

Gause, Isaac. *Four Years with Five Armies*. New York, NY: The Neale Publishing Company, 1908.

Godfrey E. S. "Custer's Last Battle / By One of His Troop Commanders." *Century Magazine*, January 1892.

Godfrey, E. S. *The Field Diary of Edward Settle Godfrey*. Portland OR: Champoeg Press, 1957.

Goldin, Theodore. *With the Seventh Cavalry in 1876*. N.p.: privately printed, 1980.

Gordon, General John B. *Reminiscences of the Civil War*. New York, NY: Charles Scribner's Sons, 1904.

Graham, William A. *The Custer Myth: A Source of Custeriana*. Harrisburg, PA: Stackpole Publishing Company, 1953.

Graham, William A. *The Reno Court of Inquiry: Abstract of the Official Court of Proceedings*. Harrisburg, PA: Stackpole Publishing Company, 1954.

Graham, William A. *The Story of the Little Bighorn*. Harrisburg, PA: Stackpole Publishing Company, 1959.

Gray, John S. *Centennial Campaign: The Sioux War of 1876*. Norman, OK: University of Oklahoma Press, 1988.

Gray, John S. *Custer's Last Campaign: Mitch Boyer and the Little Bighorn Reconstructed*. Lincoln, NE, and London: University of Nebraska Press, 1991.

Hadley, James A. *The 19th Kansas Cavalry and the Conquest of the Plains Indians*. Topeka, KS: Kansas State Historical Society, 1908.

Hammer, Kenneth, ed. *Custer in '76: Walter Camps Notes on the Custer Fight*. Salt Lake City, UT: Brigham Young University Press, 1976.

Harris, Moses. "With the Reserve Brigade—From Winchester to Appomattox." *Journal of the U.S. Cavalry Association*, vol. 4 (March 1891): 3-26

Hatcher, Edmund. *The Last Four Weeks of the War*. Columbus, OH: The Co-Operative Publishing Company, 1892.

Humphrey, Willis C. *The Great Contest; A History of Military and Naval Operations during the Civil War, 1861–1865*. Detroit, MI: C.H. Smith and Company, 1886.

Humphreys, Andrew A. *The Virginia Campaign of '64 and '65*. New York, NY: Charles Scribner's Sons, 1885.

Hutton, Paul A., ed. *The Custer Reader*. Lincoln, NE, and London: University of Nebraska Press, 1992.

Johnson, Robert Underwood and Clarence Clough Buell. *Battles and Leaders of the Civil War*, Volume 4. New York, NY: The Century Company, 1887.

Johnson, Rossiter. *From Campfire and Battlefield*. New York, NY: Bryan, Taylor and Company, 1894.

Jones, J. William, ed. *Southern Historical Society Papers*, Volume 2. Richmond, VA: 1876.

Kidd, J. H. *Personal Recollections of a Cavalryman with Custer's Michigan Cavalry Brigade in the Civil War*. Ionia, MI: Sentinel, Printing Company, 1908.

King, Charles. "Custer's Last Battle." *Harper's Weekly*, August 1890.

Kolakowski, Christopher. *The Virginia Campaigns, March to August 1862*. Fort Lesley McNair, Washington, DC: Center of Military History Publications, 2014.

Lyman, Colonel Theodore. *Meade's Headquarters, 1864–1865*. Washington, DC: Library of Congress (Atlantic Monthly Press), 1922.

Marquis, Thomas B. *Wooden Leg: A Warrior Who Fought Custer*. Lincoln, NE: University of Nebraska Press, 1931.

Marquis, Thomas. *Custer on the Little Bighorn*. Lodi, CA: Dr. Marquis Custer Publications, 1967.

McClernand, Edward J. *With the Indian and Buffalo in Montana, 1870–1878*. Glendale, CA: Arthur H. Clark Co., 1969.

McClure, Alexander Kelly. *The Annals of the Civil War, Written by Leading Participants, North and South*. Philadelphia, PA: The Times Publishing Company, 1879.

Merington, Marguerite, ed. *The Custer Story: The Life and Intimate Letters of General George A. Custer and His Wife Elizabeth*. New York, NY: The Devin-Adair Company, 1950.

Miller, David H. *Custer's fall: The Native American Side of the Story*. New York, NY: Dutton Books, 1957.

Miller, William E. *Battles and Leaders of the Civil War, Volume 3*. New York, NY: The Century Company, 1888.

Moore, Frank, ed. *Rebellion Record: a Diary of American Events, Documents and Narratives*. New York, NY: D. Van Nostrand, 1868.

Morris, Charles. *Heroes of the Army in America*. Philadelphia, PA: J. B. Lippincott Company, 1919.

National Archives. General Court Martial Orders no. 93, in Records of George Armstrong Custer, RG-9, September 16, 1867.

National Archives. Records of George A. Custer, RG-9, November 20, 1867.

Newhall, Colonel Frederic. *With Sheridan in Lee's Last Campaign*. Philadelphia, PA: J. B. Lippincott and Company, 1866.

Nichols, Robert H. *In Custer's Shadow: O. Major Marcus Reno*. Norman, OK: University of Oklahoma Press, 1999.

Philbrick, Nathaniel. *The Last Stand: Sitting Bull, and the Battle of the Little Bighorn*. New York, NY: Viking Penguin, 2010.

Putnam, Sally Brock. *Richmond during the War. Four Years of Personal Observation by a Richmond Lady*. New York, NY: G. W. Carleton and Company, 1867.

Ramey, W. Sanford. *Kings of the Battle-Field*. Philadelphia, PA: Aetna Publishing Company, 1887.

Reed, Colonel Hugh T. *Cadet Life at West Point*. Richmond, IN: Reed and Son, 1896.

Reynolds, Quentin. *Custer's Last Stand*. New York, NY: Random House, 1951.

Rister, Carl C. *Border Command: General Phil Sheridan in the West*. Norman, OK: University of Oklahoma Press, 1944.

Ryan, John and Sandy Barnard, eds. *Ten Years with Custer: A 7th Cavalryman's Memoirs.* Wake Forest, NC: AST Press, 2001.

Sandoz, Mari. *Crazy Horse.* New York, NY: Knof, 1942.

Sarf, Wayne M. *The Little Bighorn Campaign.* New York, NY: Combined Publishing, 1993.

Scott, Robert N., ed. *The War of the Rebellion—Compilation of the Official Records of the Union and Confederate Armies.* Washington, DC: Government Printing Office, 1865.

Sheridan, Philip A. *Personal Memoirs of P.H. Sheridan,* Volume II. New York, NY: Jenkins & McCowan Press, 1888.

Sherman, William T. *Memoirs of General W. T. Sherman.* New York, NY: D. Appleton and Company, 1875.

Spotts, David L. and E. A. Brininstool, eds. *Campaigning with Custer and the Nineteenth Kansas Volunteer Cavalry in the Washita Campaign 1868-69.* Lincoln, NE: University of Nebraska Press, 1988.

Staff Writer. "Gen. Custer's Peace Story Refuted." *Pioneer and Democrat,* October 2, 1863.

Staff Writer. "Sheridan! The Great Cavalry Expedition through the Rebel Lines." *Pioneer and Democrat,* May 27, 1864.

Staff Writer. "Grant!" *New York Herald,* June 2, 1864.

Staff Writer. "How General Stuart was Killed." *The True Northerner,* June 17, 1864.

Staff Writer. "The Last Great Cavalry Raid." *Nashville Daily Union,* June 25, 1864.

Staff Writer. "Description of the Late Cavalry Fight." *Daily Ohio Statesman,* October 15, 1864.

Staff Writer. "Shenandoah. Captures of Prisoners, Artillery, Caissons, Headquarters Wagons, Furniture, Papers & c." *New York Herald,* October 17, 1864.

Staff Writer. "Sheridan, The Rebels said to have Gone to Richmond to Reorganize." *New York Herald,* October 26, 1864.

Staff Writer. "The Vermont Troops at Cedar Creek." *The Orleans Independent Standard,* November 18, 1864.

Staff Writer. "Shenandoah. The Gallant Conduct of Our Cavalry." *New York Herald,* November 19, 1864.

Staff Writer. "Retaliation by Colonel Mosby." *Richmond Daily Dispatch,* November 21, 1864.

Staff Writer. "Cavalry Fight in the Valley." *Richmond Daily Dispatch,* December 30, 1864.

Staff Writer. "Details of General Sheridan's Victory at Waynesboro." *The Cleveland Morning Leader,* March 13, 1865.

Staff Writer. "New York papers of the 10th Instant—One Day Later." *Richmond Daily Dispatch,* March 13, 1865.

Staff Writer. "Sheridan's Progress, His fight with Early, Attack by Rosser." *Richmond Daily Dispatch,* March 13, 1865.

Staff Writer. "The Battle of Waynesboro." The *Cleveland Morning Leader,* March 24, 1865.

Staff Writer. "New York papers of the 20th Instant." *Richmond Daily Dispatch,* March 24, 1865.

Staff Writer. "Latest News." *Dayton Daily Empire,* April 3, 1865.

Staff Writer. "The Grand Review." *The Cleveland Morning Leader,* June 1, 1865.

Staff Writer. "Fetterman Massacre." *New York Times,* December 27, 1866.

Staff Writer. "Interview of Winfield S. Edgerly." *Leavenworth Times,* August 18, 1881.

Stevenson, Joan N. *Deliverance from the Little Bighorn: Doctor Henry Porter and Custer's Seventh Cavalry.* Norman, OK: University of Oklahoma Press, 2012.

Stewart, Edgar I. *Custer's Luck.* Norman, OK: University of Oklahoma Press, 1955.

Stiles, T. J. *Custer's Trials: A Life on the Frontier of a New America.* New York, NY: Vintage Books, 2015.

Taylor, William O. *With Custer on the Little Bighorn.* New York, NY: Penguin, 1996.

Terry, Alfred H. *Field Diary of General Alfred H. Terry: The Yellowstone Expedition—1876.* Bellevue, NE: Old Army Press, 1970.

Townsend, George. *Campaigns of a Non-Combatant.* New York, NY: Blelock and Company, 1866.

Utley, Robert M., ed. *Life in Custer's Cavalry: Diaries and Letters of Albert and Jenny Barnitz, 1867-68.* New Haven and London: Yale Press, 1977.

Utley, Robert M. *Cavalier in Buckskin: George Armstrong Custer and the Western Military Frontier.* Norman, OK, and London: University of Oklahoma Press, 1988.

Utley, Robert M. *Custer Battlefield: A History and Guide to the Battle of the Little Bighorn.* Washington, DC: National Park Service Division of Publications, 1988.

Vestal, Stanley. *Sitting Bull.* Norman, OK: University of Oklahoma Press, 1957.

Welch, James with Paul Stekler. *Killing Custer: The Battle of the Little Bighorn and the Fate of the Plains Indians.* New York and London: W. W. Norton and Company, 1994.

Wert Jeffrey D. *Custer: The Controversial Life of George Armstrong Custer.* New York, NY: Simon and Schuster, 1996.

Wilson, James Grant. "Two Modern Knights Errant." *Cosmopolitan Magazine,* May–October 1891.

Windolph, Charles. *I Fought with Custer: The Story of Sergeant Windolph, Last Survivor of the Battle of the Little Bighorn.* New York, NY: Scribner, 1954.

Whittaker, Frederick. *A Complete Life of General George A. Custer.* New York, NY: Sheldon & Co, 1876.

Wood, C. J. *Reminiscences of the War.* New York, NY: n.p. collection, 1880.

Wright, General Marcus. *Battles and Commanders of the Civil War.* Washington, DC: U.S. War Department, 1907.

Index